"THE
THRILL
OF
VICTORY"

ALSO BY BERT RANDOLPH SUGAR:

"THE THRILL OF VICTORY"

the inside story of abc sports

Bert Randolph Sugar

with a foreword by Frank Gifford

HAWTHORN BOOKS, INC.
Publishers/New York
A Howard & Wyndham Company

The author acknowledges that the title "The Thrill of Victory" is the trademark and sole property of American Broadcasting Companies, Inc. ABC is not responsible for the accuracy or content of this book, which responsibility rests entirely with the author.

"THE THRILL OF VICTORY"

Library of Congress Catalog Card Number: 76–56517
ISBN: 0–8015–7717–9
1 2 3 4 5 6 7 8 9 10

Contents

Foreword

For several years now I've heard the comment over and over that I've had the best of two possible worlds. As a professional football player for twelve years with the New York Giants, I played on several championship teams during New York City's heyday of pro football. Now I'm with another championship team, ABC Sports. And while my present playing "fields" range from Innsbruck, Austria, to the Far East with stops in between, my home field is still 1330 Avenue of the Americas, New York, not Yankee Stadium.

Odd as it might seem, there are some rather striking similarities between what I've found at ABC and what I discovered with the Giants back in the early fifties. I don't think it's any secret to those who follow pro football that the only route to consistent success lies in the combination of top management, coaching, and playing. The Giants were already moving in an upward direction when I arrived those many years ago. I joined the likes of Charlie Conerly, Kyle Rote, Emlen Tunnell, and Rosie Brown. Over the next few years, management supplemented that group with others you might recall—Alex Webster, Rosey Grier, Andy Robustelli, Sam Huff, Jimmy Patton, just to name a few. The final touch was added when Vince Lombardi was brought in to direct the offense and Tom Landry (the Cowboys' present coach) was added to head up the defense. The result of those many moves was a decade of winning years that produced seven divisional titles, one NFL championship, and a team that never finished worse than third.

As I mentioned, for me there are striking similarities to those championship teams and to the one I now "play with"—ABC Sports. There was also one difference. ABC was already a championship team when I joined it in 1971. But it was also a team that was built very much like my ole Giants. The "management" of my new team was Roone Arledge. His "coaches"—the Chuck Howards, Denny Lewins, and Chet Fortes—were all topflight young production people. His players were Jim McKay, Keith Jackson, Howard Cosell, Bill Flemming, and many others. Roone had built this team much as the Giants had been built—each man handpicked for an individual talent that could improve the overall team.

I really don't think it's self-serving to say that ABC's success in sports was and is an ongoing phenomenon in broadcasting. And even in this continuity of "winning seasons" I can find parallels from my "other" playing days. For instance, when the Giants began to stagger ever so slightly at the end of the fifties, they reached out and found help in the form of Y. A. Tittle and Del Shofner. This, combined with the progression of their younger players, continued the Giants' winning ways.

Roone, over the years, has done much the same to keep ABC Sports on the winning track. He plucked Chris Schenkel and yours truly from CBS and Don Meredith from the playing fields of Dallas. Meanwhile, the youngsters in this organization grew to develop the same winning habits that have permeated ABC Sports since its inception.

As I see it, "top" management has also played a key role in ABC Sports' growth. Chairman of the Board Leonard Goldenson's personal struggle over the years to make ABC the premier television network has been documented time and time again. However, I was totally unprepared for the man I met.

In joining ABC, I also took over a nightly sports spot on WABC–TV in New York. At the time our "Eyewitness News" team was a runaway winner in the New York market, and one afternoon we were all summoned to lunch with Mr. Goldenson in the Executive Dining Room at 1330. If any of us had expected a head coach's, "Let's-keep-it-up" speech, we were in for a shock. It was one of the warmest affairs I've ever attended. Speeches were missing, the pep talk nonexistent. It was just a get-together, an expression of Leonard's appreciation for a job well done. After dessert and coffee, Leonard took us all on a fascinating trip through the history of ABC. As he spoke of the difficult early years, the ups and downs that are part of this industry, everyone in that room knew that here was a man who deeply loved the organization he had built and the people who made it tick.

Though I came from the outside, I wasn't at all made to feel like an alien. But it's a rare bird that comes in from the outside at ABC Sports. Most of the production staff started at the lowest rung, even as "go-fers" on the so-called taxi squad, going from event to event yearning to be a part of ABC Sports. You watch the kids grow up to become topflight talent—secure in the knowledge that as long as they produce, opportunities are unlimited and nobody is going to be brought in over them. And the word gets around, as one can see from the hundreds of letters from job seekers that reach my desk and the desks of everyone else here at ABC Sports, that this is the mecca in sports broadcasting.

The most significant analogy between my two worlds comes from the top. It was men like Tom Landry and Vince Lombardi in football. And it's men like Roone Arledge in broadcasting. During the Montreal Olympics, Roone sent me to cover the 180-kilometer bicycle race at Mt. Royal with the instructions, "I need your impressions for a three- or four-minute piece." I had never even seen a bicycle race before, but when we returned and showed him the final product, he asked, "Can you make it six or eight minutes?" That was like hearing Lombardi say, "Nice job!" It doesn't come that often, but it's worth so much when it does.

Roone Arledge is far and away the very best at what he does. As I said recently in accepting the prestigious Peabody Award for him soon after he had been promoted to his new position of president of ABC News and Sports, "Roone Arledge is a remarkable combination of talents." I emphasized this by recalling that terrible day and night during the Munich Olympics. At the time, the only link between the outside world and the terrorist takeover of Israeli team headquarters was our ABC production quarters. While I personally watched the monitors with disbelief as the events unfolded, I also watched with admiration the work of Arledge. He had instantly changed hats from a sports producer to that of a newsman. And throughout those long hours as the entire free world waited for word, he was the consummate professional, filtering out fact from rumor, turning our massive sports operation into a gigantic news effort, all the while talking quietly but confidently into the ear of reporter Jim McKay. He never once left the control room during those agonizing hours, and he was never once less than the complete professional.

Roone is demandingly professional in everything he does. He can be working in his office with one critical eye on a video cassette of an ABC Sports show, at the same time deciding the infinite mathematical possibilities of who will go where to cover what and with whom, and still have time to call you and ask, "You remember what you said about Jack Lambert? Well, he was the number two draft pick, not the third." Now, how in the hell he'll know that is beyond me, with all of the other things he has on his mind. He's unbelievable. But just the fact that he is both demanding and has a great deal of pride in everything that goes on the air has helped me personally. For when you get into an event, I'll tell you, you better have it all together because nothing will ever slip by the Redhead.

There's nothing quite like ABC Sports. There's nothing so demanding and yet so rewarding. And it's basically the people who have made it number one. After all, as some wag once said with understated humor, "any network with commentators like Jim McKay, Howard Cosell, Don Meredith, Keith Jackson, and Chris Schenkel, and producers like Chet Forte and Denny Lewin can't be all bad." In my own opinion, it's as unique a championship team as was ever put together.

Frank Gifford

Acknowledgments

In 1978 television celebrates its thirtieth anniversary as an industry-cum-social phenomenon. Just thirty years ago the number of television sets in existence passed the one million mark, the number of television stations passed 100, and network programming passed 100 hours a week. Today, there are more television sets than bathtubs, more than 500 VHF (very high frequency) stations, and wall-to-wall programming by the networks.

The medium has come a long way from those so-called thrilling days of yesteryear—the dark ages of Uncle Miltie, J. Fred Muggs, and the Masked Marvel—leaving an indelible impression of its own. And nowhere has this imprint been greater than on sports. It has provoked—and merited—words, interests, debate, and passion in excess of anything that has touched one of our most sacred institutions dating back to that magic year of 1948, when the first World Series to be televised was beamed into those one million living rooms. This most dominant information element in American life and the final and most important link in what Mr. Edison's first light bulb made possible has now become translated into the electronic sports revolution taking place before our very eyes. And as we sit and stare without comprehension at the electronic orgy of miniaturized twenty-three-inch base runners going down and out for outlet passes or tennis matches between the same two players on two different networks at exactly the same moment, it becomes apparent to us that Marshall McLuhan's thesis that "the medium is the message" is indeed correct.

It is this message that we've attempted to decipher in "*The Thrill of Victory*" by focusing our attention on one network, ABC. That network, the youngest of the three and celebrating its twenty-fifth anniversary on February 9, 1978, has focused its attention on sports, achieving first its credibility and then its growth through sports.

"*The Thrill of Victory*" is a book that traces that world of electronic sports, transcending the on-the-field sports into the realm of media, business, and people—the real soul of broadcasting.

The book was not an easy one to organize nor to research. Attempting to capture over one-half the life span of television in the pages of one book was akin to forcing twenty pounds of material into a one-pound book. When Jim McKay was first asked by Macmillan to write a book about all of his experiences on "Wide World of Sports," eleven years old at that time, he knew how difficult it would be to organize it and asked the publisher if he could "just keep notes one summer." The thought occurred to us to do it the same way. But the importance and the magnitude of the topic dictated a broadbrushed stroke. Thus, while we attempted to approach events and occurrences chronologically, the reader will learn, as we did, that this was not always possible.

Inasmuch as the people involved provided the basis for the book, I am indebted to those people at ABC who unsparingly gave of their time and effort to answer any and all questions, no matter how embarrassing. They suffered none of the paranoia that those at CBS did when they were approached by a rival publisher to cooperate in a book tentatively entitled, "An Inside Look at CBS Sports," and responded that "The potential gains are not commensurate with the risks on the downside."

The names of those who cooperated and never attempted to influence either the purpose or the content of the work read like a Who's Who of Broadcasting and Communications, and so I am indebted to the following for the making of this book:

Joe Aceti, Dave Anderson, Don Austermann, Julie Barnathan, Frank Beermann, Bill Behanna, Jim Benagh, Donn Bernstein, Furman Bisher, Steve Bozekas, Tom Brookshire, Dick Buffinton, Richard Burns, Chuck Chesnut, Bob Cochrane, Bob Coen, Jeff Cohan, Beano Cook, Howard Cosell, Bill Croasdale, Fred Danzig, Gary Deeb, Bud Dudley, Bill Flemming, Chet Forte, Kay Gardella, Frank Gifford, Al Glossbrenner, John Goodman, Herb Goren, Bud Greenspan, Dick Horan, Chuck Howard, Keith Jackson, Dan Jenkins, Bill Johnson, Larry Kamm, Bern Kanner, Marshall Karp, Alex Karras, Tom Kelly, Don King, Jerry Klein, Rick LaCivita, Tim Leedy, Carol Lehti, Roanne Levinsohn, Dennis Lewin, Nat Loubet, John Martin, Jim McKay, Sam Merrill, John Monteleone, Tom Moore, LeRoy Neiman, Don Ohlmeyer, Art Paley, Ara Parseghian, Jeff Ruhe, Norm Samet, Chris Schenkel, Carol Scherick, Ed Scherick, Burt Schultz, Andy Sidaris, Simon Siegel, Jim Spence, Jeff Tallman, Marty Torgoff, Alex Wallau, Doug Wilson, David Wolf, Warner Wolf, and Ken Woodward. And, of course, Irv Brodsky of ABC and the long-suffering Sandra Choron of Hawthorn Books, who, in the vernacular, "made this book possible."

I am also indebted to another group consisting of three typists who translated tangled tapes and mangled manuscripts—Ruth Gray, Ok Galibert, and Nora Mackenzie—and two researchers, Lorraine Gracey and Michael Monbeck. Together they helped sculpt the book and make it take form and flight.

Finally, the book was created by you, the television viewer, who has spent many hours in front of the set shouting for a golfer to make a putt or a team to score as if you had 10 percent of the action. But those scenes you witnessed on your screen, contrived to please the eye and ear, are sometimes at the expense of your total understanding. It is hoped that this book will provide some of that understanding and will let you see what goes on in the world of "sportelevision"—an esoteric world just as exciting as the one down on the field.

Chronology: Twenty-Five Years of ABC

1927 The Blue Network of the National Broadcasting Company (better known as the Blue Network) formed by NBC.

1943 NBC sells the Blue Network to Edward J. Noble, chairman of Life Savers, Inc., for $8 million, largest price paid for a broadcasting entity to this date.

1944 Noble buys name American Broadcasting Company for network, replacing the Blue Network name.

1953 Merger between ABC and Paramount Theatres, headed by Leonard Goldenson, to form American Broadcasting Company-Paramount Theatres, Inc., given final approval February 9 by Federal Communications Commission. Network dates official beginning of ABC from this FCC approval.

ABC signs agreement with Walt Disney to produce seven years of programming.

1954 ABC wins rights to NCAA football, but relinquishes them after one year and loss of $1.8 million.

1955   ABC signs agreement with Warner Brothers for three hour-long shows, including "Cheyenne," setting trend for filmed shows to replace the then live programming.

1956   Howard Cosell first heard over ABC as radio commentator on the Floyd Patterson–Archie Moore heavyweight championship fight.

1958   First use of videotape, which revolutionizes the TV industry.

1959   ABC breaks into big time sports telecasts by televising the National League play-offs between the Los Angeles Dodgers and the Milwaukee Braves.

1960   Gillette becomes major sports sponsor and underwriter on ABC.

        ABC tops NBC's bid and wins rights to NCAA games for $6.2 million.

        Roone Arledge hired by sports packager, Sports Programs, Inc., as producer of NCAA football games.

        ABC acquires rights to American Football League games.

1961   Jim McKay hosts first "Wide World of Sports" program, April 19.

        Sports Programs, Inc., sold by Ed Scherick to ABC and becomes ABC sports department.

1962   Keith Jackson joins ABC sports team.

        Chuck Howard, after serving as production assistant on NCAA and AFL football, becomes producer on "Wide World of Sports."

1964   ABC sports department becomes ABC Sports, Inc., and Roone Arledge is made vice-president.

   ABC telecasts Winter Olympics from Innsbruck—its first Olympic coverage.

1965   World's first commercial communications satellite, *Early Bird*, launched, providing two-way television communications between Europe and North America.

   ABC attempts merger with ITT but is unsuccessful.

1966   ABC acquires rights to Professional Golf Association tour.

   First live boxing bout on "Wide World of Sports"— Muhammad Ali vs. Henry Cooper from London.

   After a four-year separation, ABC reacquires rights to NCAA football for $15.5 million.

1968   ABC televises Winter Olympics from Grenoble and Summer Olympics from Mexico City.

1970   "Monday Night Football" successfully debuts, inaugurating a weekday sports night.

1972   ABC televises Summer Olympics from Munich.

   Jim McKay wins the George Polk Memorial Award for "outstanding television news reporting" for his coverage of Munich Olympics.

1974   Keith Jackson replaces Chris Schenkel as principal voice of NCAA football.

   Delayed telecast of Evel Knievel Snake River jump attains highest rating for "Wide World."

1975 ABC acquires rights to Kentucky Derby.

1976 ABC televises Summer Olympics from Montreal.

1977 ABC attains rank as nation's number one network for entire season.

"THE THRILL OF VICTORY"

1
The Bionic
Network

Remember the old comic-strip body-building ad in which a ninety-eight-pound weakling grows to eventually overcome the sand-kicking bully? Well, something equally incredible, but undeniably real occurred at the end of 1976. When all of the year's ratings were added up, ABC was no longer the "ninety-eight-pound weakling" it had been for so long. For the first time in history, the American Broadcasting Company was the nation's number one network.

Almost immediately buttons and T-shirts began to appear at ABC headquarters in New York. They read: "We're Number One! and Things May Never Be the Same Again. ABC—America's Leading Television Network." For ABC staffers and management it was the almost impossible dream come true. The years of being a third place also-ran were finally and gloriously over.

* * *

The American Broadcasting Company started life as the Blue Network, a second six-station radio network established by the National Broadcasting Company to compete with its already existing Red Network. History offers two explanations for the companionate names Red and Blue. One holds that those colors identified the wiring that distinguished the two networks in NBC's engineering offices. The other claims that they were the colors of the pushpins used to identify the affiliate stations on maps of the country.

Throughout NBC's early history, announcers often had difficulty distinguishing the two networks. Usually they were able to get it straight before they went on the air, but not always. In fact, one Sunday morning an announcer who was still feeling the effects of the previous night's party flipped the "on" switch and told the world, "Good morning. This is either the Red or the Blue Network."

Whatever the derivation of its name, the Blue Network was formed on January 1, 1927. Today, more than fifty years later, blue is still the predominant color in the network's color scheme and still used to identify ABC in Nielsen rating reports.

It soon became evident to all, but most particularly to the Federal Communications Commission, that the Blue Network's primary reason for being was to run interference for NBC's far more prestigious Red Network against its competition, CBS. In a decision later affirmed by the Supreme Court, the FCC found that NBC's maintenance of the two networks was monopolistic and that it would have to divest itself of one.

By 1942, in preparation for a divestiture, NBC divided the facilities, the staff, the studios, and the stations between the Red and Blue networks. They incorporated the Blue Network as an independent subsidiary of RCA and set an asking price of $8 million.

During the summer of 1943, just as the Allies were marching toward Salerno, Edward J. Noble, the sixty-one-year-old founder and chairman of Life Savers, Inc., former undersecretary of commerce and first chairman of the Civil Aeronautics Authority, met the asking price, beating the offer of $7.75 million by the investment house of Dillon, Reed & Co. It was the largest price to that date ever paid for a broadcasting entity. On October 12, 1943, the FCC approved Noble's purchase, commenting that the transfer would serve "the public interest, convenience, and necessity." Two days later Noble took control of the National Broadcasting System's Blue Network, its 168 affiliates, owned and operated stations (O & O's), and 715 employees.

One year later, to the day, Noble purchased the name American Broadcasting Company from the owners of WOL in Washington, D.C., and at 8:14 A.M. on June 15, 1945, Jimmy Gibbons, WMAL's morning wake-up man in Washington, D.C., made history when he announced, "This is the American Broadcasting Company" to the now 197 affiliates.

But the $8 million proved only to be the price of admission. The American Broadcasting Company was making some small inroads into the radio market, including signing up Bing Crosby as its first big-name star and increasing its number of radio affiliates to 355. But the name of the game was changing rapidly from radio to television.

For example, ABC broadcast the second Joe Louis–Billy Conn heavyweight title fight in June of 1946 to a 67.8 Hooper rating, the highest for a single radio network broadcast. But NBC's *telecast* of the same fight caused the *Washington Post* to proclaim, "Television looks good for a thousand-year run." ABC, which had found itself third in the radio field, now found itself third in the television field. It was to be a costly game of catch-up ball.

Meanwhile, the government was playing cameo roles in the developing ABC story.

* * *

In Scottsdale, Pennsylvania, a small Gibbsville-type town in southwest Pennsylvania, on December 7, 1905, Lee and Esther Goldenson gave birth to a son, Leonard. Lee ran the local hardware store and desired great things for his talented and intelligent son. In 1923 Leonard was sent to Harvard and then on to Harvard Law School. However, Leonard Goldenson emerged from Harvard in 1930 in the midst of the Depression with an LL.B. and no prospect of finding a job. He went to New York City looking for work and, in his own words, "found no job in New York and went back to Pennsylvania to take the bar examinations."

Initially he had wanted to work in Senator Knox's law firm in Pittsburgh. But when two other Harvard classmates, one the son of a local judge, took positions in Senator Knox's firm, he went back to New York and "pounded the pavements" for nine more months in search of a job. The nine months proved to be a proper gestation period for Goldenson's ambitions. He eventually found employment in the firm of Charles Franklin, who represented a number of railroads including the powerful Southern Pacific. Another of Franklin's clients was Paramount Pictures, the film giant run by Adolph Zuckor.

As is frequently the case with young and ambitious junior partners in law firms, Goldenson left the employ of Franklin in 1933 to become counsel for his client, being brought over to reorganize Paramount's bankrupt New England theater operations. He was so successful at it that by 1937 he had become assistant to Y. Frank Freeman, vice-president in charge of theater operations for Paramount Pictures. He was promoted the following year to overall head of operations for the theater part of the film company. Four years later he became vice-president of Paramount.

But the times, thanks to the government, were changing. Immediately after the war the Anti-Trust Division of the Justice Department brought actions against eight of the giants in the film industry. These companies controlled both the making of films and the distribution of them in their wholly-owned theaters. The ensuing case, *U.S. v. Paramount, et al.*, went all the way to the Supreme Court, which affirmed the lower court's ruling that ordered an end to the monopolistic practices of controlling the distribution of films. The court further ordered the eight film companies—including Paramount, MGM, RKO, 20th Century Fox, Warner Brothers, Columbia, Universal, and United Artists—to divest themselves of their theater holdings. The 1948 decision initiated the fadeout of the big studios. And it was the start of a new beginning for Leonard Goldenson and Paramount Theatres.

Under a consent decree entered into by Paramount with the government in March 1949, the company agreed to separate its film-making and film-exhibiting operations. The 1,298 wholly or partly owned theaters became the property of one of the two successor companies, United Paramount Theatres, Inc. whose president was Leonard Goldenson.

By 1951, United Paramount had sold off several of its

theater chains. With its coffers overflowing from the proceeds of these sales, it immediately sought to invest in something that was a natural extension of its primary source of business. Goldenson, who firmly believed that television was "one of the greatest inventions to come down the line," was painfully aware that in markets of TV's greatest penetration movie attendance was dwindling and theaters were closing by the hundreds. His farsighted vision saw television as an allied endeavor in the entertainment business. So, in early 1951, Goldenson opened negotiations with Edward J. Noble and the cash-starved American Broadcasting Company.

* * *

Television is more defined by the laws of physics than by those imposed by government. Scientifically interlocked, there are but a limited number of channel availabilities before side-band interference from one channel begins to interfere with another channel's signal, making it look like venetian blinds. Thus, the closest channel 3 to the channel 3 in Philadelphia is the one in Hartford, Connecticut, and so on, across the country. Moreover, there are only about 200 television markets in the United States. The phrase *television market* is an engineering term, not a commercial one. Properly constructed, the television station allocation table looks like a giant jigsaw puzzle put together by a somewhat tipsy carpenter.

The carpenter in this case is the Federal Communications Commission, whose job it is to allocate television licenses based on the laws of physics. Shortly after World War II, the FCC began to issue licenses for channels in the VHF (very high frequency) spectrum for civilian broadcast stations. The FCC licensed channels 2 through 13 and reserved channel 1 for military use.

By 1948, the FCC had issued 108 licenses in some of the nation's largest cities before it called a "freeze" to study interference. According to a master's thesis written in 1959 by the now president of ABC Entertainment Fred Silverman:

The majority of choice stations were divided up among NBC and CBS before ABC began operations in 1948. These new channels in one- and two-station markets which had their choice of all three networks favored affiliation with the two older companies. This was understandable, for CBS and NBC, because of the extent of their financial resources, had been able (particularly in the early days of television when large losses were incurred) to give their affiliated stations a better program service than that supplied by ABC. . . . Consequently, in one- and two-station markets (and they included all but thirty-five markets in 1953), stations had a basic television affiliation with either NBC or CBS . . . and ABC could not possibly compete with its larger rivals. . . .

By the time the merger negotiations began, ABC had just fourteen "live" or primary affiliates, five of which it owned. In other instances it had a secondary affiliation with some sixty-seven other stations for some sort of a delayed telecast. But this was before the advent of videotape in 1958.

ABC was fast becoming the "Almost Broadcasting Company." It desperately needed cash, programs, affiliates, and sponsors, all interconnected in a vicious merry-go-round. Although Noble only partially recognized it, ABC also needed Goldenson's acumen and his knowledge of the entertainment world. It was to be a marriage of two orphans formed in a divestiture storm.

An agreement was reached between Goldenson and Noble that included the exchange of United Paramount Theatres, Inc. stock on the basis of 36/100ths shares for each share of American Broadcasting Company, Inc. stock. The agreement also included the prepayment of the $7,662,000 debt of the American Broadcasting Company. The existing corporation was to be known as American Broadcasting–Paramount Theatres, Inc.

When Goldenson brought the agreement before the board of directors of United Paramount Theatres in early 1951, the members proved reluctant to endorse it, for ABC's debt almost equaled its purchase price eight years earlier. According to Goldenson, "They argued 'til late at night," and then adjourned. But Goldenson, fired with his desire to acquire a broadcasting company and with his belief that the merger would propel his company into the forefront of the entertainment field, called Harry Haggerty, vice-chairman of Metropolitan Life, late that night.

Haggerty, in charge of Metropolitan Life's finances, had previously lent CBS money for expansion. He responded to Goldenson's passionate plea and pledged the necessary capital. In Goldenson's words, "Haggerty didn't think in their lifetime there would be more than three networks."

With this new financial support, Goldenson went back to the board the very next morning. It was the makeweight that "tipped the balance." The board of directors approved the merger and presented it to their stockholders on July 27, the very same day that ABC asked its stockholders for their approval. Both obtained the necessary consent and prepared to present the merger to the FCC. Goldenson vowed before the FCC that "we are going to build a third competitive force in network television."

On February 9, 1953, the FCC found that "the merger will provide ABC with the financial resources to carry out its plans to strengthen its programming and improve its physical plant and thereby provide substantial competition to the other networks."

The very next day an ad appeared in *Sponsor Magazine* that served as both a message to all that ABC was going to be a factor in the industry as well as a little whistling in the dark to show it wasn't afraid. The ad read: "ABC intends to be a leader in radio and TV and it intends to grow like an oak, not a mushroom."

Almost concurrent with the submission of the merger to the FCC for approval, the mysterious and wondrous hand of government intervened and indirectly blessed ABC. In April 1952, in its "Sixth Report and Order," the FCC ended its so-called "freeze" and announced that it would consider applications for a possible total of 562 VHF stations and seventy channels—14 to 83—in the UHF spectrum. It was "allez, allez, all-in-free," and the biggest beneficiary was to be ABC.

The new entity, American Broadcasting–Paramount Theatres, Inc., inherited a network lineup of fourteen "live" stations covering just 34.0 percent of the United States, gross billings of $21 million or 9.3 percent of the total network billings, and programming of less than twenty-four hours a week. Its programming schedule included "Ozzie and Harriet," "The Stu Erwin Show," "The Lone Ranger," and several less than memorable shows—like "Rootie Kazootie" and "Texas Wrestling"—that were cancelled by the end of the season.

With $30 million of United Paramount Theatre's capital flowing into the new corporation, radical and immediate improvements in programming, facilities, and personnel were made. In rapid succession ABC signed Ray Bolger, Danny Thomas, Georgie Jessel, Paul Hartman, Sammy Davis, Jr., and Joel Gray. And all of them, with the exception of Davis and Gray, appeared in the fall of 1953, the first television season after the merger.

However, ABC's primary thrust was still not aimed at creating programs. The network was far more interested in attracting sponsors. At that time most sponsors produced their own television shows and bought time on the television networks, much as they would buy space in a magazine. U.S. Steel brought forth the aptly named "U.S. Steel Hour," du Pont produced "Cavalcade of America," and Kraft bought the 9:30–10:00 Thursday night slot for the "Kraft Television Theatre." Although there was almost a 100 percent increase in sponsored programming over the preceding premerger season, 38 percent of programmed time still remained without a sponsor.

Advertisers held the purse strings and ABC became their handmaiden for precisely the same reason that Willie Sutton robbed banks: 'cause that's where the money was. It had been that way since 1941, when WNBT, the first commercial TV station licensed by the FCC, ran the very first commercial—a shot of a watch face and a voiceover intoning: "Bulova Watch Time—ten minutes after 10 (P.M.)." The cost to Bulova was $9.00. From such small acorns, mighty expensive oaks are grown.

* * *

Far above the merger, 1953 was an important year for ABC in another respect. Again it was Goldenson who played the architect. Realizing that ABC had to widen its base of operations, he foresaw that with most television markets operating as two-station VHF markets, the only way for ABC to gain access would be to pry one of the two away from NBC or CBS or acquire a UHF station. This access, of course, translated into added income, for once ABC had increased the number of stations carrying a particular program, it could increase its rates.

Before Goldenson arrived on the scene, Hollywood had come to view television networks with the same amount of affection that European countries lavished on invading Huns. Television was their sworn enemy—a far cry from today, when it is the rent payer. It had closed theaters and threatened Hollywood's very survival. The film studios had clauses in their talent contracts that actually prevented actors and actresses from appearing on television. Like the proverbial ostrich, they believed that if they ignored the one-eyed monster, it would go away. But Goldenson was not an enemy; he had come from their own ranks. He was family. This was his entrée—and ultimately ABC's entry into TV's competitive arena.

Walt Disney had never been a member of the movie moguls' club. He was a maverick and survived because of it. He had already produced a successful hour-long Christmas special for CBS and had been exploring the possibilities of producing a television series. Disney offered a package to both CBS and NBC, and both had turned it down out-of-hand because they viowod it as totally "unconscionable." At a time when the industry standard was thirty-nine original programs and thirteen repeats, the Disney package included twenty originals (half of which were movies), twenty second repeats, and twelve third repeats. His "deal" also included the financing of a dream he had harbored for years—the construction of an amusement park known, for lack of a better name—or maybe *because* it was a better name—as Disneyland.

Goldenson was then on the West Coast with ABC President Robert Kintner in tow, trying to woo Hollywood into developing and producing properties for TV. Goldenson not only saw the wisdom in pursuing the deal as laid out by Disney, but also the necessity of it if ABC were to become anything more than an also-ran. So, Goldenson lent Disney $500,000 to help finance the construction of Disneyland and in return received a 34.48 percent interest in Disneyland Incorporated. More importantly, Goldenson had acquired a weekly one-hour series and first-refusal rights for all other Disney products over a seven-year period. It was to be the deal that not only gave ABC its first hit, but also several more.

"Disneyland," the name of the show as well as the park, was scheduled for 7:30 on Wednesday night, the first time ABC had counter-programmed, pitting what they called a "kidult" show (appealing to both kids and adults) against news and musical shows. Station after station gave ABC clearance at the asked for time. The show was an instant success, immediately becoming ABC's first program on the all-important Nielsen top ten list. Just as importantly, it created a ripple effect. Audiences and advertisers suddenly became aware of ABC. Other Disney shows, like "Zorro" and "The Mickey Mouse Club," were to follow. Most important of all, the "majors," seeing the success of Disney and the manner in which he promoted his movies—like "Twenty Thousand Leagues Under the Sea"— now wanted in on the action before they were closed out forever.

Warner Brothers had been the first major studio to introduce sound into movies in 1927 when they produced *The Jazz Singer*, a revolutionary film that changed the face of Hollywood. Now, because of Leonard Goldenson's close friendship with Jack Warner, they would once again break ranks and become the first "major" to come to terms with the enemy—television.

The agreed-upon Warner Brothers package consisted of forty one-hour programs produced at a cost of $75,000 per show. All were to be produced for the 1955–56 season under the umbrella title "Warner Brothers Presents." The format was to be a trilogy consisting of three rotating series, each one based on an existing property—"King's Row," "Casablanca," and "Cheyenne"—with a ten-minute trailer at the end of each show called "Behind the Cameras," showing the Warner Brothers' stars at work on soon-to-be-released films. "King's Row," "Casablanca," and the trailer were soon dropped. But "Cheyenne," starring unknown Clint Walker, became an overnight hit. It was not only the beginning of the western, but the first realization that stars didn't make TV series, TV series made the stars.

Warner Brothers started pumping out westerns for ABC—"Sugarfoot," "Colt .45," "Lawman," and "Maverick." It ground out film after film while the other two networks were concentrating on live shows letting the horse chips fall where they might. But it soon became obvious that ABC was turning TV into a horse race and the rush was on as major studio after major studio staked a claim on TV's gold. Thus came into being "Wyatt Earp," "Gunsmoke," "Tales of the Texas Rangers," "Death Valley Days," "Wagon Train," "Frontier Adventures of Jim Bowie," and so on, ad nauseum.

Based on the success of "Disneyland," "Warner Brothers Presents" sold out to sponsors, sight unseen, and was put on at 7:30 on Tuesdays on the "live" affiliates and delayed on other stations that gave it clearance. With "Disney" on Wednesdays and "Warner Brothers" on Tuesdays, ABC was now two-sevenths of the way toward becoming a full-fledged network.

ABC now turned its attention to Saturday evenings. Charitably speaking, ABC's Saturday programming was weak. Nothing to compete with NBC's "Sid Caesar." No lead-ins. No lead-outs. No real programming, period. In 1955, Dodge brought a program to ABC which they wanted to put on. The program was "The Lawrence Welk Show," and it had met with modest success on the West Coast. But both CBS and NBC had turned it down for prime time. Although ABC got nothing more from Dodge than its out-of-pocket production costs and the money to compensate the stations for carrying the program, it scheduled it for Saturday night just, in the words of Julie Barnathan, then Supervisor of Ratings, "to open up Saturday night." It was a slow make. The first Nielsen figures showed that Lawrence Welk had a paltry 7 rating and a 13 share. But it built slowly, became a success, and ABC had broken through one more night.

It was like that on every other night as ABC slowly, inch by inch, became competitive. Sundays were built with "Maverick"; daytime with the "Mickey Mouse Club"; Thursdays with "Rin Tin Tin." It was guerilla warfare on a corporate level.

One trouble spot remained, however. Monday night. The lowest-rated show on ABC, the "Voice of Firestone," epitomized the Monday night schedule. Firestone had broadcast the "Voice of Firestone" since 1928 on first CBS and then NBC radio and television. The show was a tribute to Mrs. Firestone, who had written the memorable opening song ("If I could tell you of my devotion . . ."), and the family ritualistically gathered at the appointed hour to listen to, or in later years, watch, the program on Monday night. In realigning their nighttime schedule for the 1954–55 season, NBC replaced "The Voice of Firestone" with "Caesar's Hour." They offered the tire company other time slots, as did CBS, but Firestone rejected all of them, wanting to keep it on at the regular 8:30 P.M. time period on Mondays. ABC, with much time available and few programs, attracted Firestone and built Mondays around it.

By the 1958–59 television season, it had become one of the lowest-rated shows on television, managing only a 6.4 rating. It jeopardized the rest of Monday evening's schedule. When ABC decided to bolster its scheduling for the 1959–60 season, it went to Firestone and requested that the program be shown on Sunday afternoons. The Firestone family turned down the offer, claiming they couldn't get together to watch it at that time. (At a previous presentation by NBC to shift the program to Sundays, one of the Firestones had said, "Who watches TV on Sunday afternoon? They're all out playing polo.") So the "Voice of Firestone" was canceled. And with the last stumbling block to rearranging its scheduling removed, ABC was finally moving into the big time. Leonard Goldenson stated, "The ratings were down to nothing, it's been killing our whole Monday night schedule, and the audience that liked it— mainly older people—isn't the audience we want anyway. Now we can fill that time with a solid adventure show that'll pull a bigger and younger audience."

That statement was a sound marketing observation from a man who was to be called "a retailer, the Sears, Roebuck & Company of entertainment." No matter. Sears was a success. Why not ABC? And so, as the "Voice of Firestone" faded, ABC programmed more and more adventure shows for the so-called younger audience whose preferences were more fickle and who might just give ABC a "look-see" and stay with them.

ABC continued to invest money in the acquisition of talent and production of properties to further strengthen its schedule. Warner Brothers, Screen Gems, Desilu, Ziv, and several others were turning to ABC with a dizzying rapidity, upgrading the bill of fare and attracting greater audiences, more sponsors, and more stations. "The Donna Reed Show," "Dick Clark's American Bandstand," "Tombstone Territory," "The Real McCoys," "Make Room for Daddy," "Wyatt Earp," "Sunset Strip" and "The Untouchables" made it. "The Ray Anthony Show," "Polka-Go-Round," "The Mike Wallace Interview," and "The Frank Sinatra Show" didn't. Another show which didn't make it was a philosophical program featuring Bishop Fulton Sheen. It was counterprogrammed against Milton Berle. Sheen, who was also a Berle fan, lamented, "Now I can't even watch my favorite show."

Another failure was "The MGM Parade." Goldenson had announced the joint ABC–MGM venture as "a recognition of the present day joining together of Hollywood and television into a powerful force for entertainment." But "The MGM Parade" consisted only of old film footage publicizing MGM releases much like a thirty-minute version of "coming attractions." Although it didn't work, it indicated that Goldenson was willing to outbid both NBC and CBS for talent and for properties. ABC was on the right track, even if its misses outnumbered its hits.

ABC was still low man on the totem pole, and advertisers looked to it only when they were shut out of the other two networks or could buy time at bargain rates. Yet ABC's billings were slowly going up. From $21 million in 1953, representing but 9.3 percent of the total network sales, they reached $103 million in 1958 (18.2 percent of total network sales). By 1959, they would reach 20 percent. They were still behind, but it was now a two-and-a-half network race.

* * *

The success of any corporation can usually be traced to its leadership. Leaders usually make the corporation in their own image, and ABC executives were no different.

The first man to run the ABC Broadcasting Division under Goldenson was Robert Kintner. But friction soon developed between the two men, primarily because Goldenson albeit the description of many of being not only a gentleman but also a "gentle man" was dissatisfied with the progress of the network, despite its isolated hits. In October 1956, Kintner left, citing "irreconcilable differences" and taking with him a goodly grouping of his staff, became the president of one of ABC's rivals, NBC.

The next man appointed by Goldenson to head up the TV side was Oliver "Ollie" Treyz. Prior to becoming head of the Television Bureau of Advertising, Treyz had been at ABC in the sales and research departments. He was brought in by Goldenson not as president of the Broadcasting Division, Kintner's old position, but as vice-president of the Television Network, leaving the yawning vacuum of the network presidency open for Goldenson. Treyz was an ebullient man with a rapid and retentive mind. But he had a problem. In the words of one advertising agency executive, Treyz "would rather cut a deal with you than sell from the rate card." Treyz by some accounts was never happier than when he was working out some special arrangement with a sponsor or negotiating a multimillion dollar deal. The trouble was that some of his deals put ABC into difficult situations.

Yet, according to a former co-worker, Treyz "was really needed by ABC" at the time he was there. He changed the face of ABC's business, organizing things that had not been attended to by his predecessor and generally overseeing all elements of the operation. But, again, according to his then director of sales, "unfortunately, unlike Harry Truman, he did not grow in his job."

Treyz was on the spot to bring ABC further up the ladder in

its struggle from poverty. The major capital undertakings initiated by Goldenson started taking effect under Treyz. With a major infusion of capital, the entire schedule was revamped— including an $11 million face-lifting for Monday night alone— and some big guns were added, like "The Untouchables." Treyz's cut-rate wheeling-and-dealing started bearing fruit and billings went up, from $83 million in 1957 to $190-plus million in 1961, over 25 percent of total network billings. And ABC was still garnering affiliates, and for the first time held the lion's share of the audience in the cities where all three networks competed with equal "V" facilities. Treyz proudly proclaimed: "ABC has unlocked the dial. The day of the two-network economy is over." *Newsweek* magazine observed, "By 1961 ABC was just about even in the ratings war, thanks entirely to its arsenal of bowie knives and dum-dums."

It wasn't to be that easy, though, for Treyz or for ABC. The established formula of action-adventure shows and westerns began to get shot off one by one. The so-called "bread and butter" programming of ABC no longer provided consumer advertising sustenance as ABC began experiencing difficulties in rounding up a full slate of advertisers. Successful shows of previous years were no longer on the "Most Wanted" show list. And to top it all off, Treyz had locked ABC into several onerous contracts with program suppliers like Warner Brothers and 20th Century Fox. The contracts were exclusive with many production companies to insure their faithfulness, but they didn't guarantee the quality of what those "canning factories" produced. Viewers were offered such forgettables as "The Islanders," "Stagecoach West," "Hong Kong," "Guestward Ho!" and "Harrigan and Son." All of these shows proved to be failures during the disastrous 1960-61 season. Together they were largely responsible for Ollie Treyz's downfall.

In life, imitation is viewed as the sincerest form of flattery. In television, imitation is a way of life. The other networks followed the beaten path with more cowboys and private eyes. If westerns were a hit, the airwaves were flooded with westerns. If detective action-adventures were successful, there were detectives running all over the sets with guns drawn. And if situation comedies (called sitcoms) were "in," then the laugh tracks on all three networks were turned up to the highest level. There was safety in playing follow-the-leader and not being too innovative. It was always better to let your competitor make the first mistakes. Westerns and action-adventure shows were the first of many follow-the-leader games to be played in television programming throughout its first quarter century. But interestingly enough, the leader this time was ABC.

As it happens, ABC, NBC, and CBS were all founded and more or less developed by Jewish businessmen: David Sarnoff (NBC), William Paley (CBS), and Leonard Goldenson (ABC). And while all three were men of vision, they were also extremely pragmatic. They knew that in any business, especially in the highly visible world of broadcasting, the image a company projects is enormously important.

For a variety of reasons, all three felt that the best type of person to project an image for their networks was someone cast in the white Anglo-Saxon Protestant, Ivy League mold. Leonard Goldenson found just such a man in Tom Moore, whom he hired to be ABC's new vice-president of Television Programming and Talent.

Born in Meridian, Mississippi, in 1918, Tom Moore was a soft-spoken Southerner who exuded charm yet had a "ballsy" and determined way about him. Although not an Ivy League graduate, Moore was a gentleman of the old school who had all the necessary polish and sophistication. Unfortunately, none of his past experience had prepared him for the urban-Jewish culture that surrounded him in New York. And, in truth, even this would not have been noticeable had the network's general manager been anyone but Julie Barnathan. Julie was a no-bullshit kind of executive who not only came from Brooklyn, but *was* Brooklyn, through and through. When the two men stood side by side the scene looked like a Parisian conversing with a Corsican. It highlighted the differences between New York and Meridian.

Today Tom Moore bears a striking resemblance to Burl Ives,

sans beard, although the resemblance is tempered by an affable, open manner that puts you at ease the moment you meet him. Now the head of his own production company, Tomorrow Entertainment, viewers and critics know him best through such highly acclaimed programs as "The Scottsboro Boys." That particular show won not only critics' kudos, but also a pardon for one of the last surviving members of the group of blacks convicted more by racial prejudice than by evidence some forty years ago.

Although he couldn't have known it at the time, Leonard Goldenson set the network on a different course the day he asked Tom Moore to fill the spot vacated by Ollie Treyz. Moore was eventually to become president of ABC, but perhaps Jim McKay summed it up best when he said: "Tom Moore is most responsible for ABC going into sports with both feet. Somebody said he's crazy about two things—sports and shooting craps. When he's shooting craps with a sports show, he's in seventh heaven." In fact, for technical and governmental reasons, ABC once made a point of choosing channel 7 for its owned and operated stations in any market where the number was available. ABC's main phone number is LT 1–7777, and the extension of the chairman of the board is 7777. When you're aware of all that, McKay's remark is even more on target.

But the network presidency and ABC's dominance in sports programming were all in the future. The moment he became vice-president, Tom Moore faced the perplexing problem of recouping the losses brought on by the disastrous 1960–61 season.

First there were the affiliates. Moore and Barnathan personally went out to get any type of clearance for their shows to build up their bulk circulation. New primary affiliates were added in Syracuse, Rochester, Grand Rapids-Kalamazoo, Raleigh, and New Bedford-Providence, as the network's prime coverage rose to 93 percent of all TV homes. Then there was the programming. "Wagon Train" and "McHale's Navy" were added to the new schedule.

And so was Jerry Lewis. Once again Goldenson had sought

out high-priced talent to showcase in a variety show. The 1962 Annual Report, issued in the spring of 1963, proudly announced: "Since some shows in the current season did not measure up to anticipated audience levels, the network has already planned important innovations for the 1963–64 season. Jerry Lewis, one of the most popular and creative stars in the entertainment arts, will host an unprecedented two-hour variety show each week." ABC needed a big explosion, being deservedly third among the three networks, and figured Jerry Lewis was "it."

To set the charge, ABC bought the old Capitan Theatre on the corner of Hollywood and Vine, renamed it the Jerry Lewis Theatre, and even redecorated the bathroom with initialed "J.L." tiles—all to the tune of four hundred thousand dollars. In the middle of the preparations for the show, Edgar Scherick, then head of programming, remembers: "I can get very little dialogue about the content of the show from Jerry. The producer is walking around with this thick, black notebook and he keeps saying, 'It's all in here; it's all in here. The sketches, the dialogue, the monologues. . . . It's all in here.' Now as the show gets closer—and I've seen nothing—I'm in Lewis's office and he screams at another of his producers because the matchbook covers that said The Jerry Lewis Show hadn't come back yet. That's when I said to myself, 'We're in serious trouble.' "

And they were. The show that called itself "The most revolutionary show in TV history" featured Jack Jones's singing, Mort Sahl's jokes, and Jerry Lewis's conversational corner. It was a two-hour unrehearsed, unwritten, unmitigated disaster, and it was gone by the end of 1963 after a run of less than thirteen weeks. One ABC executive remembers that because they bought out Lewis's multimillion-dollar contract, there were no Christmas bonuses for that year.

In order to salvage Saturday night, the theater in which they had invested so much money and their reputation—which at this time was in a shambles with all the wags saying "ABC can't do anything live"—Moore and Scherick decided to replace it with "The Hollywood Palace," using a rotating host every week, like Bing Crosby and George Burns. While never reaching the expectations held out for the "Jerry Lewis Show," "The Hollywood Palace" valiantly filled the void for five years. It was also the first show on which ABC used live color cameras.

* * *

As ABC moved up in the entertainment world, it also moved out in the world. When the merger took place in 1953, the ABC corporate offices were still housed at 30 Rockefeller Plaza, a throwback to the days when they were still NBC's Blue Network. Realizing that the hindquarters of broadcasting would need headquarters, Noble had initiated an expansion program some five years before when he rented the former West 66th Street arena used by the New York Riding Club. The following year ABC purchased the block-long property and began a $3 million renovation program that would provide the fledgling network with studios and facilities for its burgeoning television network. By the early fifties they were ready for occupancy.

The complex of buildings on 66th Street, soon known as "7 West" in honor of one of its addresses, was perfect for the needs of ABC. Its large doors, once used for the horses of the riding academy, could now be used for getting trucks in and out of the building. Riding rings, which provided ample room for the construction of several TV studios, included Studio A, called "the greatest TV studio in the world," large enough to accommodate the exterior shots for a "U.S. Steel Hour" show, the first "outdoors" production in a New York studio. Of course, as a former riding academy, the building did possess some distinct disadvantages. On rainy or humid days, the personnel could smell the redolent odor of horse manure, more a vestigial reminder of the former tenants than a commentary on the shows being produced there.

But even the complex of buildings on 66th Street, resembling as it did the skyline of Kansas City, circa 1900, did not possess adequate room for all of ABC. So additional facilities were purchased on West 70th Street. All of the production facilities were housed at this location—the carpentry shop, graphic arts, prop shop, costumes, design shop, and art department. The building was a renovated garage where years before the famed Texas Club, a speakeasy run by Texas "Hello, Sucker" Guinan, stood on the top floor. While ABC was not yet a far-flung network, its offices certainly were. Before long a third group of properties on 68th at Broadway was added. Located over an A&P, ("If I had my life to live over, I'd live over an A&P", remembers one former ABC staffer), the space was used by all the service departments, including research, publicity, and sales development.

But what had once been satisfactory in the early fifties was no longer adequate by the end of the decade. One executive called it bedlam and said, "Everybody was living in everybody else's lap." So Goldenson started a search for land on which to build larger facilities. For years Goldenson had been buying property around Columbus Circle, particularly the area where the old St. Nicholas Arena used to stand, across from Lincoln Center. One day he hoped to build an ABC building there to form a cultural complex that would "rub off both ways." He commissioned Charles Luckman to design a conical building, something along the lines of the new Transamerica Building in San Francisco, complete with a spire on top. But when the bids came in at between $68 and $70 million, Goldenson promptly lost his enthusiasm.

Faced with the unaffordable prospect of building his own building for ABC, Goldenson next sought a building that could be leased.

One winter day in 1964 a realtor came into the offices of Si Siegel, the treasurer of ABC, and showed him a large schematic drawing of a building that was going up on the Avenue of the Americas across the street from CBS. The only tenants that had "committed" up to that point were Meyer Brothers, a parking concern in the basement, and the Central Savings Bank. Siegel took one look at the plans, asked if he could borrow the folder containing them, and walked through the bathroom that connected his office with that of Tom Moore. "What do you think of this?" asked Siegel in a con-spiratorial tone. Moore looked at it and when Siegel told him that they only had two tenants in an entire forty-story building already under construction, Moore said, "Hell, let's buy the fuckin' thing." In a matter of weeks the negotiations had been concluded, and ABC had leased the building with an option to buy in fee simple the ground and the building for $17 million.

ABC then took possession of the completed shell that looked like a giant erector set, and promptly hired a firm to redesign the interior of the building for $3 million more. One of the things Goldenson wanted was a studio on the corner of the building, so that people could look in on the program then originating there. What he had forgotten was that there was to be no programming originating from the building. That part of the operation was to remain at "7 West." So, when ABC moved its executive offices to 1330 Avenue of the Americas (called Sixth Avenue by most New Yorkers) in the fall of 1965, one corner remained conspicuously empty. When the plan to use that space for promotion failed, it was leased to Loft's as a candy store.

The incorporation of a Loft's candy store into the new ABC Building gave rise to one of many jokes about the building. At first, because the new building was next to the CBS Building on the east side of the Avenue of the Americas, many broadcasting wags called it "The crate that the CBS Building came in." Inasmuch as many had referred to Goldenson's one-man operation as a "candy store" for years, they now found it serendipitous that an actual candy store was on the ground floor of the new building. Still others tried to hang a tag on the building that stood cheek by jowl with the other network buildings in what is called "Broadcast Row." Just as NBC was "30 Rock" and the black granite CBS Building was "Black Rock" (either because of its color or because of the picture that starred Spencer Tracy), they gave the ABC Building the sobriquets of "Little Rock" after Tom Moore's southern heritage, "Schlock Rock" after some of its programming, and even "Hard Rock" referring to ABC's continual bad luck.

Today, as ABC has moved to the king-of-the-mountain position, a second bank, appropriately enough, can be found where the old candy store once stood. And the ABC Building that straddles the east side of Sixth Avenue between 53rd and 54th like the colossus of Rhodes, is known as "Hot Rock."

* * *

The new team of Moore and Barnathan had started planning for their first big season, the 1964–65 season, right from the start of their appointments on March 17, 1962. It usually takes at least one and a half to two years to implement your own plans and turn things around. And here they were! It was heralded as "The New ABC." No more Jerry Lewises. This time ABC premiered two weeks earlier than either CBS or NBC. By getting out of the blocks with some quality shows, the first national Nielsen ratings for the new season showed that ABC had five of the top ten shows: "Bewitched" (2), "My Three Sons" (4), "The Fugitive" (5), "The Addams Family" (8), and "Combat" (9).

The season was also notable for the introduction of the twice-a-week "soaper" "Peyton Place" and a teeny-bopper show called "Shindig." The former proved that there was a place for sex, even if watered down, on TV. The second showed that ABC now fully recognized the importance of— and programmed for—the younger generation. This was to be the beginning of ABC's acquisition of a younger, more urban audience, as contrasted with CBS's rural audience, which was, even on that first Nielsen rating, showing signs of tiring. ("The Beverly Hillbillies," which had been first for two straight years, plummeted to twenty-first.) CBS, which had been taking advantage of its deep penetration into the rural areas—courtesy of its strong signal on the lower channels—had handcuffed itself to an audience that was almost unsaleable to advertisers.

But even if ABC had made it a three-way contest for the first time on a national scale, there were still some dark rumblings in the skies. Paul Klein, the venerable NBC researcher, told Julie Barnathan, "Even though we're all even-steven now, we'll still be first, because we're in color!" And he was right. The exploding color growth gave the networks that telecast in color an advantage. Once again, ABC was the disadvantaged network.

* * *

The accelerating use and acceptance of color forced ABC's hand. Competitive developments by the other networks demanded that ABC appropriate $600,000 for "designs and plans" for production facilities with live color capabilities in both New York and Hollywood as early as December 1964. Goldenson and Siegel obtained $27 million in new financing to underwrite this and other color development costs. Just when it looked as if ABC had, indeed, caught NBC and CBS, it was going to be another game of "catch-up."

Sensing that almost $113 million in expenditures was needed to finance a complete conversion to color broadcasting, Goldenson looked for another avenue of ready cash—a merger with an existing company that had enough money to bail out ABC.

While Goldenson was negotiating with several possible suitors, Norton Simon of Hunt Foods & Industries made a run at ABC. Sensing that it was his for the taking, Simon bought 400,000 shares, or 9 percent of the outstanding ABC stock. But knowing Simon's proclivity for "reappraising" the management of companies he had taken over—including the usual ouster of one or more of the executive heads—Goldenson had other thoughts on the matter.

Goldenson held off Simon's bid by denying him a seat on the board of directors while he continued actively to pursue a liaison that would not only give his company the monies it needed, but also give him the best tax advantages. That meant a tax-free stock exchange rather than a taxable cash buy-out. On December 7, 1965, his sixtieth birthday, Goldenson announced that he had found the long sought after partner: the multinational International Telephone and Telegraph Corporation.

The two companies approved the merger two months later on the basis of one share for every ⅝ share of ABC stock, and late in 1966 the FCC gave its blessings to the union by a 4–3 vote. The future looked rosy—so rosy, in fact, that ITT forwarded ABC $25 million "on account" and threw a massive black-tie dinner at the New York Hilton with Louis Armstrong performing to celebrate the marriage.

But it was not to be. The Department of Justice waited until the very last moment to throw a monkey wrench into the best laid plans of the two corporations, asking the FCC to stay the merger planned for February 1, 1967, just hours before it was to become final. Leonard Goldenson was on the West Coast in a joyous mood on the evening of January 18, 1967, when a phone call came to him in his hotel suite. A "Mr. Jenkins from the Justice Department" was calling and told Goldenson that they were investigating the merger. Goldenson excused himself from his gathered guests and went into the next room to compose himself. He ultimately reentered, but instead of being the ebullient host of moments ago, he now resembled a wilted head of lettuce.

For the remainder of the year, the Justice Department continued its investigation, basing it in part on ITT's foreign investments and the contention that such activities would compromise the independence of ABC's news coverage. The Justice Department also put forward its belief that ABC did not need ITT financing, as well as some other legal gobbledygook to fill up pages about the merger's effects on technological progress and other such speculations. In short, the thrust of their claim was that ITT might manage the news because of its multinational operations, and if necessary, they pledged to appeal the FCC approval all the way to the Supreme Court.

Coupled with this full-court stall, two other factors convinced ITT that they should call off the deal. One was a confidential study of the ABC management, commissioned by ITT's Chairman Harold Geneen. The study found that middle-ranking executives at ABC had little confidence in their superiors. The second, and most compelling factor, was the rise of ITT stock. When the merger was originally announced, ITT was selling for $72. Two years later it was around $116. The deal as originally conceived was a $388 million package. Now it was about a $620 million acquisition. Facing a "go, no-go" date, Geneen convened a special meeting of ITT's board of directors at 8:00 on New Year's morning 1968, for the express purpose of dissolving the merger.

ABC was devastated. All of their planning, their programming, and their personnel had ground to a halt pending the merger. In 1968 the network lost $20 million. It was the worst year it had ever had. Waiting for the merger to take place had seriously weakened both the network and the corporation. Goldenson, while delivering a "Let's-win-this-one-for-the- Gipper" speech to the press ("The collapse of the deal was a good thing. It made us realize that we have to make it ourselves"), kept talking to other prospective suitors, including CIT, Monogram Industries, and even Sears, Roebuck & Company, and Ford.

But while Goldenson was out shopping for a partner, a prospector was staking out a take-over claim. It was none other than Howard Hughes, the eccentric and invisible multi-millionaire, who only two years before had declined to make an appearance in a court suit against TWA costing him his holdings but netting him $350 million in cash. It was that cash that he was now using in offering to buy two million shares—approximately 43 percent of ABC—at $74.25 per share when the stock was selling for only $55 (a total of $148 million).

Hughes had calculated that ABC's weakened position would make it vulnerable. He further reckoned that because ABC was in registration for additional capitalization they couldn't discuss their financial dealings, including the take-over bid, with their stockholders. But Hughes hadn't figured on Goldenson's determination. Goldenson carefully selected the arena for the fight: the FCC, which must approve all license transfers. Hughes already owned a Las Vegas TV station and the ABC properties would put him one over the limit allowed by the FCC. He would have to appear personally. Hughes backed off. "If Leonard Goldenson doesn't want me at ABC—forget it," he said, and he remained off-camera.

The government had played a major role in maintaining ABC for Goldenson and Goldenson for ABC. Before he probably hadn't fully appreciated the true potential of what he had; however, he did now.

* * *

Like the figures issued by the Elias Sports Bureau, inscribing each player's at-bats and hits for posterity and officially providing a list of the leading hitters of any one year, the figures put out by the A. C. Nielsen Company proclaim each television season's "hits" and "errors." The pulsebeat and other vital life signs of any television show are measured by the organization that is as important to the television industry as the networks themselves. Where network TV execs are only as "good as their last Nielsen," the men from N.I.E.L.S.E.N. are so much a part of the industry that they have offices on Sixth Avenue along Broadcast Row.

Yet their methods—more a spinal tap than a complete physical of each show—are so misunderstood that even some advertisers don't fully comprehend how television audiences are measured; one agency executive even pasted the definitions over his desk much like the accountant who kept a note in his desk reading "The debit side is the side towards the window." In much the same manner as a box-office count would indicate the number who have attended a ball game, so, too, would the Nielsen sample indicate how many people were watching a given show. For the consumer is in and of himself a consumer whom advertisers are buying in number. It's a body count, pure and simple, and it's done through a statistical method known as sampling. Instead of counting each of the country's 71 million TV households, an electronic device known as an Audimeter is attached to one or more television sets in 1,170 specially selected TV households around the country. The locations are chosen so that the entire sample will reflect the income level, viewing preferences, and geographic makeup of the entire United States. Thus, each of those 1,170 households represents 60,684 TV households, and what they watch reflects the viewing preference of the entire group.

The audimeter is smaller than a cigar box, and as one Nielsen household head said recently, "may be spreading Legionnaire's disease, for all I know." Its influence on the programming of the networks is incalculable.

By turning the channel selector, which, in turn, is wired to the audimeter, the Nielsen household registers its preference for a show. That viewing information is stored for later retrieval by a Nielsen Central Office computer. The retrieval takes five seconds and is performed by simply dialing a phone number. The preferences of the 1,170 households are then expressed in ballpark figures that read like casualty counts from a gory battle; these are the "numbers" that run the industry. New numbers come out every two weeks in something called

"The Nielsen pocketpiece." They break down every show run during the previous two weeks on a quarter-hour basis.

The two most important words, as vital to the television industry as the words *sue* and *collect* are to a lawyer, are *ratings* and *share*. *Ratings* are a percentage of *all* the TV homes in the country—whether on or off—that are tuned to a given program. *Share* is expressed as a percentage of all those sets that are on and tuned to a given program. Thus, if only 50 percent of all TV sets in America are on and all are watching the film *Godzilla Eats French Lick, Indiana,* the rating is 50 percent and the share 100 percent. If there are three great Godzilla movies on at the same time on the different networks (Godzilla Meets Gidget, Godzilla Joins Weight Watchers, and Godzilla Is a Credit to His Race), and if 50 percent of all sets are turned on and ". . . Gidget" is being watched on half of them, ". . . Weight Watchers" on three-tenths of the remainder, and the other one-fifth of those remaining are tuned to ". . . Credit to His Race," the ratings for the three are respectively 25.0, 15.0, and 10.0. The shares, which make it possible to compare the ability of these three award-winning flicks to attract equally moronic viewers, are 50.0, 30.0, and 20.0.

It is noteworthy that no television executive ever just says a program is "terrific" or "sucks," but couches his reference in the accepted Nielsen phraseology, and the results are relied on totally by entire research departments at each and every network. They massage the numbers like Aladdin would his lamp, looking for any and all magic in them. To be below the magic number of 30 in share (meaning that you captured 30 percent of those who had their sets turned on at that specific time), is fatal; it is on that basis that shows are made, broken, and sold.

One Nielsen rating point on a prime time show equals approximately $1 million in commercial billing over fifty-two weeks on *that* show. A Dean, Witter study demonstrates that an entire network's margin of 1 rating point over its rivals over the fifty-two-week period can equal up to $50 million. These confusing terms, then, are important, for they represent megabucks.

When ABC announced it was canceling "Dick Cavett," his guest, Jack Paar, advised the viewers to phone or write the rating service to let them know what show they were watching. But as one executive points out, "100,000 letters are less than two-tenths of one rating point."

But if the explanation of how the Nielsens work is confusing to you, even the founder, A. C. Nielsen, had difficulty explaining it to Edward R. Murrow on the old "Person to Person" show. Murrow had asked Nielsen to demonstrate the fabled gizmo known as a TV audimeter (and pronounced "autometer" by Nielsen). Nielsen told him, "All the householder does is to drop a film clip or magazine into a slot; two quarters pop out as a reward, and the audimeter is ready to measure TV viewing again." Then, as he walked over to demonstrate it, he said, it was "so simple that even a child could do it." But it took old man Nielsen three tries. He later found out that the factory had made a group of film magazines with the directional arrow on the wrong side.

Perhaps the only person ever to have put the Nielsen figures in their proper perspective is Art Buchwald, who said, "If one Nielsen household turns off its set and goes out to visit its grandmother, I guess that means that there are 60,000 other households visiting theirs."

During the two years ABC waited for, in President Elton Rule's words, "the cavalry from ITT," everything had ground to a halt, and worse, turned to dung. Its shows were a television wasteland. The 1966–67 season was a total disaster. Of the thirty-one programs ABC put in prime time, only three (all returning series) placed in the top third of the ninety-one prime time shows in the October-November-December Nielsens. And only the old standby, "Bewitched," cracked the top twenty. They were putting "every pilot program, everything we had in development—good or bad and mostly bad—on the air." Things were so bad that replacements had to be brought up in droves that January. So many, in fact, that ABC heralded their arrival with consummate chutzpah as "The Second Season," an attempt to make chicken salad out of what many felt were chicken droppings.

* * *

The forty-story ABC building, which straddles Manhattan's Sixth Avenue between 53rd and 54th streets.

Roone Arledge, Leonard Goldenson, chairman of the board, and Elton Rule, president of ABC, greet a group of Russian gymnasts at a reception in ABC's executive offices on the fortieth floor.

Three of the early "Wide World" team—Chuck Howard, producer, Mac Hemion, director, and Chris Schenkel, announcer—assume the stance of crouching catchers to form a semicircle around a hidden camera at one of the jumps at the Grand National Steeplechase in Aintree, England.

"Wide World" host Jim McKay prepares to do the "scene set" for an upcoming IROC (International Race of Champions) event from Michigan International Speedway.

Chuck Howard.

Roone Arledge (on the phone); Phil Levens, engineering supervisor; Julie Barnathan, vice-president in charge of Broadcast Operations and Engineering; Elton Rule, president of ABC; and Chuck Howard, vice-president of Program Production, discuss some of the events to be covered in the upcoming Grenoble games.

Roone by LeRoy Neiman.

Expert commentator George Foreman with Howard Cosell (sporting the earpiece for the Interrupted Feedback communication system with the producer and director), await the start of the Jimmy Young–Ron Lyle heavyweight fight.

The dynamic duo of Muhammad Ali and Howard Cosell, each trying to "float like a butterfly and sting like a bee. . . ."

Jim McKay, host of ABC's "Wide World of Sports" since it first began in April 1961, sets the scene for the World Lumberjack Championships at Hayward, Wisconsin, while precariously balanced on a log and directing his comments to a national audience through the technological magic of the mini-cam.

Bill Russell, here with co-announcer Keith Jackson, brought something special besides his six-foot-ten-inch size to NBA basketball telecasts.

Roone Arledge giving directions to a cameraman replete with wet suit and snorkle and holding a specially devised waterproof camera for an underwater shot; one of the many unusual shots Arledge has pioneered.

Jim McKay heads a "Wide World of Sports" skiing segment with expert commentator Bob Beattie supplying the expertise.

Against a backdrop of the Lago General Paz on the Argentine–Chilean border, Curt Gowdy explains the scoring system used to judge the World Record Trout Fishing Expedition, a "Wide World of Sports" show that served as the prototype for the "American Sportsman."

ABC's "Wide World of Sports" announcer Bill Flemming conducts an interview with a wingwalker while standing atop Cliff Winters's Stearman biplane at the National Air Races in Chino, California, 1963. The next day the pilot was killed performing a stunt.

Roone Arledge presenting ABC's "Wide World of Sports" Athlete of the Year Award in 1972 to Russian gymnast Olga Korbut.

Edgar Scherick and Michael Caine on the set of "Sleuth."

ABC shows now came and went without much fanfare. As 1967 turned into 1968 and 1969, ABC was canceling shows at an alarming rate. Things were so bad that Milton Berle quipped, "If they wanted to end the Vietnam War, they should have scheduled it on ABC. It would have ended in 13 weeks."

But slowly a new formula started taking effect. It was youth-oriented and made up largely of situation comedies and action-adventure shows. The cancellations were becoming fewer and fewer, the ratings higher and higher. And suddenly ABC was a viable competitor, counterprogramming and counterjabbing the other networks to death, all the time capturing the attention and the hearts of the younger, urban households.

Two factors helped bring this about. The first was not of ABC's doing but of the FCC's. Having created ABC and its parent company by divestitures, the FCC subtly wrought the equalization of all three networks with a prime time access rule, ruling that the 7:30–8:00 P.M. period was to be returned to the affiliates. Only ABC, of the three networks, supported the FCC's decision. And for good reason. They were the only ones to gain by it. It was a time period that had been, at best, a problem area for ABC ever since it had gained an almost equal footing with the other two networks. But now ABC could free almost $20 million that would otherwise have been poured into the development and production of new programs for that time period. Now ABC could better use that money to create better prime time shows.

The second factor derived from the annulment of the ITT–ABC marriage. The merger's failure made ABC realize that if, indeed, they were going to do it alone, they were sorely in need of a managerial reorganization. A changing of the guard was called for, and Elton Rule, a Hollywood-handsome look-alike for F.D.R., was brought in from ABC's O & O station in Los Angeles to take over for Tom Moore. Moore was gracefully promoted in 1968 to a position of overseer and then let go, a marked and enthusiastic change from the public beheadings of years before.

From the time Goldenson made him president of ABC–TV in 1968, Rule began to provide sharp focus to ABC's programming. Instead of merely offering small islands of strength to be swallowed up by surrounding seas of supportive and weak programming, he turned his attention to developing sustained strength throughout the schedule. He sought an incremental ratings gain of 5 percent per year for all prime time ratings. For the first three years he attained his goal, as the prime time ratings went from 15.6 in the 1968–69 season to 16.5, 17.5, and 18.7 the following three years.

The next three seasons were anything but a success for ABC. By 1974–75, their prime time ratings had fallen back to their 1969–70 level, a 16.5. But CBS, the longtime ratings champion, had locked itself into a formula-corner, programming for older and more rural audiences with their "hicks and sticks" programming of the "Beverly Hillbillies," "Green Acres," "Andy Griffith," and "Gomer Pyle." They could be had. And ABC's youth-oriented programming was to be the alternative.

With only four of the sixteen new programs introduced in the 1974–75 season showing any strength, Rule brought in Fred Pierce, head of television planning, to become the president of the television division. Pierce, while in charge of program planning, had developed a concept known as "building blocks." His plan was to develop entire evenings around a given program that would serve both as a lead-in and a lead-out to other programming. If one show failed, the entire evening was ripped out and rebuilt until the right formula was found. Also, instead of viewing the 8 P.M. slot as the backbone of the evening's programming, Pierce saw the 9 P.M. show as the pivotal one—"Monday Night Football" was to be Monday's; "The Rookies," Tuesday's; "Baretta," Wednesday's; "The Streets of San Francisco," Thursday's, and so forth.

Pierce was begrudgingly called "the secret to ABC's whole success" by NBC's vice-president for programming, Paul Klein, as he brought to ABC—and the nation's screens—"Baretta," "Welcome Back, Kotter," and Barbara Walters. He even moved "Six-Million- Dollar Man" to Sunday nights, making it an instant success.

But it was not just his restructuring of the evening's programming that was to lead to ABC's emergence as the number one network. It was a move he made in May 1975 that was to be the catalyst that took ABC over the top. For on the twenty-first day of May, Fred Pierce announced that Freddie Silverman, CBS's ace programmer, would become ABC's new president of ABC Entertainment. Not only did this bold move give ABC an innovative and dedicated programming genius, while, not incidentally depriving CBS of his services, but it was also received on "the street" with such enthusiasm that ABC's stock rose almost two points that same day. In one bold stroke, ABC had "arrived" for all to see.

Silverman applied his special talents to the upcoming 1975–76 season almost immediately. He made Fonzie the central character in "Happy Days," spun off "Laverne and Shirley," and developed the characters in other ABC shows, including the smash hit, "Charlie's Angels." To many Fred Silverman is the man who made ABC number one.

An intense man who has been described as a hard worker, Silverman's idea of a good time is watching television, and his idea of an exciting conversation is talking about it. Tom Heath, executive vice-president of Leo Burnett Advertising Agency in Chicago, remembers having lunch with him once. Heath believed that his across-the-table companion was not paying attention to him. That is, until he made a suggestion on a kid's television program. Then Silverman lit up, "That's a good idea. A good idea." He immediately incorporated it into the overall programming. "He was not so proud that he couldn't identify a good idea and appropriate it," Heath said.

Silverman is not paralyzed by the common failing of many executives, the not-invented-here syndrome. He will take suggestions—as long as they're good—from anyone. "The product is what he's most interested in," recalls Heath. And the product is what he got. And so this man, who had written his master's thesis at Ohio State on ABC's programming from the time of the Paramount merger until 1960 and then couldn't get a job with ABC until 1975, was instrumental in taking the network over the top.

ABC is no longer the butt of all the jokes on Broadcast Row. Twenty-five years after it began, the American Broadcasting Company had arrived. The little network that could, did.

2
The Making of ABC Sports

No single factor can ever be totally responsible for a network's rise to the top, any more than a single move in chess can be totally responsible for winning a game. In both cases, success can only come from a *combination* of things. But just as a chess master can build a winning strategy around a single piece, a network can move its way to the top with a single area of programming.

In the case of ABC, that area was sports. ABC Sports was number one long before the network as a whole earned that title. Sports programming put ABC on the television map. It provided income and prestige at a time when there was precious little of either to be had from the network's other divisions. And it provided a much needed focal point for ABC's future ascent.

* * *

Of course, many people are responsible for the success of sports programming at ABC. But one who was an especially key figure in developing the area is Edgar J. Scherick.

Today Scherick is president of Palomar Pictures International, the highly successful motion picture company that produced such movies as *Sleuth*, *For the Love of Ivy*, *The Taking of Pelham, One, Two, Three*, and *Take the Money and Run*. He looks something like a cross between a mature Michael Caine with white mane and glasses and Dr. Silvana, the mad genius

in Captain Marvel. Described by many of his former colleagues as a high-strung Mad Hatter, Scherick was a combination midwife, clairvoyant, and public-address system for the
coming sports revolution on TV in the late 1950s. Today, as he
alternately sits near and paces by his California swimming
pool, he shows no signs of letting up. After more than twenty
years in the communications industry, he's still throwing off
kinetic sparks.

A magna cum laude Phi Beta Kappa graduate of Harvard,
Scherick's first job after college was as the assistant campaign
manager for Boston's mayoralty candidate John B. Hynes, who
successfully defeated incumbent Mayor James Michael Curley
in what has become memorialized in politics as *The Last Hur-
rah.* Finding no way to further his ambition of breaking into
broadcasting, Scherick came back to his native New York to
look for a job. Like most youngsters attracted to New York, he
tried everywhere, including NBC, but found no openings. And
then in that tried-and-true occurrence that takes place so frequently, he saw an ad in *The New York Times* which read:
"Time Buyer Wanted." The small type read, "Must know Nielsens." Scherick's response was "Well, I know what a time
buyer is, but where do I meet this guy Nielsens?"

The ad had been placed by Dancer Fitzgerald Sample,
one of Madison Avenue's top ten advertising agencies. Jimmy
Neale, the head of media at DFS, said, "He has no experience." But Lyndon Brown, head of marketing, said, "Don't let
that young man get out of the agency without giving him a
job." And so, Scherick insinuated himself into one of the country's foremost advertising agencies just by being there and being himself. Scherick served first as a time buyer and then as
media supervisor on the Falstaff beer account. Later, he became director of sports and special events. ("Actually, I took a
sword and dubbed my own shoulder.")

One day, as Scherick remembers, he was thumbing through
the hundreds of circulars sent out by local stations to New
York agencies—all trying to crack the computer curtain and
all crying "Buy us"—when he chanced across one from KMTV
in Omaha. It simply read: "Available locally, the Chicago Cardinals and the Chicago Bears." Scherick thought, "How in hell

can the Chicago Cards and the Chicago Bears be going into Omaha?" Investigating further, he found that in those pre-CBS–NFL days, WBKB in Chicago had made a deal with both teams to telecast their home games over a network of from thirty to forty stations, all of which belonged to ABC. Scherick went to his supervisor, the man who had hired him, Jimmy Neale, and told him of his discovery. Moreover, the area covered by the network also seemed to overlap a key sales area for Falstaff. It would be "a terrific time buy" for a beer whose basic marketing strategy was in part predicated on an association with sports. Neale liked it, and together they went to see ABC President Robert Kintner, who, according to Scherick, "didn't even know that the games were on a regional ABC network." They told Kintner that they wanted to buy half sponsorship. It was Falstaff's first taste of sports on a network basis. And Scherick's too.

* * *

Sometime in early 1954 Scherick devised a plan for his client Falstaff to sponsor baseball on network TV. They had had great success broadcasting the St. Louis Cardinals and Browns games locally. The concept was to black out the major league cities and cover only the 48 percent of the country then supporting minor league baseball. That 48 percent of the country might not have been attractive for a national advertiser, but it was perfect for Falstaff.

In presenting his TV plan to the major leagues, Scherick found them to be afraid of it. And "they were right to be." But if the major leagues were afraid of the baseball game of the week conceived by Scherick, the minor leagues were terrified. The minor leagues in 1954 were a viable and going concern. There were thirty-six minor leagues—as opposed to today's twenty—with 307 local teams playing to a combined attendance of well over 19 million, 3 million more than major league baseball. The televising of major league baseball into those minor league cities, providing *major* league games free to potential fans who might otherwise have gone to see their local *minor* league team, was to cripple baseball at its grass roots. Scherick saw this. He worked out a compensation plan to reimburse the minor leagues for the loss of potential fans.

But when he went before the Broadcast Committee of the National Association of Baseball to present his compensation plan, their reaction was, "It's spinach and the hell with it." They turned up their collective noses at the offer.

Traditionally baseball has put its head in the sand and hoped its problems would go away. But solving problems that way doesn't work and didn't this time either. Scherick, Dancer-Fitz, and Falstaff were all committed to televising network baseball, and they were going to do it—with or without the sanction of the minor leagues. So instead, they lined up the Indians, the White Sox, the Philadelphia A's, the New York Giants, and Dizzy Dean.

Dean was an authentic original, a man of tremendous baseball instincts and humor who not only broke into spontaneous a capella renditions of "The Wabash Cannonball" on the air but had a lovable homegrown Arkansas drawl as well. While to many, his constant use of the word *slud* when a player slid into base was as grating as fingernails scratching across a blackboard, it was nevertheless vintage Dean. He was an American tintype who was smart enough to do what he had to do and did it well.

* * *

Network sports was on the move. And now Ed Scherick was ready to move on to more challenging things.

When the "Game of the Week" moved to CBS in 1955, Tom Dawson, the national sales manager for the network, approached Scherick to find out whether he was interested in becoming the head of sports. Scherick admitted he was intrigued by the idea. When Dawson further asked him what he thought of the operation, Scherick brashly and truthfully responded, "it could be improved." But in the end CBS wound up hiring the head of promotions and publicity for the Kansas City A's, Bill MacPhail, and Scherick was to wait another year before he moved over to the then number one network under MacPhail.

Between the year that MacPhail joined CBS and Scherick followed, CBS attempted to acquire the rights to the NFL games. They included Dancer Fitzgerald Sample in all of their meetings as the advertising agency for Falstaff, a potentially important initial buyer of the NFL games. But more importantly, DFS, which had put together the baseball "Game of the Week," was experienced, and no one was more experienced in network sports then than Media Director Ed Scherick. And so, soon after CBS's acquisition of the rights to the NFL games, now needing someone to put the regional NFL networks together and prepare them for the sponsors, they once again approached Scherick. He was brought over as sports specialist, one of those Wizard-of-Oz–type titles that abound in the communications business.

Scherick hadn't been at CBS eight months before he became acutely aware of the time-honored problem that has always bedeviled network TV—the scarcity of sports events for airing during the first quarter of the year. Between the end of football and the beginning of baseball, it was almost a "dark" season.

The only sports programming that CBS had on during that time was Big Ten basketball. But it wasn't working and was on the verge of receiving its pink slip from the network.

Scherick picked up the phone and called Bill Reed, then Big Ten Commissioner Tug Wilson's lieutenant, who would, in 1961, succeed Wilson as the commissioner of the conference. "Bill, you're getting canceled by CBS. You'll never make it as a national vehicle," said Scherick, "but you can make it as a regional one and I can clear the regional network and sell it so that Big Ten basketball can have a very fruitful and long life." An agreeable Reed appreciated Scherick's assessment of the situation and gave him his verbal authorization to do what he could to set up that "regional network." And not incidentally, launch Scherick on a new career.

* * *

And so in 1957 Ed Scherick once again heard the sound of his own drummer and picked up his stakes, leaving CBS to form the Big Ten basketball network. He first contacted Dick Bailey, who had left ABC to set up his own corporation to provide facilities for away sports events. Bailey's expertise in ordering and scheduling long lines from AT&T to carry the audio and video portions of the broadcasts back to networks gave him the reputation of being a "linesman." But Bailey had never done any original programming. Only feeds. His new associate, Ed Scherick, was to provide it.

Taking the name Sports Programs, Inc., because it sounded similar to Bailey's Sports Network, Inc., and taking "sparse" office space at 11 West 42nd Street, Scherick started clearing stations throughout the Big Ten midwest area—Chicago, Grand Rapids, Detroit, Rockford, Lansing, and Omaha, among others. He knew that if he offered Big Ten basketball to stations in that Big Ten hotbed, they would preempt anything that their networks were feeding them in order to carry the program.

Scherick and Sports Programs would order the telephone lines, connect them, set the pick-ups, hire the equipment, and finally, produce the show that went out to a network of some thirty midwest stations. But one important ingredient in the construction of a successful network was still missing—a sponsor. So one morning, filled with hope and *chutzpah*, Scherick flew to Chicago. He knew that Wes Nunn, the legendary advertising manager of Standard Oil, arrived at his office each morning at eight. So at 8:30 on the nose he picked up the phone and called him.

Scherick remembers saying, "Wes, I can deliver thirteen weeks of Big Ten basketball to you, one-half in the following markets." He rattled off his list of thirty markets. "At these prices. . . ." He went through another list in Gatling gun fashion lest he be interrupted. There was a pause. Then the voice on the other end of the line said, "Where are you?" Scherick told him—the Sherman House on Michigan Avenue. Nunn said, "Be at my agency, N. W. Ayer, at ten. I'll alert them you're coming." By four that afternoon, Scherick was back on a plane for New York with a written order for half sponsorship for each of the season's games. Sports Programs, Inc. was in business.

The remainder of the games were sold back to the stations for them to resale as local co-op advertising to local sponsors. Jack Drees was hired as the announcer, and through a percentage arrangement, the Big Ten made almost as much as they had before CBS canceled them. But now they had something far more important than money—they had their own program and their own network. And Big Ten basketball prospered.

But Ed Scherick had his moments before he, too, prospered. In one of the first games he produced that first year—before he hit upon the revolutionary idea of "banking" commercials to put in whenever there was a break in the action—there was a particularly trying game at the Indiana Field House. The game was taking on the semblance of a long-distance marathon race up and down the court with no breaks in the action. Scherick panicked. He saw his small profit, even his shoestring existence, being wiped out if he couldn't get the called-for commercials on the air. Then he had an idea. He raced from the broadcast truck into the stands and got a seat directly behind the Indiana bench. As the teams continued to race up and down the court, Scherick started to scream at Branch Mc-Cracken, the Indiana coach. "Call time-out, they're exhausted! Look at them, they're exhausted! Call time-out, they're exhausted!" And sure enough, the pseudo-suggestive powers of the fan-producer worked, as Indiana took the much-needed break. Of course, it was not needed so much by Indiana as it was by the producer.

* * *

At about this time ABC's affiliates were literally screaming for some kind of sports programming. But, for a while at least, nobody at 7 West seemed to know how to provide it. Fortunately for both parties, James Aubrey, then head of Programming and Talent at ABC, had met Ed Scherick earlier in his career. In light of the desperate need for sports programs, it was only natural for Aubrey to contact his former acquaintance at his fledgling company.

Aubrey liked what he saw, and before long Scherick was retained as an outside consultant with the assignment of negotiating and producing all of the network's sports events.

Things worked very well, and, when Aubrey departed for CBS, Scherick continued to bring ideas for potential properties to his successor, Tom Moore. One of those ideas was the acquisition of the rights to televise something called the Bluegrass Bowl, a postseason game played for the first, and only, time in Louisville, Kentucky, in November 1958. Pickings were rather slim in those days, and ABC welcomed the opportunity to have a bowl game—any bowl game.

What they got was not just any bowl, but an all-time television curio piece. It was the last broadcast of Harry Wismer, one-time sportscasting giant, and it was the first national sports telecast of a newcomer named Howard Cosell. (As Scherick recalls it, "I flew down with Howard on the plane, and I had to listen to him tell me for three hours that he is the greatest announcer in the history of the world.")

Then there was the field. Although a preliminary survey had been made by an engineer, Scherick wasn't prepared for what he was to see. It was an 8,000-seat stadium, with the stands all on one side of the field. The field was frozen solid, with mounds of leftover refuse—cups, paper napkins, and uneaten hot dogs from a previous game—frozen to the ground. The weather was just above zero, and the two teams were also-rans—Florida State and Oklahoma State.

The logistics demanded that a pipe tower be built on the open side of the field for the cameras and the announcers. The tower would permit them to shoot *into* the crowd. At game time, with only 2,100 people in the stands and the weather at six degrees above zero, they were climbing up the pipes. That is, all but one. Wismer refused to go up. Scherick remembers saying, "Harry, if you don't go up there, there won't be any telecast." So Wismer climbed up the pipes. Slowly.

Scherick recalls: "Here is the first football game I ever televised or produced for ABC. We televise a game in six above zero between two nondescript college teams. The players wore sneakers, and they slipped and slid all over the field, facing empty stands of 2,100 people. On either side of me, two of the greatest sports characters in the history of sports broadcasting were sitting   It's got to be the low point in my life!"

Who won the game? Cosell thinks Oklahoma State did. The Florida State athletic department doesn't have the game in its records. And nobody cared—then or now. The only thing that anyone remembers is that, according to Cosell, "Eddie and I got cystitis."

* * *

Such were the tentative beginnings of ABC Sports. But it was not the Bluegrass Bowl that would serve as the moment of birth. It was two separate events, both of which occurred in 1959, which would mark the official start of ABC Sports and the first steps in the network's climb to the top.

The first of the two events was a luncheon held at "7 West" in the spring of 1959, with Leonard Goldenson, Ollie Treyz, Tom Moore, and John Daly, the head of ABC News, Special Events and Public Affairs, in attendance. The subject under discussion was how to make the evening six o'clock news more saleable, thereby generating more money to make some much-needed changes in the news department. After a few minutes the discussion turned to other things. Moore began to wonder aloud about the "lousy sports programming" and volunteered his belief that ABC could get clearances if they had exclusivity to some interesting sports events. Daly acknowledged that he didn't want sports, much less understand them, and he wanted out of the sports operation. A silence, which would be described in literature as a pregnant pause, fell over the table. Then Goldenson, in the absence of anybody speaking up, turned to Moore and said, "Tom, you got sports."

The other event, which could be classified as the single date marking the beginning of sports at ABC, was Monday, September 28, 1959. That was the day the Milwaukee Braves and the Los Angeles Dodgers met in a play-off for the National League pennant. As it turned out, it was also the day that sports became what it has been ever since—the thyroid gland of ABC.

The race for the National League pennant had been a three-team race for the last month of the season. With less than two weeks left in the season, only one game separated the San Francisco Giants, Milwaukee Braves, and Los Angeles Dodgers. The contenders jockeyed back and forth, and then, with only seven days left in the season, the Braves and the Dodgers became locked in a head-to-head dash to the wire that resulted in a photo finish. By Monday of the final week it became obvious to all that the third play-off for the pennant in National League history was more than an outside possibility—it was a real probability.

One of those who sensed that baseball history was about to be made was Ed Scherick. Another was Tom Moore, then ABC's vice-president of Programming and Talent. Although both had had considerable experience in broadcasting sports events, neither had ever tackled anything like a National League play-off. But that was soon to change.

By Wednesday or Thursday, just two games separated the Milwaukee Braves, the Los Angeles Dodgers, and the San Francisco Giants. The Giants went on to lose seven of their last eight games, or as Charlie Dressen pronounced, "The Giants is Dead!" It was now between the Dodgers and the Braves, as first one and then the other pulled ahead in a seesaw race that saw both teams enter the last five days of the season deadlocked. And when each won their final game on the last day of the season, Sunday, September 27, it guaranteed that the third play-off in National League history would begin the next day, with the first game being played in Milwaukee on Monday and the next two in Los Angeles Tuesday and Wednesday.

Although baseball was a split package in 1959, NBC owned the rights to televise the World Series. But they hadn't foreseen the contingency of a play-off, although there had been precedence for one occurring, as it had in 1946 and 1951—when the Dodgers lost first to the Cardinals and then to the Giants.

Moore, acting on Scherick's suggestion, called Walter O'Malley, the president of the Los Angeles Dodgers, née the Brooklyn Dodgers, on Thursday to sound him out on the feasibility of ABC being able to poke its nose into major league baseball's tent. And although O'Malley had not yet met Moore—they were later to become close friends—his reception was surprisingly cordial. "I'm glad you called." Moore delicately broached the subject of the games and how much O'Malley wanted for them. "$125,000 a game." Moore was shocked to hear O'Malley say next, "I've got to offer them to NBC first." Moore only remembers that he muttered, "Well, forget it then."

But there was one interesting addition to their conversation. Fully thirteen years before night baseball was introduced into postseason play, O'Malley wanted the two play-off games from Los Angeles to start at 5:00 P.M. PCT, which was prime time in the East. Moore could easily preempt his Tuesday and Wednesday night schedules, which included "Wyatt Earp" and "The Rifleman" on Tuesday and "Hawaiian Eye" and the "Wednesday Night Fights" on Wednesday, giving him better counterprogramming to NBC's "Wagon Train." Moore ended the conversation, "All right, you let me know if there is any chance I can make a bid on them." But as he hung up the phone, he felt that NBC would probably wind up with the games, even if they didn't have the contractual rights to them.

The next day, Thursday, O'Malley called Moore back after calling Tom Gallery, the head of NBC Sports. He told Moore, "Gallery won't clear the two night games, but he will clear the Monday game, and he'll give us $150,000 for the opening game in Milwaukee in the afternoon." O'Malley then asked Moore, "Will you want the two night games?"

Moore told him, "No, we've got to promote and sell the whole deal." And then, taking a chance, he ventured, "We want the whole thing or nothing!"

O'Malley plumbed the water like a riverboat captain, "You'll give me the night games then?"

Moore answered in the affirmative, having already decided to preempt his two evenings of programming. And O'Malley, assured of getting his pet project, night games, agreed to $300,000 a game for the three-game play-off, whether it went two or three games.

ABC was in business. Well, almost. First they had the play-offs *if* indeed there was a play-off. Secondly, they had to sell the games to sponsors in the intervening four days, two of which were the weekend. It was, as Moore recalls, "A tough sell, especially when you've never been in sports and don't know who to call." Moore was buckshotting it, calling anyone he could get. He called Danny Seymour, president of J. Walter Thompson advertising agency and told him what they had. Seymour replied, "We'll be interested." Others told him, "We'll get in touch on Sunday afternoon if there's a tie."

Just as soon as Bob Buhl had retired the last Phillie in their Sunday afternoon game in Milwaukee to match Roger Craig's earlier victory over the Cubs, ABC had its play-off. Or so they thought. Within hours after Milwaukee had assured themselves of a tie, National League President Warren Giles made the announcement that there would be no nighttime play-offs.

Moore thought to himself, "Oh, hell. There goes my whole ball game right back to NBC." He turned off his set and called O'Malley. "You're going to have to play in the daytime."

O'Malley, then as now a power to be reckoned with in baseball, replied as only O'Malley could, "The hell I am!"

Moore told him that it wasn't ABC's doing, but Giles's and asked that he call Giles. O'Malley abruptly hung up, leaving Moore to believe he was "out of business."

By now Moore had spent more time on the phone than Don Ameche. But still he needed one more call to complete a five-day round of furious and seemingly futile round of negotiations. The phone rang. It was a more mollified O'Malley calling back to tell him that they were going to play in the daytime and, more importantly, that the games would belong to ABC.

From that day on ABC would never again take a backward step.

* * *

The first game was scheduled to go on the air at 1:30 P.M. Milwaukee time, Monday, September 28. The twenty-four hours preceding the first game of the play-offs and the last game of the season were pure comic opera, consisting of station clearances, announcers, sponsors, mobile pick-up units, commercials in place for the feed, and a production team. It was more chaotic than Patton's dash through France. And far more frantic. ABC, with its best daytime programming since it had run the army-McCarthy hearings six years earlier—again because it had nothing else—was gaining clearances from stations throughout the country, many of whom were not even ABC affiliates. The first three-quarters of the sponsorship had been spoken for on a contingency basis. They were firmed up, together with the sale of the last quarter to Schick. Scherick called a station manager in Milwaukee to arrange for the rental of a mobile truck. His production assistant, Jack Lubell, was sent out to handle the production. And the reel of commercials was sent to Chicago.

But problems soon started to erupt like boils. First, the commercials weren't in the right place and had to be reorchestrated to coincide with the cue sheets and logs—a time-consuming operation. Then there were the announcers, or more accurately, there were *no* announcers. Dizzy Dean had been flown in, but because of a sponsor conflict with a regional beer that bought half of the games, couldn't do the broadcast. Jack Brickhouse was contacted. But he, too, had a sponsor conflict, being under contract to Gillette.

And just when it looked as if everything was working against ABC's big-time sports debut, something starting working for them. The skies opened up and a pregame shower mercifully fell like manna from the heavens. In the ensuing rain delay, the commercials were properly arranged in the right order in Chicago. Scherick, on the phone to Lubell, instructed him to go through the County Stadium stands and find someone who knew baseball and could describe the action. Anyone. In a scene reminiscent of discovering Lana Turner at Schwab's soda fountain, Scherick remembers he had heard that George Kell, the former third baseman for the Tigers, was somewhere in the stands. "Find him!" shouted Scherick. Kell was dug out of the stands by Lubell like one of those grounders he used to field and put on the phone with Scherick. He agreed to try his first announcing assignment. It began with a forty-seven-minute rain delay. Kell had to "fill" dead air, something even experienced broadcasters have trouble doing. He was magnificent. Jack Gould of *The New York Times* gave him rave notices, and George Kell's career—like that of ABC—was under way.

The play-offs ended the second day as the Dodgers wrapped it up in two straight games, cheating ABC of its "free" third game. But pressure had served as a tremendous incubator for ABC's start in big-time sports programming.

* * *

ABC's success in broadcasting the play-offs led, indirectly, to a second giant step. But this time the deal for broadcast rights was even more complex and, well, "intriguing." In fact the story has many of the elements found in best-selling novels of the thriller genre. For ABC, it all began with a razor blade, a series of fights, and a secret deal with one of its competitor's sponsors.

The razor blade was made by Gillette, now the leading

name in shaving products. But it wasn't always thus. At one time there were over 3,000 brands of razor blades on the market. That was in the 1930s, and at the time Gillette had only 16 percent of the market.

The Gillette Company, of course, would have preferred to see the numbers transposed. They would have liked to have 61 percent of the market instead of just 16. But to achieve this they needed to promote their product. And promote it they did—by sponsoring sports events on radio and later on television.

They achieved astonishing results. Gillette's sponsorship of the 1939 Yankees–Reds World Series, for example, nearly tripled its sales with the same basic product and a special "World Series" overwrap. The company created "The Gillette Cavalcade of Sports," an entire marketing program dedicated to sponsoring sporting events, including baseball, football, and boxing. But their most popular staple was their Friday night boxing bouts. It not only appealed to their target audience, but not incidentally, increased sales. And, as such, was the backbone of their marketing strategy.

But then, in 1959, the ratings of the Friday night fights began to fall. NBC, wanting to free the time period for other programming, now considered the prospect of dropping Gillette's "Cavalcade" and communicated that desire to the powers that be at Gillette.

The "Cavalcade" and the fights had been exceptionally good for Gillette. They were largely responsible for carrying the company to a commanding 60 percent share of the shaving products market. Understandably, Gillette was more than just a little concerned over the prospect of losing the linchpin of its advertising program. So, through its advertising agency, Maxon Advertising, it began to explore ways to continue to air the fights. ABC, which at that time had just successfully broadcast the National League play-offs, was an obvious possibility.

Six weeks after the play-offs, Tom Moore received a phone call from Lou Maxon. Although Moore didn't know Maxon, he knew the name. As the president of the advertising agency that handled the Gillette account, Maxon was a man of no small stature in the New York advertising community. "Will you come over to our apartment?" began Maxon. "I want to talk sports with you."

Moore knew that invitations like that were hard to come by. He wasted no time in saying yes. On his way he went by the new offices of Sports Programs, now more conveniently and comfortably located in the Time-Life Building, and dragged Ed Scherick to the meeting as well.

Maxon's apartment was in the old Park Lane Hotel, since replaced by the American Brands Building on Park Avenue. Upon arriving, Moore and Scherick found not only Lou Maxon, but A. Craig Smith, Gillette's director of advertising; Boone Gross, chairman of the board; and Art Zeigler, then a top officer of the corporation and ultimately the chairman of the board.

After the few perfunctory salutations, Maxon got right to the point. "Look, we've just been kicked off of Friday night fights. NBC is going to carry no more fights." After that had sunk in, Maxon continued with the hook, "Because our whole marketing strategy is built around boxing, if you'll give us your whole Wednesday night fight package, we'll give you all the rest of our money. . . ." Then he added, "With the exception of the World Series, you've got everything else."

Moore gulped. Then he asked incredulously, "You mean we can agree on what we're going to spend it on?" meaning that ABC would have some control over the programming, not having to rely on sponsor-provided programming, as they had in the past.

Then he bit the bullet and asked that hardest to ask of all questions: "How much money is that?"

Maxon turned to the Gillette advertising manager and asked, "How much is it?"

"Well, after the fights, it's $8 million," replied Smith.

Eight million dollars! That was more than ABC had bid on sports in all of its years in existence, more than ABC's total profit for its television and radio operations in the entire year of 1959. It was their passkey to the big time.

But before he left, Moore wanted to make sure of the depths of Gillette's support. Knowing he had Gillette where he wanted them, he said, "If you want to get it," meaning the fights, "you've got to support us." Then he ticked off a list of events he wanted for his network that only minutes ago were figments of wishful thinking. "This is what we want . . ." and Moore listed NCAA football then on NBC, the baseball game of the week then on CBS, and several other events. The Gillette foursome agreed with an "OK, you've got it."

But one other thing was obvious to Moore. Before he left the room he extracted the additional promise that everything that had been said in the room was to be privileged. If the word got out that ABC had a war chest of $8 million, they wouldn't have the additional element of surprise needed if their overall plan were to succeed.

Assured of Gillette's dual pledge of money and secrecy, Moore and Scherick left, six feet off the ground. They raced back to ABC's offices and immediately got on the phone to Brown & Williamson and Miles Laboratories to somehow get them off ABC's own Wednesday night fights, so they could schedule one fight a week—Gillette's. They gave the two sponsors "anything and everything in the world" to free the time and get their hands on that $8 million. By dint of more pleading and horse trading than shrewd negotiations, they were able to move the two incumbent advertisers off the fights to other shows on ABC. The $8 million now belonged to ABC. What to do with it?

* * *

One of the prime reasons for the secrecy surrounding the Gillette-ABC entente was that ABC wanted the rights to NCAA football. These rights had been held by NBC since 1952, with the exception of one year, largely because of one man, Tom Gallery, NBC Sports director. Gallery was a large, balding Irishman who had been a writer, a publicist, a cowboy movie star in the Rin Tin Tin series, and a Hollywood fight promoter. But above all else, he was a social creature with an umbilical cord attached to the powers that be at the NCAA. And if word of their sudden largesse were known to Gallery, ABC's chances would be severely minimized. For, as Scherick remembers, "The NCAA was used to the crème de la crème, NBC, and viewed ABC as a guttersnipe organization, third at best." And Moore and Scherick intended to keep it that way—until the day when the NCAA accepted sealed bids for the rights to their games for the next two years.

The day of the bidding was set—Monday, March 14, 1960, at 1:00 P.M. The sealed bids were to be received in a suite rented for the occasion by the NCAA at the Manhattan Hotel on Seventh Avenue and 44th Street on the west side of Manhattan. Bidding specifications were sent out by the NCAA to all three networks. But not all three were expected to bid—at least not expected to by ABC. Moore and Scherick reasoned that CBS would not be bidding because of their recent acquisition of the NFL rights. But Tom Gallery would be there to bid for the rights for his network. Scherick's instincts told him that Gallery would have two, maybe three, sealed envelopes in his pocket. If there was no one present from the other two networks, he would drop the envelope with the low bid on the table, probably containing no more than the standard 10 percent increment over the previous $5 million bid. However, if his antennae were stimulated or he spotted a recognizable member of the alien forces, he would hand over another envelope containing a higher bid. "It was simple common sense," says Scherick. "What I would have done. If nobody else is going to bid against me, I'm going to put in a low bid. If I think there is someone else bidding against me, I'm going to put in my high bid."

And so, in as secret a covert operation as James Bond ever starred in, Moore and Scherick went about landing the most important rights their network ever had—the rights that could give their network the big sports breakthrough they had foreseen when Gillette opened up their $8 million Pandora's Box.

Moore, as head of programming, took the proposal to the ABC board of directors and got their approval to bid $6,251,114 for the rights to the NCAA games. "The $1,114 was put in to give the bid character," remembers Scherick.

Even the typing of the bid was done in absolute secrecy. Scherick had only recently hired Jim Colligan, who had once been Billy Rose's secretary. Rose as a former shorthand champion had delighted in sitting opposite Colligan while they alternately gave each other shorthand drills. But now, in his

Sports Programs offices late the night before the bids were to be accepted, Scherick dictated to Colligan the letter that was to contain the bid with the portions mentioning the amount of the bid left blank. They would be added in ink just before the actual delivery of the bid. ABC even had to verify that they had the money to make the bid, reverting to an antiquated legal procedure known as affixing the seal in order to, in Scherick's words, "prove we were good for the money."

But how was the bid to be delivered at one o'clock so that Gallery wouldn't have time to revert to his envelope containing the high bid? "If Tom Moore or I had gone anywhere near the Manhattan Hotel, we would have been a red flag and blown it," says Scherick. So now their mission impossible was to find someone unknown and innocuous enough to insinuate himself into the room without being noticed by anyone—particularly Gallery. As Moore and Scherick sat in Moore's office at 7 West, Scherick mentally combed through the personnel in the company on a floor-by-floor basis "looking for the most innocuous person we could find" as a carrier. He got to the second floor and eureka, a lightbulb went on! "Stan Frankel," shouted Scherick, half rising from his seat. The man Scherick had selected for the espionage mission was the assistant controller for ABC, a six-foot-one, stooped-shouldered, extremely lean young man about thirty-one years of age who wore horn-rimmed glasses, had a large nose, and thinning black hair with a bald spot atop his head, and could have been played by Franklin Pangborn. To Scherick's fertile mind, Frankel may have been an assistant controller by day, but in the dark of the bidding night, he was to be Super Courier.

Moore called both Frankel and his boss, Mike Bolin, the controller, in to brief them on their mission, a la 13 Rue Madeleine. Scherick ran through the step-by-step raid on NBC's home territory. "This is what you'll do. . . ." began Scherick to Frankel and Bolin, outlining the bombing strike. "At 11:45 you will both have in your possession exact duplicates of the same letter, which is a letter addressed to the NCAA. You'll both go downstairs to the lobby. There will be two Carey limousines waiting for you. Identical limousines," Scherick stressed. "You will each get into those separate limousines, and one will follow the other to the Manhattan Hotel. You will go to the NCAA suite."

Scherick directed his next set of instructions to Bolin. "Now, Mike, when you see Stanley enter that suite, your work is done. You can turn around. Get in the car. Come back, you're finished. But if he stumbles and breaks a leg, you do not even pause to ask him how he is, you walk right past him and go into the suite."

Through with Bolin, who would serve as the all-important backup, in case, Scherick went on, "God forbid, Stanley should have a heart attack," Scherick once more turned to Frankel. "Stan, these are your instructions. When you get into the room, you have a difficult job ahead of you. Stay out of the limelight. Walk over, look out of the windows, melt into the drapes. Anything!" Scherick emphasized, "But try not to become obtrusive. However," and here the moral part of Scherick won out, "If you are asked any direct question, *do not tell a lie*. If they ask, 'Who are you?' tell them your name. If they question, 'Why are you here?' tell them who you are. Don't volunteer anything." And then Scherick repeated himself, "Don't volunteer. You don't have to tell them what you're going to do until 1:00. But don't tell a lie that would damage our reputation or invalidate our bid." Scherick spoke slowly, "Do you understand?"

"Yes," said Frankel.

"Now," said Scherick as he warmed up to the moment of truth, "the man you have to watch for is Tom Gallery."

Frankel asked his first question, "How will I know what he looks like?"

Scherick, glad to see that he was getting some response to his briefing and that his subject was paying the proper amount of attention, went on, "He's a rather large Irishman with a bald head. But he will be immediately obvious to you because he will be the kingpin of the meeting. Everybody will be talking to him. You can't miss him. He's Mr. Big," said Scherick, using a term that made him sound like Mr. Bigdome in Little Iodine, but knowing full well that Gallery would be playing his moment in the sun to the hilt.

Scherick covered one last base before taking Frankel up to

the implanting of the bandolero. "There may be a guy from CBS there. There may not be. You can't do anything about that. That's beyond your control. But," and here he returned, licking his chops, "your target is Tom Gallery. He probably has two bids with him—one high and one low. Now your entire task and the success or failure for you, us, and our company depends on Tom Gallery putting his envelope on the table *first*." Scherick wound up emphasizing the word *first* as if enunciating the word to a first-grade classroom. "If he gets up first, we have a very good chance of being successful. If he is aware that you're there, our chances are significantly diminished."

"Now," Scherick said, "Do you understand?"

And Frankel dutifully answered, "Yes, I understand."

The first leg of the perilous journey began as the men got into the two rented Carey limousines and pulled away from West 66th Street. Frankel made the midtown run in fifteen minutes and strode into the Manhattan as if he owned the world, as indeed he might in just one hour. Bolin peeled off, seeing that Frankel had been successfully and safely deposited. Frankel had no trouble finding the room, the draperies, or Gallery, who was sitting in front of the room, straddling his turned-around chair with the back of it serving much like the horn of a saddle. In between his stomach and his legs were three envelopes, color coded, and visible to all in the room. Frankel melted into the furnishings in the back of the room. No one in the communications crowd bustling around the room bothered to communicate with him, and so Frankel had to answer none of the questions he had been alerted to.

At one o'clock Asa Bushnell, head of the NCAA, stood up and said, "We're ready to start the bidding." Gallery started peering around the room, looking for CBS or any familiar face. No one. Bushnell again spoke, this time directly to Gallery, "Tom, we're ready." It was as if Bert Parks had asked, "The envelope, please."

Gallery, this time hearing the invitation directed to him, got up, looked around once more, and seeing no signs of movement, picked up an envelope and put the others in his pocket.

The moment the envelope hit the table, Stan Frankel began

walking forward. "My name is Stan Frankel and I represent the American Broadcasting Company," he said. And twenty seconds after the NBC bid had been put on the table, it was covered, in more ways than one, by the bid delivered by Frankel.

There was a stunned silence as the room became a replica of Mount Rushmore. Finally, Jim Corbett, the athletic director of LSU, suggested that the NCAA group adjourn to an adjacent room to discuss it, off camera. For the next forty minutes they were gone, discussing the unforeseen bid by ABC. How were they going to deal with this? The ABC bid was obviously the high one, by some $1,051,114. While they couldn't dismiss it out of hand, some of the discussion did focus on how *not* to give it to the high bidder. Finally, they came back into the room and made the only announcement they could make: "The NCAA rights are awarded to the American Broadcasting Company." Frankel called Moore and Scherick, who had been sitting in Moore's office counting beads, and said succinctly, "The American Broadcasting Company now owns the rights to the NCAA football games."

It was the culmination of the hoped-for dream and the beginning not only of a long continuous relationship with the NCAA but the start of ABC's almost unchallenged ascendancy to the top of the sports mountain. It was also the beginning of the end of Tom Gallery's reign at NBC.

* * *

As convoluted as the story of ABC is, it seems as if the same set of characters are continually appearing and reappearing, as in a repertory company, merely playing different parts. So it was now, as enter left, Harry Haggerty—the same Harry Haggerty of Metropolitan Life who had seen the wisdom of the merger almost ten years earlier and authorized a loan to Goldenson's Paramount Theatres.

Haggerty was now approached by another entrepreneur, asking him if he could set up a meeting between ABC and his group. The man who came to Haggerty was Harry Wismer, who had been the director of sports for ABC when it had been a radio network. The idea was something called the American Football League.

Haggerty called Goldenson to set up the meeting, and Goldenson referred the matter to Moore in a corporate version of Tinker-to-Evers-to-Chance. Moore met with Wismer and Lamar Hunt, who had been rebuffed in his bid to join the NFL and together with other millionaires—and Wismer—had formed another league. They had already been to see both NBC and CBS and found a surprising amount of indifference to their new league. Their last chance was ABC.

They met at the Ambassador Hotel and discussed the possibilities of ABC taking their package. Moore told them he was interested but offered nothing more in terms of a commitment. They agreed to get together again soon.

The second meeting was held at Wismer's apartment in the old Park Lane Hotel and was attended by Wismer, Hunt, Bud Adams of Houston, Max Winter of Minneapolis, Frank Leahy of Oakland, Billy Sullivan of Boston, and Baron Hilton of Los Angeles; along with Moore and Scherick. All of the attendees were directed by Wismer to arrive at staggered appointed times to prevent any detection of their meeting in what Moore called "cloak-and-dagger stuff." Wismer started the meeting by asking for $2 million. Moore responded by telling him that "we were talking about two hundred thousand, at most." Thereupon, Wismer banged his fist on the table and screamed that he was "absolutely insulted" and that if Moore and Scherick didn't leave the room, he was going to.

As Moore turned to talk to Bud Adams, they heard Wismer get up, turning his chair over, and march to the door. But instead of opening the door and walking out, Wismer walked into a closet in his own apartment. Everyone in the room knew it was a closet and just sat and waited. Ten minutes later, he opened the door and came back out as if nothing had happened. The meeting resumed.

A deal was eventually agreed on that would give the American Football League a ballpark figure of $8.5 million for five years, with several contingent factors thrown in to act as prophylaxes for ABC, including a sliding scale for ratings and sales slippage. Moore estimates that the first-year rights amounted to somewhere in the neighborhood of $400,000.

Moore then arranged for Sullivan and the new AFL Commissioner Joe Foss to meet with the Gillette brass at Boston's Algonquin Club in an all-day and all-night meeting. It was set. Gillette would also underwrite ABC's expenditure for AFL football.

* * *

By now sports had become important at ABC. The department was sane and workmanlike compared to the rest of the network, which resembled a group of bright young people performing like a ragtag army performing like a network. Where chaos continually seemed to come out of chaos, sports alone was within the limits of solid corporate citizenry. And because it was ABC and because there was no structure—with Goldenson extremely receptive to, in the words of one of his former associates, "an adventure,"—sports became all the bigger than it could possibly have become under a Paley.

Sports also provided Tom Moore with a showcase and talking point, for at this time, outside of sports, the network wasn't making it—prime time, daytime, anytime. Nothing else was working.

Ed Scherick was also the beneficiary of this freewheeling structure. He was an outside consultant who had become a power within the ABC structure, such as it was, operating on a free-lance basis. He had absolute carte blanche to run through the offices at 7 West and was always in the station clearance or sales departments checking up on them and on anything else that might have a bearing on the success of his programs. For it was his adventure as well as Goldenson's, an adventure that could only have taken shape at the ABC of that time.

Scherick's Sports Programs had had to grow to mirror the growth of ABC Sports, operating in the vacuum that the sports department's lack of personnel and expertise created. He now sought to fill that vacuum by hiring personnel who could operate as the designated pinch hitters for the so-called sports operation. One of the first people he brought over to Sports Programs was a young media man from Dancer Fitzgerald Sample, whom he had hired there just a few years earlier.

When Scherick was the media director on the Falstaff account, a friend of his who was the manager of Guy Lombardo's band had called him to request a favor. "Listen," he said. "I've got a friend who is dying to get into the broadcast business. Can you do anything for him?"

In his usual open reception to all such entreaties, Scherick said, "Sure, send him in to see me."

The young man was Chet Simmons, then working for an uncle who ran a string of private hospitals on Long Island. After an interview in the form of an open-ended discussion, Scherick found a job for Simmons as an assistant media buyer at DFS.

Now, by 1957, it had become fairly obvious to Scherick that he needed help with his added responsibilities: pregame and postgame shows, Big Ten basketball, etc. He followed the path of breadcrumbs he had left back to his old agency to look for the urgently needed help. After talking to several of those in the media department, he hired the man he had brought to the agency three years earlier as his administrative assistant for the munificent sum of $75 a week. At the time, Scherick remembered, some of those he had interviewed had turned up their noses at $75 a week believing "hell, he's not going to last." But now the laugh was on them, for that $75-a-week man eventually became director of NBC Sports with a salary well into the six-figure bracket.

But even with Simmons and Jim Colligan, whom Scherick hired in 1959 (another call from another friend, "There is a guy who used to work on Welcome Travelers for Procter & Gamble who is a terrific guy who knows a lot about sports. . . ."), much more help was needed, especially since the NCAA and Friday night fight packages had just been acquired by his client, ABC. Helpful hints from friends and associates continued to pour in about people he "should see."

One day the director of Television Programs, Ted Fetter, accosted Scherick, who was then on one of his traditional forty-yard dashes through the offices at 7 West. "Please speak to my secretary, she's got a problem."

Scherick, never one to miss an opportunity to talk to anyone about anything, asked the secretary what her problem was. It seemed that the secretary had a boyfriend who was a management trainee at the Chase Manhattan and hated what he was doing. "Do you think you could use him?" she asked. "Sure, send him in," replied Scherick.

The management trainee was Chuck Howard, a recent graduate of Duke, who yearned for a job—any job—in sports. He had interviewed for a position as assistant to the then publicity director of the New York Yankees and was ready to pick up and go wherever the siren call of sports beckoned. He had visited Scherick at his old offices at 11 West 42nd, but nothing more concrete had come of it, although Scherick had mentioned, "Sometime soon I'm hoping to expand this operation. You may hear from me again."

Now, some nine months later, with the NCAA package and the fights coming up in the fall, Scherick called Howard. "Are you still interested in a job in sports?" That was all Howard needed. He left the bank with interest in his principal calling and was hired in August 1960. The world didn't lose just another bank officer, it gained what was to become a damn good producer. And—oh yes—the secretary who had recommended Howard became his wife shortly thereafter.

The Sterling Drug account at Dancer Fitzgerald Sample was like an agency within an agency. As a longtime client, Sterling Drug was handled by a special group headed by Malcolm "Bud" Spence, the account supervisor. Spence called Tom Dawson, vice-president in charge of sales for CBS, to set up an appointment for his nephew, who was a recent Dartmouth graduate and who, like one of a walking army on the streets of New York, was interested in sports. He also called Bill Mullen, head of sales at ABC, and set up an appointment with Scherick. Spence first went to CBS, where he was interviewed by Bill MacPhail, head of CBS Sports. After the session, MacPhail suggested that it might be worth Spence's while to spend some time with a production assistant named Chet Forte. Spence spent about an hour with the former Columbia all-American, who told him, "Don't quote me, but if you want to get into TV and sports, ABC is the place to go."

On the day of his appointment with Scherick, Spence took a seat in the reception area of the Sports Programs offices. After an hour, from somewhere inside the small group of offices, he heard a booming voice hollering, "Spence, come on in here." Spence followed the trailing off sound of the voice and found Scherick standing up at his desk. Spence sat down across from the desk and began pulling out some clippings he had submitted to *The New York Times* and United Press, but Scherick stopped him. "I don't want those. Put those away. I don't want to read anything. Just tell me about yourself."

After a half hour of recounting his noncareer in school and in the army, Spence found Scherick staring at his green Dartmouth socks. "I like your socks," said Scherick. Then he went on, "We're looking for a production assistant. This is not a permanent position; it's temporary, through the football season. We're hiring you to do two football score shows. Are you sure you want this job?"

Spence remembers replying, "Yes sir."

"'OK, go out and see Chet Simmons and he'll get you squared away."

Spence then dutifully went out to see Simmons, much as if he were going through an army physical.

Simmons asked, "When do you want to start?"

Spence eagerly replied, "Now is fine."

In the loose-knit atmosphere that prevailed, Simmons only said, "Go out to lunch and come back at two." And with that, another member of the DFS mafia had been added to the payroll of Sports Programs.

But if, according to that old mystery film, The Postman Only Rings Twice, Scherick's phone seemed to be ringing off the hook. An old acquaintance called him to set up an appointment to look at a show he had an interest in. The old friend was Pat Hernon, whom Scherick had known when he bought the ten o'clock news on KPIX–TV in San Francisco for Falstaff. Hernon, who later did some sports, including the memorable reading of a football score as "Los Angeles 34, San Francisco 49," had migrated to New York and was working for NBC and doing some outside work. "Ed, I want you to see a pilot we made of a half hour sports magazine show."

Scherick asked what it was.

Hernon responded, " 'For Men Only.' When can you see it?" it?"

Hernon told him to come over to NBC at 3:30 the next day, Tuesday. And he did.

"It was another attempt to do a sports magazine show," recalls Scherick. "There were pretty girls in it and everything. But it was done with a nice flair and I liked its production." The lights came up after the screening and Hernon said to Scherick, "I'd like you to meet the man who produced it, Roone Arledge."

3
Roone Arledge: The Man Who Gave You ABC Sports... and Howard Cosell

On the evening of May 17, 1976, the lobby of the posh Century Plaza in Los Angeles was overflowing with teeming hordes of TV executives and well-wishers all bustling about in a never-ending ceremony of backslapping and handshaking. It was just minutes after the ritual known as the annual Emmy ceremonies had taken place across the street at the Shubert Theatre. There seemed to be almost as many well-wishers as winners. Except in one category, sports, where one network dominated as no other organization ever had. ABC had captured thirty-two of the thirty-four statuettes awarded in the sports arena on the national TV awards show, and Roone Arledge had been on the stage almost continually for twenty minutes receiving the awards given by the National Academy of Television Arts and Sciences.

Over on one side of the lobby, Grant Tinker, the husband of Mary Tyler Moore and producer of MTM properties, a CBS program supplier, was overheard commenting to a top-ranking CBS executive, "We really have got to do something about this Roone Arledge. He's embarrassing. We either have to get rid of him, get him over to CBS, or get the sports awards put on with the technical awards the day before so they won't be on prime time."

In a field devoted to fashioning halos for personalities,

Roone Arledge wears a special nimbus. He is that rarity in American television, a behind-the-scenes superstar.

Ever since his star started rising in the East, many have attributed God-like qualities to him—some real, some folklore. But his stature rests not so much on being a one-man laboratory for the discovery of new forms, as in being a master of theory and techniques who has made important contributions to the development of both.

However you look at it, he has made ABC Sports the biggest jock on the broadcast block and has had a fertilizing effect on all of televised sports.

The man who has received mail addressed to Rue Knowledge was born with the unlikely handle of Roone Pinckney Arledge II on July 8, 1931. He is the second in a short line of three Roone Pinckney Arledges, along with his father and son. Once asked where the name Roone came from by *Sports Illustrated* writer Gilbert Rogin, he replied, "It doesn't mean anything. It seems to be the most ridiculous name imaginable." But if the root derivation of the name Roone is unknown, his middle name, Pinckney, is apparently a lineal throwback to the southern ancestry of his father, who was a lawyer from the Carolinas. The middle name has long since been discarded; the name Roone is weird enough.

Shortly after his birth, Arledge's family moved out to Merrick, Long Island, where he experienced "a typical Long Island childhood." After graduating from Mempham High School in Merrick, Arledge matriculated at Columbia College. On his way to a B.B.A. in 1952, he stopped along the route to become president of his class, president of his fraternity, and editor of the yearbook. He also joined the wrestling team and began to nurture the desire to be a writer. Unable to "decide whether I wanted to write sports, government, philosophy, or theater," he enrolled instead at the Columbia School of International Affairs. After a brief stay in graduate school, he took a job with the old Dumont television network as a production assistant, or, as it's known in the trade, a go-fer—as in go-fer coffee, go-fer papers, go-fer pencils, and go-fer anything anyone else wants. After one year, his on-the-job training was interrupted by his entry into the service, where he spent his time at the Aberdeen Proving Grounds in Maryland, producing and directing radio programs.

Upon being mustered out of the service, he continued his J. Pierpont Finch career with NBC, working his way up the ladder as stage manager, director, and then producer. Along the way he did remotes for the local New York station, WNBC–TV, including the covering of such monumental events as the Christmas tree lighting at Rockefeller Center.

By 1958, he was producing his own shows for the local New York NBC station. His first show was "Sunday Schedule," a show which ran from 7:00 to 11:00 on Sunday mornings. *Variety* called it "an abdication of program responsibility." His second show met a better reception. It was a local New York television program entitled "Hi, Mom" starring Shari Lewis and a cast of puppets, running from 9:00 to 10:00 every weekday morning, immediately following the conclusion of the "Today" show. His flair for production won him an Emmy, the first of many that were to decorate his mantlepiece like epaulets on the shoulders of full generals.

After six years at NBC, Arledge sought other challenges and consequently developed the format and pilot for the hour-long show entitled "For Men Only." After presenting it to the powers that be at NBC and being turned down, he looked for other possible avenues. The announcer on the pilot, Pat Hernon, suggested one—Ed Scherick at Sports Programs, Inc.

Scherick had left "For Men Only" on a "don't-call-us-we'll-call-you" basis, but was impressed with the production values he saw in the pilot produced by Arledge. He invited the 28-year-old producer to his office to discuss the possibility of his producing the NCAA games.

"Look," Scherick said once they were seated, "I have the rights to the NCAA football games, and I'd like to talk to you about them."

Scherick's office walls were laden with sports pictures, featuring both his TV exploits and his heroes. It was a patchwork quilt of photographs that could easily have passed for the wall of a neighborhood bar and grill. Scherick had already decided that Arledge had the skill to produce the NCAA games. However, before hiring him, he wanted to put Arledge to the supreme test.

"Do you know anything about sports?"

Arledge told him that he was a sports fanatic.

"All right," said Scherick, jumping up, "Goddamn it, here's the test." And with that he began waving at the pictures on his walls with all the gusto of a traffic cop in Rome. "Who's that?" demanded Scherick. And Arledge would answer. "Who's that?" And, again, Arledge had the answer. This rapid fire game of "Show-and-Tell" continued until every picture on the wall was pointed out. Arledge correctly identified each and every one.

Scherick sat back in his seat and said, "I think you *can* produce these games."

Arledge was flattered by the praise and excited by the challenge. He accepted on the spot. And with a handshake, the two men who would turn out to be the most important characters in the electronic sports revolution came to a tentative agreement.

One minor piece of business remained—Arledge's salary. Scherick offered Arledge $10,000 to produce the NCAA games. Arledge sent over his attorney, David Braun, to negotiate for him. Braun asked for a one year's signed contract for his client. The never-placid Scherick answered this request with a roar, "You tell him that if he's got to have a signed contract, forget about it!" And the lawyer promptly forgot about it.

* * *

Roone Arledge, known to many of his associates as the Redhead, possesses the disarmingly friendly appearance of a redheaded Pillsbury Doughboy, his round bespectacled countenance often split by a grin. His personal appearance is as informal as his manner, usually trending toward open-collar, vertically-striped sports shirts, worn not with the avidity of a Bill Veeck or a Ted Williams, but with a casual, stylish appearance. On out-of-town trips, of which there are many, he has been known to don cowboy boots, jeans, and a somewhat tattered shirt, wearing it in the style of a man who could affect such a shirt and is comfortable with his own success. His modish hair style goes with his sometimes upbeat "Hey-baby-it's-great" style that has endeared him to many as a gifted *salonniere* who enjoys the company of notables and travels in his own ratpack of confidants, the closest of whom is Bob Beattie. Dan Jenkins, sportswriter and friend of Arledge, views him as "the most sociable of men," and "fun to be around."

But not many people have been around him. For while Arledge has been able to maintain a high profile in the press, he has also been able to keep a low personal profile, almost an invisibility to those outside his inner circle. Lee Grosscup, who has worked as the color commentator on NCAA football for seven years, has yet to meet his leader. Even Jim McKay, the voice of "Wide World" and the Olympics, had only seen Arledge once in the five months after Montreal—and that passing him in the halls.

For years he has cultivated a mystique, one in the best traditions of Greta Garbo, Howard Hughes, and even Lamont Cranston. Called No-Show Roone by many members of the press to whom he is unavailable except when he wants to be, Arledge has almost attained a high level of anonymity by another standard, *The New York Times's*. With a picture morgue of those in the news reputed to be the most complete in the world, there are just fourteen pictures of Arledge on file, one-third as many as most of his fellow television executives and half of those are the "Gee-I-can't-help-it-if-I'm-in-this-picture" variety.

Roone's storied aversion to the press stems not only from the fact that being right is important to him and he is frightened of being misquoted or misrepresented in the press, but because of an incident that took place early in his career. An incident which nearly ended his career before it began.

Hired by Scherick to produce the NCAA games, his capacity was generally unknown, particularly by the client, Gillette. It had generally been assumed that Jack Lubell, a former CBS producer called the Iron Major (because of his fanaticism about his physical condition) would be the producer of the series. Lubell was to distinguish himself in later years by running out on the field during an AFL game and demanding the teams have another kickoff because he had missed the first one.

During one of those interminable meetings that preceded the first game of the first NCAA season, a reporter from one of the many gossip sheets that purport to cover the New York communications industry chanced to be in Sports Programs's offices. During the course of the meetings, which tended to be more of a strolling troubadour affair than a structured meeting, the reporter from *Show Business* was able to glean that Roone Arledge was to be the producer of the NCAA games. He wrote "Unknown 29-year-old freckle-faced kid named Roone Arledge, who produced a local kiddie show for NBC, to produce NCAA games for ABC." No sooner had the newsletter hit the desk of Ed Wilhelm, account executive for Maxon Advertising Agency, who, according to Scherick, "controlled the account, lock, stock, and barrel," then he called to demand, "What's this?"

The facile Scherick told a lie and shot back, "It's not true. I'm going to do it and Roone's going to report to me."

Wilhelm, Maxon, and Gillette were pacified, and Arledge did, in fact, produce the games. But that incident instilled a healthy suspicion of the press, adding to the privateness of this very public figure.

Called by Cosell, "the executive producer of more shows he has never seen," TV's version of a missing person is more often not at an event than he is. Three years ago he called up producer Don Ohlmeyer on a Monday afternoon to find out where the Monday night game was. Ohlmeyer said, "I guess that means you won't be using the suite we got for you."

One reason for his absence is the sheer physical impossibility of getting to all of the shows while also running the store. Another cause is what Chet Forte calls "a Roone Arledge personality trait. There was a point when he used to go to all the Monday night football games. He doesn't do that any longer. He lives his own type of life."

Arledge himself perpetuates the myth. On one occasion when his good friend Davey Marr was signing out after finishing his round of golf at the Pebble Beach course, he chanced to look up at the Del Monte Lodge overlooking the eighteenth green. There he saw Arledge standing on the balcony in front of his room waving for him to come up. Picking up Frank Gifford on his way, Marr and Gifford went to Arledge's room and knocked on the door, not five minutes after the signaled greeting. No answer. More knocking. Still no answer. Then Gifford put his fist and finally his shoulder to the door, almost knocking it off the hinges. Finally, after a few minutes, the frustrated twosome retired. Later that afternoon, they called Arledge's room, and in the course of setting up dinner told him they had come up to his room and couldn't find him. Arledge merely said, "I wonder where I was."

During the days when he was highly visible, Arledge would spend as much time selling the network to advertisers and affiliates as he would producing. "But somewhere along about 1970," according to Dan Jenkins, author of *Semi Tough* and other books, "Arledge got overcliented. There are only so many hands you can shake." And he returned to his real love—producing better shows.

But even in his physical absence, his presence is all-pervasive throughout ABC Sports. Sam Merrill, who interviewed Arledge for *Playboy,* observed, "Making allowances for the kiss-assing that goes on, just because they want to get a nice quote about their boss into the magazine, still you could see that they really have more than the usual boss-employee relationship. He's mysterious to them. They really think he knows things that they don't know."

Because Arledge came up the same route his staff did, as a producer and director, there is tremendous respect not only for his accomplishments, but for him as well. You can hear it when Chuck Howard says, "You can't con him, because he knows," and when Chet Forte says, "It may take three to four days to reach him, whether he's in Hawaii or Long Island or Europe, but that decision is held until Roone makes it. Roone is the guy who makes major decisions."

But even if Arledge is not at an event, he is only as far away as the Red Roone Phone in the remote control truck, an umbilical cord from Arledge to the producer. Not infrequently, the phone will ring and a disembodied voice, like John Forsythe's on "Charlie's Angels," will come over the line asking the producer for history cassettes of the just-concluded show. Or, during the event itself, he will get through to instruct the producer, who stands next to the red tie-line, to plug this or that upcoming show; or, on one occasion, "I can't hear any crowd noises. You sound like you're broadcasting from a morgue. Get the crowd level up." He has even called through to tell the producer to get one of his announcers to "shut up, he's talking too much."

Those who work for Arledge don't feel that they have to trick him into thinking they're better than they are or that they have to impress him. Their most cherished "perk" is neither their expense account nor title. It's their sense of satisfaction in a job-well-done commendation from their leader, who is a great respecter of artistic and creative ability. And like an Arabian potentate with many wives, he makes everyone feel that they are the *only* one.

* * *

Tom Moore, from the very first day Ed Scherick introduced Arledge to him, was a Roone Arledge fan. "Roone was great in his total control of the whole situation. That is, the acquiring of the rights, the administration of the office, the hiring of personnel, the packaging of the product, the delivery of a good product, and the scheduling and promotion." Moore, who once discussed the prospect of Arledge's taking over as head of programming after the 1964 Winter Olympics, an offer Arledge could—and did—refuse, summed him up by remarking, "Roone's greatest asset, which very few people know, is people. Listen, he's got the goddamndest troop of people over there you've ever seen!"

If Roone Arledge is the head of ABC Sports, its people are the heart. Marion Harper, when president of McCann-Erickson Advertising Agency, said, "At five o'clock all the company's assets go home." This is almost true of ABC Sports. Except, they don't go home at 5:00 or 6:00 or even 7:00, or at any normal hour. Instead, they mainline tension, working super-human hours, all with a tremendous pride in their product and in the team's efforts. That teamwork is reflected in Arledge's continual use of the collective pronoun *we* and in his installation of an *esprit de corps* that would be the envy of any organization, even the Oakland Raiders. Chet Forte recently turned down an offer to return to CBS, where he had been until Roone lured him away in 1963, because "there is a family here, one I'm very happy with." Larry Kamm, a director who joined ABC as a production assistant on the "Voice of Firestone" fifteen years ago, feels "it is a desire to continue what it is that so many who have gone before and who are still here have built up. There is a professionalism represented in the end product at ABC Sports that just isn't exuded on CBS or NBC."

Added to that pride is the knowledge that ABC Sports has always promoted from within. Those working there won't come to work tomorrow to find somebody brought over from one of the other networks planted on top of them. Most of those who join as production assistants, or PA's, the lowest level on the corporate totem pole, know they can move up within the organization. They stay because there is a pride in what they do, an opportunity to learn, and the belief that if they stick it out they will receive fair treatment and a chance for advancement.

Moreover, there is surprisingly little movement from ABC Sports to the other networks. For years, Arledge was proud of the fact that "we've never had a single person leave—well, perhaps one—and darn near everybody from both other networks has come here for jobs." Ironically, within the last two years, more have left ABC Sports—four—than in the preceding fifteen. One, Arledge's assistant Dick Ebersoll, particularly wounded his boss when without talking to him he merely left a "Dear John" note on his desk. In a family situation, where a very personal relationship exists and Arledge really cares about those working for him, that hurt deeply.

＊ ＊ ＊

Roone Arledge's turf extends through the whole of sports. In the jungle atmosphere that prevails in network negotiations, he has been called a claim jumper and opportunistic by those from the "so's-your-old-man" lobby at the other two networks. Those at his own network view him as a man of single-minded perseverance who got what he wanted because he stayed at it. Even so-called media watchers like Frank Beermann of

Variety view Arledge as "a more forthright guy in dealing, who's going to go out and get everything he can for ABC." But whatever his marks, he left his indelible stamp on all major and most minor sports by spending with a lavish and imaginative verve.

Perhaps his most famous negotiating ploy was something that came to be known as "the ABC Closer." As in almost any business, negotiating and bargaining play a pivotal role in broadcasting. For example, when a network wants to buy the rights to a particular program, it will usually sit down with the program's packager or promoter. The network will make an offer that is usually lower than the price it would be willing to pay. The promoter will respond with a figure that is higher than he really expects to get. And so on back and forth, with each side inching toward the other until they meet on mutually satisfactory ground.

"The ABC Closer" creates a definite roadblock to the customary bargaining procedure. When ABC wants to close a certain deal, it will frequently make a first offer that is substantially higher than the promoter expects a first offer to be. The network will then give the promoter a firm deadline to either accept or reject the offer. It's all or nothing! There are no counteroffers. No comebacks. No negotiating. And it is an extremely effective negotiating technique, for the promoter is usually too stunned to shop for a better price.

At first glance it may look as though ABC is giving away the store. But that really isn't the case. Usually the price ABC pays is considerably lower than it would have had to pay if it had encouraged negotiations. For in many cases, negotiations over price, especially the price of a desirable property, can end with the three networks trying to outbid each other while the promoter cheers them on.

Of course, it's a gamble. The program promoter may feel that he can get a higher price elsewhere and refuse ABC's offer. But in the masterful hands of Roone Arledge, "the ABC Closer" can be very effective indeed.

Arledge has often said, "The bane of this industry is that we have to buy rights to an event before we can produce anything." From the day he first gained the rights to the AAU events for "Wide World," Arledge was to become the proud possessor of more rights than Joe Louis had in his prime.

In one of the most creative of all fields, television rights negotiations, where the chase is sometimes as thrilling as the capture and mounting of the trophy, the Olympics, World Series, Kentucky Derby, pro and college football games are all tributes to the ability of Roone Arledge. In the words of Tom Moore, "Roone is a good salesman. He just bores in. He's a good talker and flatters them. He knows how to 'hype' them, and it's a great world in which to 'hype.'" To the NCAA, he promised that "ABC is going to do the best job in football." To the Olympics organization committees in Mexico City, Innsbruck, Munich, Lake Placid, Montreal, and all points East, West, and South he convinced them that ABC was best for them and laid rights monies on them. He is to television negotiations what Theodore Kheel was to labor negotiations, a man who knew how to close a proposed deal that worked for all.

* * *

Arledge and Moore drew up a must list of fourteen events that they just had to get if ABC was, indeed, to become the recognized leader in sports around the world. "There were," according to Moore, "just so many events, and you weren't going to create any more. There was the Rose Bowl in college football. There wasn't going to be another one like that."

And so Roone set off after the Rose Bowl. But he only succeeded in what Moore called "running up the price for the other guy—quite a bit." Ditto the Cotton Bowl. But after weaning the Sugar Bowl and the East-West game away from NBC, Arledge trained his sights on the Orange Bowl.

"I negotiated the deal with Roone," recalls Moore. It was "$300,000 for a three- or four-year deal." But the ABC board of directors "was in a grumpy mood. It was a tough time of the year for them, and they turned it down—the only time in the whole history of sports that our board of directors turned down something that Roone and I recommended."

Horse racing is a sport that drew 51 million to thoroughbred tracks during 1976, more than the totals of major league baseball, pro football, and pro basketball *combined,* and yet horse racing is totally invisible on the tube—with the rare exception of three races, the Kentucky Derby, the Preakness, and the Belmont, racing's Triple Crown. And while three races do not a season make, that's almost it for television. That's why the Kentucky Derby is not only one of America's premiere sporting events, but easily made the list of fourteen that Arledge and Moore had drawn up.

Eight years before ABC finally landed the Derby ("We had actually made a deal for both the Derby and the Preakness. And, in both cases, they backed out.") Moore reconstructs the bidding like a bridge grand master: "Every time we'd go down to Louisville, they'd say, 'Gee, your money's good. We hate CBS, they're pushing us around. But that goddamned station of yours in Louisville. . . .' Our station in Louisville was just a UHF, channel 89 or something. They couldn't get a signal down off the goddamned antenna in their own control room. It was that bad!" So Arledge devised what Moore called "a master stroke." On the first Saturday in May, all stations in Louisville would carry the Derby. That turned the tide. But then the sports department of the Louisville *Courier-Journal,* which owned the CBS affiliate, WHAS–TV, learned that ABC had made a deal and after CBS found out, it was called off. Plans for the Preakness, contingent upon ABC's getting the Derby as part of the Triple Crown, were also canceled.

Every year thereafter Arledge returned to visit Churchill Downs like one of the faithful at Lourdes, waiting to be blessed. Bill MacPhail, former head of CBS Sports, remembers "looking up and seeing Arledge having lunch with Wathen Knebelkamp, the president of Churchill Downs. For all I know, Roone was trying to steal the Kentucky Derby from me right before my eyes." He was right. In the biggest luncheon heist since Horn & Hardart's raised its price for a cup of coffee to 35¢, Arledge ultimately landed the Derby for ABC in 1975, ending a reign of twenty-six years for CBS, and then added the Preakness in 1977.

* * *

Another of those magic fourteen events was the Masters Golf Tournament. While the word *prestigious* has been used to describe almost every major golf tournament with the same frequency and for the same purpose an aging lady of the streets applies rouge to her cheeks, one that has truly merited it—together with the U.S. and British Opens—is the Masters. Almost from its inception in 1934, this by-invitation-only tournament has brought together the crème de la crème of golf—without the addition of coffee-skinned golfers, until recently. As the first major outdoor sports event of the season, shot against a backdrop of dogwoods and azaleas, it was as all-American as the quilt spread it was played on, the Augusta National Golf Course, designed by golfing great Bobby Jones. And it was a must for ABC in its attempt to be first in sports and first in golf.

Golf has not always been popular. As late as 1955, when televised golf tournaments were suggested to him, Tom Gallery, then head of NBC Sports, had said, "Golf isn't a spectator sport." But stimulated by the front-page treatment golf was getting in the Eisenhower years—even to the behind-the-scene headline in those pre-*Penthouse* days when the *Richmond Times-Dispatch* ran a headline over a story of the president at Burning Tree: *Ike Loves His Putts*—thousands were turning to it in a variation of that old game called follow the leader.

One man who had seen its potential was Walter Schwimmer, a former advertising agency owner, who packaged a concept called "All-Star Golf" and sold it to ABC's programming chieftain, Tom Moore. The premise was a simple one: twenty-five big-name tournament golfers would play a total of twenty-six rounds for $2,000 a round plus expenses, with the winner going on to the next round in a king-of-the-mountain approach, until beaten.

Gone were the days when one golfer turned to a cameraman on the eighteenth hole and muttered through clenched teeth, "The next time you take my picture when I'm putting you're going to get my putter in your mouth." Golfers had now somehow managed to sublimate their old prejudice against cameras and cameramen breaking into the funereal silence that surrounded golf, where any sound—a sneeze, a whisper, or a camera—could distract them. Now they only heard the sound of money. And they didn't care how loud it talked, so long as it did.

Soon, the most noticeable thing on your TV screen after commercials for "new-improved-fortified-Steel-belted" products was the proliferation of new golf tournaments. It seemed that every star of stage, screen, and TV who had everything else was given a tournament: Here a Bing Crosby Pro-Am, there a Dean Martin Tourney, everywhere a Sammy Davis or Glen Campbell. And everywhere, too, were TV cameras, because golf had become a television staple. Not only had "TV golf been the biggest factor in increasing the popularity of the game," according to Jimmy Demaret, but advertisers and advertising agencies, like McCann-Erickson, believed "golf tournaments represent an excellent vehicle to present corporate messages to an upper-income male audience." And, even if HUT levels (homes using TV) were down in the warm weather months, there was no accounting for the number of members at local country clubs in front of the sets at the bar watching the tournaments on weekends. Golf alone was independent of the ratings guillotine.

And so the networks teed up for golf; but none more so than ABC. To those hundreds of tournaments that dotted the landscape like Christmas tree lights, it was a blessing for all seasons. Though in the beginning, it was pure chaos. With no central clearing house for rights, each tournament negotiated its own. Tom Moore remembers, "They were all over. To talk to the Crosby, you had to talk to the Los Angeles Junior Chamber of Commerce. You'd talk to whomever...." The solution? Moore and Arledge told the Professional Golfers Association, "You go out there and get your TV rights back and you guarantee us so many players out of the top money winners and we'll give you a series. We will give you fifteen to twenty golf tournaments a year."

The PGA began chiseling away at the formless mass and soon sculpted order out of chaos, taking over each tournament's television contract after it expired. Then, with control over the TV rights, they hired a television representative to sell the PGA tour as a package.

But the rights to the PGA tour didn't just "fall through the crack," as Tom Moore remembers them doing. Their sale to ABC came only after one funny incident best recounted in

William Johnson's delightfully witty book, *Super Spectator and the Electric Lilliputians.*

One afternoon in 1966, CBS Sports Director Jack Dolph glanced idly out of his office window in the CBS skyscraper and gazed, as he often did 'to rest my weary, weary eyes,' across the narrow canyon of 53rd Street into an office of the ABC skyscraper—an office occupied by one unsuspecting Barry Frank, Director of Sports Planning for ABC. There, to Dolph's amazement and profound curiosity, he saw sitting at Frank's tweedy elbow one Martin Carmichael, the television representative for the Professional Golfers' Association. Now this might not have piqued Dolph's curiosity or offended his sense of fair play quite so much had it not been true that only hours earlier CBS had made an offer to Carmichael to buy the rights to the PGA tour. As Jack Dolph stared between the skyscrapers—no longer idly—he found that though he could not read lips he had a very clear idea of what was being said. "I'm afraid only Marty was over there shopping our bid." says Dolph. "He spilled our offer and figured ABC would top us by a few bucks, and I suppose Barry was encouraging that to its fullest extent."

But no matter who saw whom do what to whom, in a cross between an old Alfred Hitchcock movie and the continual game of one-upsmanship that goes with the television territory, ABC got the tour. And the same Barry Frank, who today is head of sports at CBS, was "moved to the other side of the building."

Arledge soon followed up ABC's acquisition of the PGA tour with another approach shot to make ABC the number one carrier of golf. That same year, 1966, he negotiated a contract with the United States Golf Association for the U.S. Open, the U.S. Womens's Open, and the U.S. Men's Amateur Championships, taking them away from NBC, as they had the PGA Championship from CBS. There was no longer any doubt about whose green was buying the rights to golfing's Grand Slam—the PGA, the U.S. Open, and the British Open.

The only one of the four tournaments grouped into the

Grand Slam they did not have the TV rights to was the Masters. "We broke our pick to get the Masters," remembers Moore, in his colorful southern idiomatic way of speaking. "We spent a lot of goddamn time down at the Reynolds Company with Cliff Roberts, who controlled that thing. Roone and I would go down there every two months and have lunch with him. And he'd say, 'Oh, I like you guys and I'm going to do it with you.' But his was one of the few events in the world that not only had the event, but he also had Cadillac, Travelers Insurance, and Arrow Shirts. And they all belonged to the club and were all on the board of directors of the Augusta National. All he wanted," recalls Moore of the now-departed Roberts, "was a carrier. He didn't want your money, because he didn't want to gouge his friends. But," concluded Moore, with a cheerleader's allegiance to his old alma mater, "we'll get the Masters."

* * *

By 1964, Roone Arledge had been appointed vice-president of ABC Sports. In 1968, as the lame duck president of the network, having been relieved of his duties, Tom Moore called Leonard Goldensen and said, "Can Roone be made president of ABC Sports?" And so in a parting gesture, Tom Moore not only made his favorite disciple the president of the sports division, but also made the division a separate entity within the company. An entity that continues today, with its own controls and expense accounts, responsible first to itself and then to ABC.

* * *

Nobody has yet come close to competing with the Arledge product. The amateur chef has combined carnival pitch, personalization, total story, and technical virtuosity and mixed them together in a unique blend that comes out one part entertainment and one part news reportage.

When he first joined the staff of Sports Programs, the prevailing attitude was one which the commissioner of baseball, Ford Frick, held: "The view a fan gets at home should not be any better than that of the fan in the worst seat in the ballpark." This myopic approach to the televising of sports was straight out of the Neanderthal "if-God-had-wanted-you-to-fly-he-would-have-given-you-wings" school of thought. And yet those televising sporting events adhered to the principle, believing only that their many millions of dollars bought them a seat in the house, nothing more, for their television cameras. cameras.

Arledge took Ed Scherick's fundamental concept of "bringing the fans to the game, not the game to the fans" and embroidered it with the then not recognized Arledge touch. He prepared a mammoth loose-leaf notebook, still legendary in the corridors of ABC, which said that covering a televised game should be just like being a spectator at the game; you not only looked at the game in front of you, but at other people in the stands, the players on the sidelines, and the action around you, whether that be cheerleaders or marching bands or personalities in the stands. It was a simple forthright approach, heretical up to that point, that television was not in the ticket-selling business, but in the business of projecting a game with all its color to the fans.

It has long been held as a truism that those on the FBI's Most Wanted List could escape detection by either becoming the vice-president of the United States, the captain of a whaling vessel, or an interior offensive lineman. Using a hand-held camera to capture players on the sidelines with their helmets off, Arledge revolutionized the ground rules of sports coverage by personalizing the game. It was a monumental moment, the close-up, and had the same effect that first met the classic one-minute rendition of *The Kiss,* starring May Irwin and John Rice. We were fully present with no more need to turn away than our grandfathers did from this first rendering of that private act of affection. We were there. And Arledge had captured the action away from the field as well as on it. "The greatest contribution we can make," he said ten years ago, "is getting people aware of production. We tried making it easier to see the event on television than in person."

Arledge sensed that football and television were perfect partners, symbiotic in what they could bring to each other and the viewer. The shape of the field lent itself to television coverage, with the play always starting in a known area of the field and then flowing continuously to other predictable portions. This fairy tale of fact was given a balletlike reality by Arledge—who not incidentally was a ballet fan—by slo-mos and instant replays, which further stylized the real action. The fan in the stands wasn't privy to these rare studies of intensified action down on the field, and the fan at home would soon reverse his preferences and his habits.

Through Arledge's direction and eyes the camera's report was as real as it was innovative. In a grace shot, the pass goes long and there, reappearing on our screen as if by magic, is the receiver. How did he get there? What pattern did he run? Where is the defender? Sure, some of us want to fancy what happened, like we did when Charlie Chaplin in *City Lights* whispers in his fellow boxer's ear and leaves the screen. Where did he go? What did he do? We know. But that doesn't necessarily work in a football game. And so the iso's and the slow-mos give us the receiver on a down-and-out or post pattern, showing a visual of what really happened without the announcer having to illustrate it.

And as we watched, we unknowingly became fans of Arledge's innovations and fully expected to see replays and isolates when we attended the game in person. We wanted to see the same incontestable reality Arledge had pioneered when we saw the game at home. But, irony of ironies, that reality wasn't there when we went in person. It was as different as a stage play and a stage derivation made into movies. What we saw at the stadium was stilted and unreal compared to what we witnessed on our twenty-three-inch cathode tube, and we would have to wait, like the head coach, to see the game film to understand fully what had transpired. This was the measure of Arledge's contribution to sports; he had transcended the mere bringing of the game to the fans—he had brought the fans to the game.

This one-man electronic revolution has attached small portable cameras to everything from skis to racers in the Grand Prix. He has used cameras underwater and developed missile-tracking devices to keep cameras fixed on a sky diver falling at over 150 mph. And he has placed microphones in more places than J. Edgar Hoover ever thought possible—wherever discretion and rules allow. We have been able to hear the thwack of the bat, the thud of the punt, the screech of burning rubber, the calls of the officials and the umps, and just about every other allowable sound imaginable.

But the real test of his success in bringing the "feel" of the action to the audience, much like "Smellovision" in Aldous Huxley's *Brave New World*, is that at several events covered by ABC, most particularly golf, newspapermen can be seen covering the actual event going on just a few feet from them by watching the monitors in the press tent. But while it was like eating a ham sandwich with the wax paper on for the newsman, Arledge's approach shots have become the television viewer's bread and butter.

* * *

Roone Arledge is somewhat of a stargazer, viewing the celebrities around him as celestial beings, rather than mere human beings. But he is not immune to the siren call of fame himself, and would like to be as well known as some of the celebrities he's surrounded by. He'd like to be known by the brightness of his own star, not theirs.

His first step toward acquiring that much sought-after and elusive commodity known as fame came when he attached his own personal coda to the end of every one of his shows. To many viewers he became known as Roone-Arledge-Executive-Producer. Tom Moore, unaware of the closing credit addition, ran into former CBS President Bob Wood on the street one day. Wood greeted him with "you're creating a monster."

Moore didn't know what he was talking about. "What the hell have I done?"

"You've got that goddamned Roone Arledge on the end of all those shows," groused Wood. "And now every time we hire a guy he says, 'I want to be listed as the executive producer on my shows.' "

The nonplussed Moore, hearing about it for the first time, only said, "Give it to them. What difference does it make?" But it made a difference to Roone and to those who now knew the name and could identify the faceless man who had begun to make ABC Sports a going entity.

* * *

As success begot success and the name Roone Arledge Executive Producer appeared on show after show, it seemed that it would never be associated with a failure. But not every Arledge venture met with success. One, in fact, must be counted as a real disaster.

The biography of Roone Arledge in the 1976–77 edition of *Who's Who in America* contains a dazzling list of accomplishments. Tucked in amongst them is the line "producer entertainment spls, including 'Frank Sinatra, The Main Event at Madison Sq. Garden.' " And hung proudly on Arledge's office wall is a picture of the star of the show, The Chairman of the Board himself.

But neither on his walls nor in his biography can any mention be found of his other "entertainment spl."—"Saturday Night Live with Howard Cosell." Several reviewers suggest that authors Dan Jenkins and Bud Shrake have patterned their main character, in their recent novel *Limo*, TV programming chieftain Frank Mallory, after Roone Arledge although Jenkins disagreed. But the reviewers found the similarity in a programming cross to bear Mallory was given by the president of the network called "Just Down the Street." The program was a three-hour-long live program, which looks like the Loud family series, yet brings back memories of Arledge's only programming debacle. In the book Mallory-Arledge brings off "Just Down the Street" by instilling it with a combination of controversy and programming gimmickry. But "Saturday Night Live with Howard Cosell" failed because of its lack of those two ingredients.

When Arledge telecast the major league baseball games back in 1965, he discovered an overly ambitious, somewhat pushy announcer named Howard Cosell. But there was something in his manner that recommended him to Roone. Maybe it was his vast storehouse of knowledge, spun out at the slightest oral stimulus of a name or fact like a memory bubble of a computer. Maybe it was his ability to command an audience and an interview and ask questions that coming out of others' mouths would create pure embarrassment, but out of his more oft than not were incisive. Or maybe it was his ability to put on as well as put down anybody—celebrity and non-entity alike. Whatever it was, Arledge was taken with this man who, in a world where everyone is just five people away from knowing everyone else, seemed to be just one away—himself. Over the objections of many in the clubby world of broadcasting, Roone championed the cause of Cosell and found that anti–New York and anti-Semetic feelings were negotiable commodities. It was to be his greatest find and the beginning of a love-hate relationship that would have done justice to the Corsican Brothers.

For "Saturday Night Live. . . ," Arledge conceived a show that was modeled after the old "Jack Paar Show." Instead of using Cosell as a communicator, which would have been, as one of those in the programming section of ABC said, "a marvelous melange that Howard could do wonderfully and with ease" of all the important matters from the previous week in the worlds of show business, human interest, and even politics filtering through one studio, Arledge envisioned a show where anything could happen—some great and some ridiculous. "Where people would," according to Arledge, "be saying, 'Boy, I better not miss this tonight because Lord knows what will happen.' "

And so at 8 P.M. on September 20, 1975, Arledge's special opened with a scene reminiscent of a 1930s Hollywood premiere—complete with spotlights sweeping the Manhattan skyline and celebrity after celebrity tumbling out of their rented limousines onto a sidewalk filled with rubberneckers. In front of the aptly named Ed Sullivan Theatre, the tuxedoed Cosell stood, mike in hand, to announce to a nationwide audience which had been bombarded with promos that it was "Saturday Night Live with Howard Cosell," featuring Frank Sinatra, John Denver, Shirley Bassey, the Bay City Rollers, Jimmy Connors, and Paul Anka—and, of course, Howard Cosell.

Sinatra walked on and wished Cosell good luck, cracking, "This show will be a millstone on American TV." Paul Anka sang a duet with his doubles partner, Jimmy Connors. And the Bay City Rollers were shown by satellite from London. But the ingredient that Arledge had really wanted, something or somebody to make people sit up and take notice, never happened. F. Lee Bailey, the attorney for the just-surfaced Patty

Hearst, was lined up to come on the show and be interviewed about the case. But, in light of a restraining order from the presiding judge—even considering Bailey's willingness to bend it—ABC's lawyers vetoed the idea. *Variety* reviewed the show as one which "looks like the 'Wide World of Show Business.' But at its base 'Saturday Night Live with Howard Cosell' has a stronger kinship with the 'Ed Sullivan Show.' The tendency to present its roster as slick vaudeville turns seemed to ignore the reason its predecessor, the Sullivan series, finally went down the drain, namely the cold mechanical flavor of an act doing its turn without time to project some personal warmth to the viewer. The presence of Cosell, even under wraps as he was on the preem, does not seem destined to bridge that gap."

* * *

The second show was to feature LaBelle, a recycled black singing group that had once been Patty LaBelle alone, which had hit the pop charts with something called "Voulez-Vous Couchez Avec Moi?"

The group had wanted a guarantee that they would sing two songs. When it got near the end of the hour, it became patently obvious that there wouldn't be time for two songs, just one. They walked off and left Cosell with an open segment. Cosell came over to Arledge and asked him what he should do.

Arledge told him, "Go out there and blast them."

Cosell, for once in his life squeamish about making waves, defensively responded, "What about the law suits?"

Arledge, hot on the scent of something that would "happen" on his show told Cosell, "Don't worry about the law suits. Leave that to me. This is the kind of thing we've been waiting for."

But instead of blasting them, Cosell made some innocuous remark, refusing, Arledge believes, "to take the abuse he would have to take to make the show work." It was at that point Arledge began to feel that "deep down inside Cosell believed the show would fail and didn't want to go through the hate mail he would have to endure" by being himself. For this, Arledge blamed Cosell in part for the show's demise.

While the first week's ratings were marginal, the second week's were what is known in the industry as "disaster-ville." Saturday night, long a burial ground for variety shows, was once again eating its young. Now all those in the research department whom Arledge had kept at bay with his hit shows started assaulting him with their memoranda telling him "who really watches television at 8:00 on a Saturday night." Arledge saw what he described as "little bits of paper" telling him he would have to have "tigers jumping through hoops and Kate Smith" to appeal to those stay-at-homes. For the first time in his life Arledge was involved in a failure and lost control of his show. He crumbled and, instead of relying on his intuitive feel for programming, listened to those people who read out of a computer what is supposed to be a show based on who's supposed to be watching.

Things began to deteriorate. Arledge lost confidence in "Saturday Night Live with Howard Cosell" and began to feel that the concept of the show had slipped away from him. Whereas he blamed Cosell for part of the reason for the failure, he now blamed himself for the rest. Word got out that the show was going to be canceled and the downhill plunge was on. Before its thirteen-week commitment, "Saturday Night Live with Howard Cosell" was dead. It was to be Arledge's only failure.

* * *

Roone Arledge conquered almost every other mountain he has tried to scale by a combination of negotiating genius, a feeling for people and properties, a delight in hard work, and a passion for technological innovation. But still, after having climbed all the peaks he has, he can look back with more affection for "Wide World of Sports" than any other accomplishment. It is the show that made him what he is. It's not that the Olympics weren't important, but most of the concepts used in Olympic coverage were first developed on "Wide World." It's not that "Monday Night Football" wasn't a milestone, but its personalization and developmental story outline are outgrowths of "Wide World's" focus on people, making the event more than merely an event. Everything ABC Sports does is an offshoot of the "Wide World" production syndrome and Roone Arledge. Regardless of whether "Wide World" was the "doing" of Ed Scherick or Roone Arledge, the very existence of "Wide World of Sports" is a tribute to the many talents of Roone Arledge. He did indeed create it, as we know it today.

* * *

The man who had wanted a contract from Sports Programs when he first joined them in 1960 decided that he'd rather be without one when his own six-figure contract expired in August 1975. Tom Moore, who had worked with Arledge for eight years, gave this insight into the man: "He never wants to come to grips with his own decision. He wants to have all his options open. In plain language, he'd rather not have a contract." And so, by design, he didn't. Now he could pursue all of those avenues available to him.

One such avenue was NBC. Bob Howard, the president, conducted a long series of discussions with him, making what someone at NBC said was "a fantastic offer . . . a combination of the presidency of the sports division and a participation in the entertainment area." But Arledge finally decided that "if it were sports, what the hell could he do to top what he's already done?" He would have to start all over, and his performance at ABC would always be the measuring stick. He investigated organizing his own production company, even co-producing a movie starring John Denver. Arledge was at the crossroads. Clearly, while he remained faithful to ABC, he wanted new horizons to conquer. "I'm at a point where I have to come to some career decision," he told TV writer Kay Gardella. "What direction to go in is the question."

Meanwhile, back at Hot Rock, ABC was in a bind. Obviously Arledge couldn't be given a position commensurate with his talents in the entertainment area, an area run by Fred Silverman with all the efficiency and success of a Vince Lombardi, producing winner after winner. There would have to be some *other* avenue, some *other* option in the words of one reporter. And while Arledge was, in the words of Cosell, "throwing up smoke screens," ABC was seeking a way to keep him by creating a position that would synergistically work for both Arledge and ABC. On December 28, 1976, they finally found that position. In a scene right out of *Network*, Elton Rule, the president of ABC, Inc., announced that ABC News, previously an autonomous department reporting directly to Rule, would be placed under the supervision of Fred Pierce, president of ABC Television.

And then on May 2, 1977, the other shoe dropped. Pierce announced the long-rumored appointment of Roone Arledge as president of both ABC News and ABC Sports. Here was an opportunity for Arledge to once again work his magic, to breathe life into a division that had suffered share and morale slippage, the worst two maladies imaginable in the world of television. ABC News was running third out of three and losing ground, despite the addition of Barbara Walters. ABC might have tolerated that in years past. But no more. And Arledge would *never* tolerate it.

* * *

You could almost feel a new day aborning for ABC News on that Monday morning a redheaded, informally attired man made his way from office to office on the news floor, introducing himself to everyone with a quiet and warming, "Hi, I'm Roone. . . ."

4
Spanning the Globe with "Wide World of Sports"

A small man with twinkling eyes, a thin tie, and a Bob Halde-man crewcut stood in the rain in Franklin Field and spoke into a microphone: "Today's exciting show launches ABC's 'Wide World of Sports,' a new and exciting global concept of sports. Each Saturday for the next twenty weeks we'll be taking our cameras to the scene of the famous sports events all over the world." The event was the Penn Relays. The date was April 29, 1961. The show, of course, was "Wide World of Sports." And the announcer? Jim McKay, the man who has been associ-ated with the "Wide World of Sports" as its host since its inception that rainy April day seventeen years ago.

* * *

"Wide World of Sports" was not born out of a creative explosion. It was, as the old saying goes, born of necessity. During the summer doldrums, the ABC affiliates were literally crying for sports programming to fill some of the open week-end spots that pocked their schedules like bomb craters. What, they asked, could be sensibly programmed to 100 percent of the then 100-plus ABC affiliates during those dog-day summer weekend afternoons? Baseball was out of the question. Not only did the "ABC Game-of-the-Week" in previous years not do well—but all major league areas were blacked out. There were no other so-called major sports available to fill those weekend afternoons that were fast becoming TV ghetto areas. A program would have to be created, one which was not subject to blackouts in 52 percent of the country, but which could, instead, go out to all of the affiliates.

In the late 1950s and early 1960s, CBS had a documentary type sports show on Thursday nights called "CBS Sports Spectacular," a program that was resuscitated in recent years on the weekends. Ed Scherick believed that a similar package could be built for ABC, featuring events of less than overwhelming importance in terms of their newsworthiness but that had visual appeal. A sports fan would not seek out these events the next day in the daily newspaper but would enjoy them at that moment. And so, in December of 1960, with no great pride of authorship in the idea, he went to see Tom Moore, ABC programming head. "Tom, the only way we can program this network to 100 percent of the affiliates is to do it with taped programming of events that people are willing to watch on a delayed basis." Moore, by now a complete devotee of sports and sports programming, agreed and gave Scherick the go-ahead.

Although the program was tentatively set to go on that April as a summer replacement, it had neither content nor form. Scherick went to his new producer, Roone Arledge, and asked him "to put something down on paper" so that he could go out and sell advertising. "We've got a schedule, but we don't know what the fuck we're doing," he explained.

Arledge, in turn, called in his production assistant, Chuck Howard, and told him to compile a list of sports events, from April through September, on a week-by-week basis and then list the best ones.

Howard just stood there: "How'm I going to do *that?*" he asked incredulously.

Arledge, remembering his old alma mater, NBC, answered, "I'll tell you exactly how you're going to do it. Go over to the NBC library and take the microfilm of old copies of the *New York Times.* I don't know how long it will take you to go through the microfilm of the sports sections everyday from April to September, but do it."

One last question from Howard, "How'm I going to get in?"

Arledge replied, "I can get you in on Pat Hernon's name." Why Pat Hernon's name? Because he made no use of the library facilities and therefore wasn't known there.

And so, in just two days, a long working list for the program that was to become known as "Wide World of Sports" was conceived in the NBC library.

The working schedule derived from *The New York Times*'s sports pages was nothing more than a guide, hardly written in graven stone, and changed as exigencies and suggestions dictated other events be pursued. Suggestions were welcomed from any quarters: Tom Moore suggested a winner-take-all head-to-head match between Arnold Palmer and Gary Player at St. Andrews golf course in Scotland; Carol Scherick, Ed's wife, long an afficionado of rodeos, suggested either the Calgary Stampede or the Cheyenne Frontier Days Rodeo; and so on. While the suggestions kept coming in, Arledge and Howard worked frantically to lock up the rights to the events they had culled from the newspapers. But they ran into two major obstacles. First of all, they couldn't commit to any event, because the show was only tentatively scheduled as a summer replacement. And, just as troublesome, most of those contacted had never heard of the proposed show and merely responded to the opening thrust, "We'd like to do your auto race on our news sports show called 'Wide World of Sports' " with a resounding "What?"

Slowly Arledge hacked away at the thicket and began lining up events one-by-one for the twenty-week series. In order to expedite their acquisition of rights, Arledge and Scherick agreed that they should approach someone who had the rights to a multiplicity of events and could provide them programming on a wholesale basis. Immediately the AAU came to The AAU not only sponsored many of the events that would meet Scherick's original premise for the show—that very few sports fans would read the agate type in their daily sports pages to find the results of an event, but would enjoy them at the moment when seen—but also the US–USSR track meet that was coming up later that year in Moscow. Scherick sent Arledge to the Plaza Hotel in New York, believing that it would be better if Arledge presented the case for ABC, since "a Jew didn't go in to talk to the AAU at that time and Arledge had a much nicer name than I did."

For Roone Arledge, it marked his first big negotiating triumph, as he landed the rights for the AAU events for 1961, including track and field, gymnastics, swimming and diving, and the Russian–American track meet. For the "Wide World of Sports" it formed the backbone of their first year, providing them with almost half their programming. For Ed Scherick, who felt a "little ashamed" of his actions, it proved that his instincts had been correct in sending Arledge. It also proved to be one of the last things he was to do for "Wide World of Sports."

* * *

The show-to-be was still without a name. It soon had one. Just as the show itself was formulated out of an already-existing idea and did not jump full-born out of someone's head like Athena out of Zeus's, the name was also less an inspiration than an adaptation. At that time NBC had a program on called "Wide, Wide World of Entertainment." One day Chet Simmons, Scherick's administrative assistant, approached him with, "Why don't we call this program the 'Wide World of Sports.' " Scherick responded, "That's a terrific title. Let's *not* call it the 'ABC Sports Spectacular.' " Thus the bloodlines for "Wide World of Sports" came out of CBS, and the show was sired by the NBC microfilm library.

In later years, Bill MacPhail, head of CBS sports, used to say to Scherick, "Edgar, there's a great deal of similarity between the Wide World of Sports and the CBS Sports Spectacular." Scherick never responded, "Bill, how could you say that?" He merely chose to ignore the remark.

A funny thing happened to Ed Scherick on his way to the "Wide World of Sports" inaugural. By the time the show aired on April 29, 1961, he no longer owned Sports Programs, "Wide World of Sports," or any of the other properties developed by his company. In fact, he no longer worked there. As an outside consultant (and sometimes insultant) Scherick had more than met ABC's expectations. He had brought in shows, sponsors, and success upon success. His small company, Sports Programs, was not only a profit center, but ABC's sports department as well.

Both Scherick and Sports Programs had been the subject of some discussion among ABC executives, and both were on their "Most Wanted" list. Right after the completion of the NCAA season, Tom Moore approached Scherick, who had gone to the West Coast to establish yet another venture—the importation of sailboats from Yugoslavia, dubbed with a certain admixture of class and *chutzpah*, Sailing USA. Moore broached the subject of Scherick joining the network in an executive capacity. He had already discussed it with Ollie Treyz, the president of the network, and wanted him to become vice-president in charge of sales. But Scherick the entrepreneur had never been a vice-president of anything. And besides, he asked, "What am I going to do with my business?" Moore was ready and answered, "We'll merge your business into ours." Scherick left to "think about it."

But Scherick, who was actively involved in getting the "Wide World of Sports" together for its tentative air date of April 29, didn't have time to think about it. Two months passed and nothing happened. The next words he heard were those of Ollie Treyz resounding from coast to coast: "Tell Ed we'll be tilling another field soon if he doesn't do something about this."

By now Scherick was giving the offer, as well as his future, a lot of thought. He had come to that point when men start reassessing their accomplishments, their present situations, and their futures, and he had come to realize that there was something more important than merely pointing the camera at two teams who ran around playing a game. He decided to take ABC up on its offer and negotiated a deal with Si Siegel, treasurer of ABC, whereby ABC purchased Sports Programs, Inc., and all of its properties—including 100 percent of "Wide World of Sports"—from Scherick for half-a-million dollars in stock, thereby making him the second largest individual stockholder in ABC. In March of 1961, Sports Programs, Inc., became the official sports department of ABC and Ed Scherick became the vice-president in charge of sales. Jim McKay remembers: "On a Friday Ed Scherick walked out of the office, like he did every other Friday, and he never came back."

* * *

From the very day Ollie Treyz introduced him to the ABC salesmen with the opening line, "Meet your new sales manager" (while the previous one sat in attendance, publicly beheaded), Scherick was excluded from any further participation with the sports department he had built. It was as if a latticed portcullis had dropped down and separated him from his own creations. The umbilical cord had been cut, and Scherick was no longer permitted to be a part of it; it was now the property of ABC—lock, stock, and "Wide World of Sports."

But Scherick did return to the Sports Programs offices one last time. As head of sales, Scherick was to continue to play a major role in getting "Wide World of Sports" on the air. Scheduled as a replacement for the fourth week in April, there was still a go, no-go decision to be made. That decision depended upon the one element Scherick was now in a position to do something about: advertising. The show did not have a sponsor, and with the cutoff date of March 31 fast approaching, it had begun to look as if the "Wide World of Sports" would be stillborn.

Gillette had already requested that one-half of their full sponsorship in the college football games for 1961 be sold off to other sponsors by ABC. Scherick, as head of sales, had no difficulty in finding sponsors for the games, selling one-quarter to Amoco. Suddenly he found two major cigarette brands clamoring for the final one-quarter. But with no sponsor interest in "Wide World of Sports" and the executive dictum that one-half would have to be sold before March 31, which was less than a week away, he decided to "package" the sale of the two programs together, using the NCAA as leverage. He played the two agencies for R. J. Reynolds and Liggett & Meyers, William Esty and J. Walter Thompson, off against one another and was finally able to get Esty to commit for one-quarter sponsorship in the NCAA games and one-half in "Wide World." At 4:30 on Friday afternoon, March 31—just thirty minutes before the deadline—Scherick was seen running into the Sports Programs's offices—the only time he was to set foot in them after he sold his equity—waving a piece of paper over his head, screaming, "It's a go! It's a go!"

* * *

Sports Programs now came under Tom Moore's aegis as programming head. Moore had been the catalyst in the entire development of the sports operation, the man who had been the sounding board for Scherick's genius. Together they sparked and kindled and changed the face of electronic sports. His bête noire had been Ollie Treyz, who never truly understood or cared about the potential importance of sports to ABC.

Moore understood. If he hadn't sensed it before, he discovered it during the telecast of an American Football League game that previous fall. Independently watching a game between the New York Titans and the Dallas Texans, it became obvious to both Moore and Scherick that the game bore little if any resemblance to football. All that the teams in the AFL could do was throw the ball downfield in a never-ending cascade of "Hail Mary" passes. Rarely, if ever, were any of the passes completed. The referees suffered from the same infirmity, never being able to get the ball back to the line of scrimmage on less than three bounces. Watching this charade, Scherick called Moore and told him, "We've got trouble."

Moore knew the trouble. Disney came on at 7:00. As he watched another referee kick the ball upfield, he said, "Let's talk about it in ten minutes." But ten minutes later it had only gotten worse. When Scherick and Moore conversed again, Moore uttered the deathless line, "Who could be watching this piece of shit?"

Mutually they decided to take the game off the air at 6:58:30, whether it was over or not. As the game faded from the screens the switchboards at all the ABC affiliates throughout the country lit up like fields of fireflies in August. At this precise moment, six years before the infamous Heidi game, Moore became aware of just how important sports was to the American viewer—and to the American Broadcasting Company.

Scherick had, for all intents and purposes, left the ABC sports department—née Sports Programs, a name it kept until 1962—in the hands of his administrative assistant, Chet Simmons. But once it merged with ABC, it became a division under Tom Moore and his to do with as he wanted. But whether he wanted to create a division in his own image and not only remove Scherick, but all vestiges of him, including the reminder of Scherick in Simmons, or whether he merely supported another in a fight for top post in the power vacuum, the results were the same. And the next two years at ABC Sports would be spent playing the executive game called power struggle.

Late in 1960, Scherick introduced a young, freckle-faced man-boy to Moore as "the producer of 'Wide World of Sports' . . . and doing a good job of it." The young producer, of course, was Roone Arledge. Moore was taken with him and saw in Arledge the ability to attract and lead men (such as the man whom Moore referred to as "Roone's secret weapon," Production Assistant Chuck Howard), negotiate for rights, and most importantly, produce outstanding sports programming. In short, Moore saw in this redheaded leprechaun with glasses the man to head up the department. And while, according to Julie Barnathan, "It would be normal that Chet was the guy who was going to be running the department," others saw the dual positioning of two top young executives, one the administrator and the other the producer, as "an impossible situation", which "wasn't going to sit long." The ensuing executive struggle between Arledge and Simmons for king of the mountain was no contest. Arledge's "priest" was going on to bigger and better things at the network, and Simmons's was all but gone. One executive-watcher said, "Roone wasn't going to have Chet standing in his way." And by 1963, he didn't. After coming to work one day and finding that his desk had been cleaned out, Simmons solved the impasse by leaving to join NBC, where he was to go on to become vice-president in charge of sports. Tom Moore soon succeeded Treyz as president of the ABC network and named Arledge his vice-president in charge of ABC Sports.

ABC Sports and the "Wide World of Sports" were to be the

lasting legacies of Ed Scherick. But in a larger sense, they were also to be monuments to the efforts and contributions of Roone Arledge, who was to develop them by adding production and programming muscularity to everything bequeathed him—far beyond the hopes of Moore and the dreams of Scherick.

* * *

Probably no man has a higher standard of excellence than Jim McKay—particularly when the English language is concerned. He speaks in complete sentences and prefers, among other precise uses of the queen's English, the term *commentator* over the word *announcer*, professing to be less of the "tell-it-like-it-is" school than the "tell-it-*as*-it-is" school of journalism. Although McKay had been the "commentator" on Sports Programs's first telecast dedicating the new Roosevelt Raceway, he hadn't received many other assignments from Scherick. When he would request that Scherick find him "a good sports show," Scherick, half in jest and half in truth, would respond, "You're too literate for this stuff, Jim."

With the "Wide World of Sports" elevated from its tentative holding pattern to landing a permanent position on the summer replacement schedule, there was need for just such a literate commentator. After Chuck Howard tracked down McKay, who was in Augusta, Georgia, serving as the anchorman for CBS on the Masters Golf telecast, Arledge called him in the middle of the tournament and asked McKay if he was interested in being the host for the twenty-show series. Arledge then threw in the most classic understatement since a Crow scout told Colonel Custer that there might be trouble along the Little Big Horn: "It involves a good deal of travel." Yes, McKay was interested. The next day Arledge called back and said, "You're our guy. How much money do you want?" McKay tried to put him off by telling him that he was in the middle of a golf classic; couldn't this wait until he returned to New York? But no—"we have a press conference in half an hour and we'd like to announce who the host of the show is." And for McKay, it's been that way ever since.

* * *

Jim McKay is an American institution, as enduring as the faces on Mount Rushmore and the Statue of Liberty, and more familiar to Americans than both. His face, with twinkling eyes and thin lines outlining them, is the face that has graced television for almost four-fifths of its adult life, more than Ed Sullivan and Milton Berle combined. And the man who goes with the face has won a six-pack of Emmys, the George Polk Memorial Award for the outstanding television news reporter of 1972 and has been called "as much a historian as Arnold Toynbee."

And yet, sad to relate, Virginia, there is no Jim McKay. For the man we watch every Saturday and Sunday on "Wide World of Sports" is in reality Jim McManus, a former city-side newspaperman at the *Baltimore Sun* who traded in his typewriter for a microphone when the *Sun* called on him as one of the army of recruits they needed for the coming television explosion at their new TV station.

For two-and-a-half years, Jim McManus served as a news and sports commentator, whose duties included covering such major Baltimore civic events as wrestling. After graduation to a three-hour afternoon "strip" show called "The Sports Parade," he emceed the first and third hours and filled with interviews and songs. During the second hour, he directed the show "pushing my own buttons."

In 1950, CBS invited him to New York for what he thought was a sports show. He found out "they were talking a variety show." He auditioned for two-and-a-half hours one Sunday morning at the old Leiderkranz Hall on 58th Street with a piano player and a girl singer, just seeing "how long you can go." And McKay, who sounds like George Burns in drag and can use any three words of any sentence to break into an impromptu song, went and went and went. CBS bought his act and he came to New York.

It was then that CBS dusted off one of its old names, Jim McKay, stored somewhere in the back room between props and scenery for the twenty-seven-year-old McManus. Long a radio tradition, which had carried over into the antediluvian days of TV, stock names were owned by the station or the network in case there was a contract dispute with the talent or the so-called name personality upped and quit. There had been an unbroken string of Galen Drakes throughout the history of radio, all unrelated in blood or looks, merely alike in voice. And now there was to be another voice in a string of Jim McKays, albeit *this* Jim McKay was to be the last of the line.

The show Jim McKay was to host was to be called "The Real McKay," a takeoff on the old bromide "the real McCoy." After the first introductory lines; "Brighten your day with the real McKay, here's a show just meant for you. We're going to chase all your blues away, going to make you feel just like the real McKay. We've got old songs, and new songs . . . a little conversation, too. Now is the time to introduce to you . . . The Real (drum roll bruuuuum) McKay (drum roll bruuuuum)"— he spent most of the time singing duets with either his piano player or the lead girl singer. The song always seemed to be "Angry," remembers producer Doug Wilson as McKay breaks into one of his free association song shticks. "Angry, please don't be angry, 'cause I was only teasing you."

McKay had always been interested in singing and had once aspired to be another Bing Crosby. Once, during a talent search by a local Baltimore station, McKay and a classmate showed up to represent their school with a rendition of the Bing Crosby–Johnny Mercer song "Lazy Bones." But just before they were to take their place in front of the mike, the "Johnny Mercer" partner succumbed to tension and fled the studio in fright, leaving just McKay to handle both parts. Ever the trooper then as he is now, able to leap embarrassing situations in a single bounce, he filled in and did both parts. When he got home that night, his parents greeted their star performer with words of praise. But his father threw in the kicker. "You were fine, but frankly I can't say much for the kid that sang the Mercer portion."

All the while he was doing "The Real McKay," McKay was doing a five-minute sports summary on WCBS–TV in New York, the first such late-night sports summary in the country. Then, after a brief stint as the host of a courtroom drama, entitled "The Verdict is Yours," McKay took his talents and his name to the sports side and became one of CBS's sports stable, specializing as the commentator on golf matches.

For the past seventeen years, Jim McKay has become identified as "the Voice" of "Wide World of Sports." In fine tuning our perception of little known sports, he has become "The Man of a Thousand Places," both figuratively and literally. And McKay is one of the few announcers who follows the insights of Ernest Hemingway, who, when asked by the Parisian *Review* "how does one become a good writer" answered "have a typewriter with a built-in shit detector." McKay is that detector for the viewer, as he "tries to find a little broader meaning in everything than just going around the globe watching jocks win and lose games."

Starting with the first show on April 29, 1961, with Jim McKay in Philadelphia to broadcast the Penn Relays and Bill Flemming in Des Moines for the Drake Relays, that first year was a smorgasbord, with twenty-five different events in fifteen different sports telecast in the twenty-week series.

The show lived up to its energetic "Wide World of Sports" billing by going to Mexico City for tennis; Le Mans, France, for auto racing; London, England, and Norman, Oklahoma, for football; Scotland for golf; Seattle for hydroplaning; and Nagoya, Japan, for baseball. The events were not, as James Michener calls them in his book *Sports in America*, "oddball" events, but were, in the main, solid sporting events telecast with technical wizardry. "You'll find very little of the basket-weaving-type thing in "Wide World'," said Arledge. "However, some sports do not have mass appeal. For this reason we have never done jai alai, badminton, dog racing, curling, and archery." Arledge was able to delicately wed "whatever it is that makes those events fascinating" to both the participants and the spectators with the action to come up with a documentary-type show that was not only wide-ranging but totally imaginative. Shot "live on tape" for airing the week after, its immediacy and fast pace made it the most interesting sports show on television from day one.

The technical virtuosity for which Arledge was to become legendary in years to come evinced itself during that first year as he sent an engineer to the bottom of the pool at the National AAU Swimming and Diving Championships, took a skeleton crew and seventeen tons of equipment to Moscow for the one-day US–USSR track meet, and employed expert commentators to bring the fine points of unusual games, like British football, to the viewer.

But it was all for naught. The ratings hovered between 5 and 6, and the decision was made to cancel the show at the end of its run, September 9. ABC had thrown a mammoth party and nobody came. "Wide World of Sports" was going to be just another of those summer replacements that prompted a California repair shop to advertise: "TV Sold, Installed, and Serviced Here. Not Responsible for Summer Programs."

The reason for its cancellation was almost as multifaceted as the show itself. For openers, there was no room at the TV inn; the show had nowhere to go. Scheduled between 5:00 and 6:30 on Saturday afternoons, "Wide World of Sports" would have been preempted for the next three months by NCAA football on Saturdays and AFL football on Sundays had it been continued. Secondly, many advertisers had pulled back on their budgetary allocations in the face of the uncertain business climate and market slump, exacerbated by Kennedy waving the governmental big stick at the steel industry. And, most importantly, the local affiliates wanted the summer time slots back so they could use them themselves.

And so, the president of the network, Ollie Treyz, decided to cancel the show over the strenuous objections of his programming vice-president, Tom Moore. In a fateful showdown in Leonard Goldenson's office attended by Treyz, Moore, Scherick, and Julie Barnathan, the matter was thrashed out. Treyz opened the meeting: "No point in continuing this disaster." Moore, who had originally given the show its Promethean spark of life, fought for its continuation on Saturdays in the fourth quarter of 1961 and on Sundays in the first quarter of 1962. Barnathan, general manager of the network, was against this flip-flopping of days, feeling that it gave the stations an excuse not to clear the program. He wanted to establish a viewing habit for the show. Besides, he was having trouble clearing "Maverick" with certain affiliates on Sunday at 6:30 and felt he would lose them. But in face of the objections, valid though they might be, Moore's fervent argument to "give me one more thirteen-week shot, just one more!" won the day. Goldenson decided that "Wide World" was worthy of another chance and extended it for the first quarter of 1962.

If anything, the second year of "Wide World of Sports" was better than the first. It began with the Sunday, January 7 telecast of the AFL All-Star football game and then segued into more traditional "Wide World" programming, like barrel-jumping, water skiing, track and field, and auto racing. By the time the "Wide World of Sports" had hit its fifth show, it had also hit its stride with the International Surfing Championships and the National Skiing Championships, giving it a thirty-eight share. The most successful franchise in sports had finally taken off, and yet no one at ABC was certain of just what they had.

* * *

Over the succeeding sixteen years, through the end of 1976, the "Wide World of Sports" has featured 1,871 events from ninety-eight different sports on 800 shows, an average of almost two-and-a-half events per show. This giant maw had to be filled with prime events that could be scheduled and rescheduled, but most importantly, were of interest to the viewer. Where could they be found? They couldn't continue to sneak into the NBC library to cull them from the sports pages of the *Times*.

There was little trouble obtaining the rights to events in the beginning. Some of the events would even have paid to be on national television, and "Wide World" was the only game in town. The Gold Cup Hydroplane Championships were one case where "Wide World" just went to Seattle and covered it, without worrying about the rights. Another was the Oxridge Horse Show in Darien, Connecticut, at the club where, not incidentally, Tom Moore was a member. And still another was the Queen's Cup Polo Match from Windsor Great Park in London, England, featuring Prince Philip as one of the players. A friend of the prince's had a show that Tom Moore wanted and as an accommodation to the friend, the polo matches were picked up for two years.

But ABC would occasionally look a gift horse—or dog—in the mouth. For years the Westminster Dog Show people had literally hounded ABC to put their show on "Wide World." Many prominent people in the advertising world and with the affiliates were dog-fanciers and tried to put pressure on ABC. One, Henry Kaiser, was not only one of the major sponsors of "Maverick," but also raised poodles, five of which were entered in the upcoming Westminster Show. He had his agency call Tom Moore. But Moore resisted the overtures and opportunes and neatly sidestepped, arranging instead for ABC news to carry an interview with Kaiser and his five poodles. That got him off the hook, especially since all of the dogs lost. To this day "Wide World" has never carried the Westminster Dog Show.

The majority of those approaching ABC do so because they see the road to television paved with gold. Over one hundred people a week call and write to offer ABC the "chance of a lifetime"—to put on their event. Those offered have included motorized bar stool racing in San Francisco, a rat decathlon organized by a group of college kids at a California junior college, and several other such wondrous events. One table tennis group even sent all three networks bid specification letters, demanding that they send in their sealed bids by a certain deadline date "or they would not be eligible for the rights." All three passed.

Perhaps the most classic case of what the Italians call *ballista* occurred during the second year of "Wide World," when a crew went down to Acapulco for the taping of the International Water Ski Championships. As Arledge and the crew reached their hotel, they were met by a local man named Raul Garcia, who represented the water skiers. When he was asked by director Dick Kirchner if everything was all right, he answered, "Oh, everything is fine." And then he added, "By the way, I've got the divers."

"Wait a minute," said Kirchner. "What divers?"

Garcia pointed to the now-visible eighty-seven-foot cliffs overlooking a shallow inlet, where one of the divers was doing a swan dive into the water. And although both Kirchner and Arledge immediately saw it as adding a little local color to their scene set of Acapulco, they still hadn't asked the most important question, "Quanto?"

Garcia, without batting an eye, replied, "One hundred thousand dollars."

Arledge and Kirchner both told Garcia it was out of the question and started to leave.

"Un momento," said Garcia and scurried away to consult with his "clients." Within a minute he came back, "It's all right. They compromised."

"Compromised?" said Kirchner, "It's still way out of range."

Arledge then asked, "What did they compromise for?"

Garcia proudly announced, "They've agreed to $10 a dive."

And so, for a price that sounded like a dance-hall request of the thirties, Roone Arledge had his greatest negotiating coup. But the divers meant to keep him to his part of the bargain and wouldn't make any rehearsal dives without being guaranteed $10 for those, too. ABC was to find out in their quest for events that nothing was free.

* * *

"Wide World of Sports" became the *Guinness Book* of the airwaves as it continued to spew out a cornucopia of sports events that ranged from A to at least W: auto racing, bobsled runs, computer fights, demolition derbies, Eiffel Tower climbs, fighter interceptor rocketry meets, grand national steeple-chases, high wire walks, ice skating championships, and everything else imaginable on the spectrum down to wrist-wrestling from Petaluma, California. It covered everything from the wild cheering at Madison Square Garden and Wembley to the sedate grandeur at Wimbledon.

Sometimes "Wide World" seemed to cover a sport for the same reason Sir Edmund Hillary climbed a mountain—"Because it's there"—but more often there was a pattern. Haunted by a sense of the public's fickleness, "Wide World" shifted the pace of television programming to accommodate their audience's short attention span, an outgrowth of the television age. Faced with the viewer's number of multiple choices, including the perpetual game of musical dials, as well as popular divertissements around the house, "Wide World of

Sports" became a potpourri of events, as the cameras flicked back and forth, showing very little in its entirety. To some purists, it was a blasphemy; to others, a sensory overload. But to most viewers, it was a veritable feast, the opening chorus from "A Funny Thing Happened"—"something for everyone tonight!"

Arledge not only covered the full-range of sports, but also the fervor of the people who participated in them. He presented the competition of man against man as well as the competition of man against himself and against the elements, bringing a dramatic quality to "Wide World" that stylistically set the show apart from anything ever done before. He recognized the inherent qualities that made these events appealing: "All sports are equal in their potential for dramatic impact on those people who know and care and are involved in the spirit of the contest, so that the atmosphere in Hayward, Wisconsin, on the day of the lumberjack championships is really not unlike the atmosphere in London on the day of the F. A. Cup Championships or in Baltimore when the Colts are playing the Chicago Bears." It was this "air of electricity . . . and this atmosphere that pervades any sporting event," which Arledge captured in a vivid and purposeful manner. It was as if he was able to convey a bird's eye view through the mirror of the electronic eye.

Throughout the years Arledge has been able to invest the viewer with a deeper insight into what makes Sammy run, catch, and throw through getting up-close-and-personal with the participants, allowing the viewers a sense of how important the sport is to the participant. Such is the macho sport of wrist wrestling, first shown on "Wide World" January 17, 1970. The matches are held each year in Sonoma County, California, not 100 miles from Calavares County, where another unusual all-American sporting event took place—the jumping frog competition. And just as Mark Twain made the jumping frog contest famous, Ernest Hemingway first wrote about wrist wrestling in his classic The Old Man and the Sea.

It was not until Bill Soberanes, the sports columnist for the local Petaluma paper, decided to organize the "boys in the back room" that this timeless bar sport took on the trappings of a competition. Now designated as founder-president of the annual contest, Soberanes recently explained what it takes to enter: "Anybody with a wrist can do it." In fact, the rules are so simple it's a wonder it wasn't organized before Soberanes did it. All you need are two competitors and a level surface. The two sit across from each other and grasp each other's right hand, planting their elbows on the surface. Then push comes to shove until one forces the other's arm to the surface. That's all there is to it. Unless, of course, you're an advanced wrist wrestler, in which case you also grasp your opponent's left hand at surface level, preventing him (or her, incidentally) from exerting extra pressure and forcing the right hand down.

It has now become big league, as far as bar sports go, with $5,000 offered in several classes, including heavyweight and two for the ladies. And through presenting wrist wrestling with enough presence and sensitivity to convey the premise that there are some sports that are more fun to participate in than watch, ABC has turned it from mere electronic trivia into interesting programming.

* * *

Dick Young, the sometimes acerbic sports columnist for the New York *Daily News,* recently asked the loaded question, "Does anybody really watch those racing cars chasing each other around and round every Saturday on ABC's increasingly 'Narrow World of Sports?' " In his effort to berate ABC and his old nemesis, television, Young displayed a smug New York provincialism that leads many New Yorkers to believe that the world ends west of the Hudson.

But there is another world out there, the world of auto racing. According to Triangle Publications's prestigious study of sports attendance, more than 49 million fans attend auto racing every year—more than baseball, football, or basketball— and more cram into the Indianapolis Speedway to see the 500 than any other sporting event in the world. And apparently they "can't get enough of that wonderful stuff," because they continue to tune in to the auto racing presented on "Wide World," whose auto racing ratings are consistently better than the competitive NBC baseball "Game of the Week."

Since its inaugural year "Wide World" has covered 317 auto

racing events ranging from "good ole boys" driving old Mercuries with "Fahrstone" decals on the doors to high-powered machinery at Indy and Monaco. The names of their locales—Daytona, Atlanta, Phoenix, Indianapolis, Lime Rock, Ontario, and Monaco—are now as familiar to sports fans as Madison Square Garden and Yankee Stadium. But if auto racing is one of the most popular "Wide World" shows amongst sports fans it is also one of the most difficult to cover—particularly the showcase of them all, the Indianapolis 500.

Chet Forte, who has directed many races, feels that the 500 is "the most difficult thing for a director to do. Say you're on the leader covering a battle for first and second and all of a sudden the producer says, 'Hey, we want to go back to sixth place.' Now you've got to change all those cameras to find sixth place. And you've got to reorient the cameramen, 'Here he comes into turn two. Be ready, camera two. Stand by, camera three.' " Add the cameras in Gasoline Alley and you have fifteen or sixteen cameras, all attempting to catch an event that appeals to the senses of sound, smell, and sight and you have one helluva logistics problem. But the biggest nightmare of all in covering Indy is condensing a three-hour-plus event into two hours on prime time TV that night. It's kamikaze time. As the program comes on the air, they are still editing the show in the truck, with Jim McKay sitting in front of his monitor to do a voice layover. It's much like changing your tire while the car is moving. But somehow it's done, and it's not only great sport but great television. And the fans remember it.

Fans also remember Chris Economaki bulldogishly chasing A. J. Foyt through Gasoline Alley trying to find out why his car was knocked out of the race. Or Jackie Stewart squeaking in his delightful Scottish burr, "Look at that. Cale's car is up on the wall . . . Richard's trying to get by him . . . oh, oh, they almost touched . . . What a marvelous bit of driving!" Or Keith Jackson, with a voice that still retains enough of that down home sound, "Only 'bout an exle-greasing away from the track he's now at," bringing the color of a stock car chase. Or Jim McKay, with his wisps of hair waving in the breeze, standing on the track, setting up the day's race. Or Chris Schenkel lend-ing his proud back-home-again-in-Indiana voice to another running of the Indy.

Some viewers will always remember Schenkel's near-brush with disaster in the 1972 Indy 500. The pace car carrying him—along with the venerable Tony Hulman, president of the Speedway, and astronaut John Glenn—had driven into the pit stop area at a higher rate of speed than anticipated. As the car hurtled toward the stands, Glenn ducked and they all followed his lead. Glenn later told Schenkel, "When you learned to fly, and a crash was imminent, you were taught to duck behind the engine. That would probably save your life." It probably saved Schenkel's life that day in Indianapolis as well. The visibly shaken announcer escaped with only a slight concussion and a cracked scapula. Those five seconds were indelibly branded on everyone's memory; they all froze—viewers, participants even the cameramen. And, as Arledge frequently reminds Schenkel, "What a shame if you had been killed. We wouldn't have been able to show it on videotape. Schenkel didn't think that was too funny—then or now.

It's all there in auto racing—the fear and the courage, the crashes and the victories, the competition and the camaraderie. And "Wide World of Sports" is there, too, to capture those ingredients and the audience as well.

* * *

In making the show insightful, ABC had more than its number of electronic thrills of victory. But they also suffered their share of agonies. Perhaps none so agonizing as trying to capture both the action of and the emotion in the Fischer-Spassky World Championship Chess match in Reykjavik, Iceland, in July of 1972.

The twenty-four-game series for the World Championship had been arranged by the International Federation of Chess, under the auspices of the Icelandic Chess Federation, which had paid $125,000 for the rights to hold the match in their capital. In an attempt to recoup their investment, they had, in turn, sold television rights to promoter Chester Fox, who then sold them to ABC.

Arledge dispatched Producer-Director Chet Forte to Iceland

to tape some segments of the match for a "Wide World" and get an interview with Fischer. Easier said than done. Forte arrived in late June and by the end of June, with the match to commence on July 11, he had sent back some footage but no interview. "The prime thing was to try to get an interview with Bobby Fischer," said Forte, in retrospect appreciating the difficulty of his assignment.

After two weeks, he called Arledge. "Jesus, Roone, I can't get anything."

Arledge, hardly sympathetic to Forte's predicament in trying to assail the impenetrable fortress known as Mount Fischer, only said, "Well, keep trying."

Forte complains of his claustrophobic existence there. "There was no place to go, nothing to do. It's daylight all day long; I couldn't sleep. I saw every movie on the island, and I'm killing my time still trying to get something with Fischer."

Finally, the day before the tournament was to start, Bill Flemming, who was to announce the match for ABC, showed up. The pair finally tracked down Fischer, a nocturnal creature who slept during the day and came out only at night, at a bowling alley and did the interview. Forte packed his things, went to the airport, and called Arledge. "Roone, I got the interview and I'm heading back."

"Chet, you can't come back," answered Arledge. "The tournament's not over yet, and we don't want to send a new guy up there." After all, Forte had gotten the interview. In Arledge's mind Forte was very close to Fischer now and all the people up there. "So stay with it!" he ordered.

A stunned Forte could only obey.

But things only got worse. First of all, there was the matter of the hidden cameras. The petulant Fischer demanded that there be no cameras in view in the auditorium where they were to play the match. Forte met him and took him to the auditorium the day before the match to see if Fischer could hear the now-hidden cameras "rolling." They shut off all the lights and just stood there in the dark for ten minutes. Forte said, "Bobby, OK? You ready? Can I turn the lights on?" No answer. Forte, with a sigh said, "Well, we'll wait." Ten more minutes. Then he tried again. "OK? Can we go now?" And he turned on the lights. But Fischer thought he heard the cameras whirring. The exasperated Forte took Fischer around to the four hidden cameras, planted out of sight for the next day's shooting, to show him that they were recessed and couldn't be heard. For the time being Fischer was satisfied.

But the next day was another story. It was the first game of the twenty-four game series. With one point given for a win and one-half for a draw, the champion needed only twelve points, for a draw, to retain his championship; but the challenger needed twelve-and-one-half points to take it away from him. Sometime during that first match, Fischer claimed he heard the cameras, and making a bad mistake on the twenty-ninth move, he lost the match. He threatened not to play again until the cameras were removed; he would, instead, go back to New York. With the cameras still in the auditorium, Fischer forfeited the second match; the first time a game had ever been lost "off the board" in world championship play.

The Icelandic Chess Federation was in danger of losing its investment. The international organization was in danger of losing its tournament. America was in danger of losing face. And Chet Forte was in danger of losing three weeks of his life. The matter was finally resolved. Henry Kissinger, using a bit of "king-sized" diplomacy, called Fischer and persuaded him to continue the match, and Forte removed the cameras from the auditorium. The third game, at Fischer's behest, was played in a backroom, offstage, and Fischer won to pull to within one point of Spassky, 1–2.

Now Arledge used an ingenious castling gambit to cover the lack of cameras. He called on artist LeRoy Neiman, the sport scene's Hogarth, and assigned him to cover the match. Neiman flew up to Reykjavik on an emergency plane as a replacement for Forte's crew. Apparently Fischer didn't mind Neiman, as he sat on the stage and sketched the participants in the fourth game. But as Neiman started to sketch with his felt-tipped marker, he noticed that Fischer was picking up its odor, so he switched to a heavy Mont-Blanc pen. But that was audible, as it scratched the paper and just as Fischer started to raise his head, Neiman quickly shifted to a graphite pencil, something he never uses, and completed the drawings. That fourth game ended in a draw, as Fischer went on to take five of the next nine games to Spassky's one, finally defeating him in the twenty-first game, 12½–8½. For ABC, too, the match had ended in a "draw."

The agonies are not always limited to the field; sometimes they take the form of unseen production battles—to get the show on the air. One such battle took place at Le Mans on the eighth "Wide World" show in 1961. The expert commentator that day was Stirling Moss, who, not incidentally, was also driving in the race. As the countdown for the race entered its final minutes, Jim McKay went out onto the track to interview Moss next to his machine.

There were no tape machines at trackside, all taping being done by machines in Paris using a French telephone coaxial cable. As McKay and the increasingly nervous Moss did take after take, it became apparent to Chuck Howard, then production assistant, that the lines connecting Le Mans and Paris were acting up and that the signal was not being received clearly. Finally, during what appeared to be a good take, the band suddenly struck up the national anthems of all the competing drivers. As the first strains of "God Save the Queen" were heard by Moss, he stopped in mid-sentence and stood ramrod straight for its duration. As the last anthem was played and the local constabulary, escorted by a cordon of twenty motorcycles, started down the track to sweep all press, hangers-on, and groupies from the track, McKay tried one last interview from the top—his seventh such attempt. The race was ready to start, the drivers were getting into their machines, and Howard and McKay were still interviewing Moss! As a motorcycle stopped nearby with its motor revving up, a gendarme got off and walked toward Howard brandishing his pistol and motioning him to get off the track. Howard, completely absorbed in getting the interview over what was now a clear line, held up his hand and waved the gendarme off. "ABC—American television," he shouted desperately. It was enough to momentarily stop the officer from interrupting what was to be the seventh and last interview. McKay finished the take, and unknown to the viewing audience, ABC had triumphed in another human drama of competition.

* * *

Roone Arledge has often said that "the greatest contribution we can make is getting people aware of production. We started using television to make it so you could see it better on television than in person." And because the television revolution wrought by Arledge has been based, in no small part, upon technological advances, it is a wonder that relatively few calamities actually took place. Videotape, sophisticated cameras, and complicated and sensitive electronic gimcrackery have all contributed to the making of the revolution; a change that couldn't have taken place ten, or even five, years before.

While they are not necessarily pointed out with pride, ABC had its share of disasters. Every now and then a taped event, such as the Tournament of Thrills Auto Daredevil Championships or the World International Target Diving Championships, will accidentally get erased and recycled in the constantly rotating videotape which gets turned over like box cars in a freight yard. Once a rodeo show actually became a piece of a "Dick Van Dyke Show"—a $40,000 error. And in 1976 the telephone company inadvertently crossed its Telco lines, causing a CBS program to come through on "Wide World of Sports." Perhaps the biggest "mux ip," though, and one that was beyond the control of any human force, was "Wide World's" first live satellite transmission from Le Mans, France. At least that's what it was supposed to be.

The world's first commercial communications satellite, *Early Bird,* had been launched April 6, 1965, 22,300 miles above the equator over the Atlantic Ocean. It was a geostationary satellite, designed, through synchronous orbiting with the earth, to be able to provide two-way television communication between the two continents. The 85-pound *Early Bird* was to beam the Grand Prix from Le Mans on the afternoon of Saturday, June 19, in what was to be the first of three satellite transmissions back to the United States from Europe that summer. The other two would be the Irish Derby and the US–USSR Track Meet.

But satellite transmission was not yet perfected. The communications satellite over the Pacific was called *Lani Bird,* and "*Lani* went looney," according to Julie Barnathan, vice-president in charge of engineering. Moreover, much depended on the ground station, which was to send the signals or the energy to the satellite.

Thus, on the afternoon of June 19, ABC President Tom Moore and the entire ABC Sports staff gathered in the main conference room at 10:30 A.M. for the transmission. But no picture. The ground station had failed. Or, more accurately, the connecting PTTs (Postal Telephone and Telegraph—roughly equivalent to AT&T in the United States) had failed, never getting the picture to the ground station to be sent. For the next hour all that was shown was a "Stand By" card, as Jim McKay and Phil Hill did an improvised radio show. Then, miraculously, as if the PTTs had a mind of their own, a picture showed up in New York twenty-one seconds after they had signed off. McKay was heard to mutter, "I've been telling you, man was not meant to send pictures through the air." And Chuck Howard the producer added, "But it didn't mention words!"

Later that evening, at 5:00, the entire show was finally aired. And the following week, the Irish Derby was beamed to the United States.

But something was gained from the foul-up, for when later that summer ABC presented the first live telecasts from the Soviet Union—the US–USSR dual track and field meet from Central Stadium in Kiev—they did so prepared for technical difficulties. Now the experienced ABC staff had two transmissions to the ground station to serve as a prophylactic against another malfunction. The Russian television system fed the signal north through Moscow to Helsinki, where it was sent south to Rome through Hamburg. In addition, Intervision, the Eastern European network, fed the pictures westward to Hamburg. At Hamburg, ABC technicians were able to select the better picture—or the only picture—for relay to Rome. At Rome, the signal was beamed to the nearby Fucino ground station, which in turn sent it to the satellite for bouncing to the United States ground station at Andover, Maine. And from there it was sent by Telco land line to New York for network dissemination. Some 55,000 miles in a matter of milliseconds!

* * *

Of the technological advances that have made "Wide World" possible, perhaps none is more responsible for its existence than jet travel, for it was humanly impossible to travel the "Wide World," let alone tape it, without the jets of today.

In his sixteen years as the host of "Wide World of Sports," Jim McKay has traveled over three million miles to serve as the commentator on almost 100 different events in forty-six states and forty foreign countries. The man who is to "Wide World" what flour is to bread has constantly been on the go since that day when he was told by Arledge that his job would entail "a good deal of travel."

For the 15th anniversary show McKay was picked up in Hartford by a specially chartered jet, which had taken off from Teeterboro, New Jersey, that morning, and flown to Cleveland for a "shoot" at the Cleveland Marina, then to Sioux Falls, South Dakota, to the Snake River where Evel Knievel did his thing, then to the Los Angeles Sports Arena, and finally, Palm Springs, California.

During a two week span in late 1976, he traveled from his home in Westport, Connecticut, to Tokyo, to mainland China for a show, then back to Tokyo, to Westport again, with a stopover in Anchorage, to Toronto to tape a Dorothy Hamill special, to Orlando, Florida, for the Disney World Golf Tournament, with layovers in Pittsburgh and Atlanta, and then back to Westport. But this was more the norm than the exception not only for McKay but for all the "Wide World" crew.

* * *

Dick Horan, one of several engineering supervisors who oversee the comings and goings of the engineering staff on each show in tandem with a manpower pool called "Tech" Records, has 500 people to draw from on the East Coast and

160 on the West Coast. In a personnel operation that rivals Patton's landing at Salerno, it is not unusual, according to Horan, "to have a guy walk through the door while you're setting up the truck in Lincoln, Nebraska, and you give him an airline ticket to Austin, Texas, telling him, 'Hey, instead of being here, you've got to be there.'"

One member of the Wide World touring company is a producer who is also the composer of songs and sometimes the composer of songs who is also a producer. Doug Wilson, with his faithful and trusty companion, a guitar, constantly composes songs whose thematic content is—obviously—travel. He has written songs including "3 O'Clock Lonely" and "My Home Time Zone Blues." Jim McKay remembers coming back with Doug Wilson and another Wide World director from Tokyo. The only way they could get home for Christmas was to fly from Tokyo to Hawaii to San Francisco and then to Los Angeles and then layover until the "Red Eye" to New York; a total of 27 hours altogether. During the layover in Los Angeles International Airport, the three repaired to the Admiral's Club when McKay "suddenly noticed Doug way over in the corner by himself. We were the only people there, and he was looking out the window playing his guitar and quietly singing Christmas carols. The bartender and the waiter came over and we all went over and started singing Christmas Carols."

Because the "Wide World" staff live out of a proverbial trunk, several of the stories they tell on themselves are travel-oriented. One man alone, a character named Joe Aceti, is the source of enough of them to fill an entire book. Aceti is, in a purely dramatic sense, a comic character. Functioning as the Associate Director of Wide World of Sports, on weekends he oversees the operations from a room filled with enough monitors and microphones to intimidate Commander Kirk or any of the other Enterprise officers.

When Aceti is on the road the stories start, most of them revolving around that most creative of all executive fringe benefits—the expense account. The most legendary one concerns the time he went to the Walker Cup Amateur Golf Tournament in 1966 in Sandwich, England for a Wide World "shoot" to be aired on a delayed basis. Upon his return he filed his expense voucher with the ABC Sports business manager, since all ABC Sports vouchers are approved in-house and not by ABC Corporate. Among all of the items he listed was one that read "$50—tree-trimming." Since time immemorial, tree-trimming had been a legitimate expense, inasmuch as ofttimes the camera's sight lines are obstructed by overhanging foliage. But it just so happened that the delayed telecast of the Walker Cup was seen by the business manager, who had Aceti's expense report in front of him. "What do you mean 'tree-trimming'? I saw the opening pan of the golf course and there wasn't a shrub on there over two inches high." Aceti, equal to the challenge, answered "Boy, that guy really did a good job. That's *now* you don't see anything!"

Another time the business manager, after poring over Aceti's expense account for over an hour called down to TV Studio No. 9 where Aceti was in the middle of some delicate editing. "Joe," said the officious administrator, "I've gone over your expense account and I figure I'm going to have to deduct $20 for cabs, $34 for entertainment, and $15 for incidentals." The unflappable Aceti only said, "That's about right. Good-bye," and hung up.

And there are hotel stories, too. On a Wide World trip to Ljubljana, Yugoslavia for a World Figure Skating Championship a few years back, Producer Dennis Lewin and Director Chet Forte checked into their rooms at the Hotel Lev. But almost as soon as Forte saw his room, he was back down at the desk. The room was actually a little closet impersonating a room. Moreover, it was a smelly little closet. And to add to its charm it was right under the dance floor of the night club on the top floor of the hotel. Forte demanded his room be changed, and it was—to the last available one in the hotel. But Jim McKay still hadn't checked in, and he was now ticketed for the Black Hole of Ljubljana. McKay checked in the next day, and during his four-day stay he couldn't even go into the bathroom without first spraying deodorant into it. Finally, after the four less-than-memorable days, as they were checking out, the female manager of the hotel had the temerity to ask: "How was your stay here, Mr. McKay?" McKay, who wasn't going to say anything, now apparently feeling the code of silence was lifted by her question, answered: "Well, as long as you've asked, I must tell you the truth. That room is one of the noisiest, smelliest, and worst rooms I've ever been in." The manager merely said, "I know!"

Not only must each "Wide World" staff member acquire an immunity to travel and hotels but because of the catch-as-catch-can world they live in, each must also serve as his own travel agent. To many the *Official Airlines Guide*, available through subscription, is not only indispensable but as one executive notes, "All of us, including Roone, only know it's the end of the month when the *Official Airlines Guide* arrives."

* * *

ABC's "Wide World of Sports" is more than just sports, more then electronic advances, and even more than Jim McKay visiting exotic and intriguing venues. It is people. And the people who have made "Wide World" what it is would cumulatively make up a Who's Who in Broadcasting. Since its inception, the roster of those who have served as announcers for various portions of the show has included Bob Beattie, Charley Brockman, Howard Cosell, Chris Economaki, Bill Flemming, Frank Gifford, Curt Gowdy, Keith Jackson, Jim Lampley, Al Michaels, Bud Palmer, Chris Schenkel, and Warner Wolf.

Working together with them are those who serve as expert commentators—whose function it is to add a new dimension to broadcasting by bringing some of the nuances and intricacies of the sport to the viewer. Some of them have succeeded admirably, like Dick Button and Gordon Maddux, who have given us valuable insights into figure skating and gymnastics and added the words *camel* and *summy* to our vocabularies. Others, like Jackie Stewart, whose high-pitched impersonation of Inspector Clouseu grows on you like a good scotch, have succeeded by bringing color to the telecasts. And the returns aren't in yet on some—like George Foreman.

One of the first expert commentators signed by ABC was Orenthal James Simpson, known to all as just plain "OJ," and to the fans of Buffalo and Howard Cosell as the Juice. OJ, who started his football career by playing for a high school team that lost thirty straight games, went on to greatness at City College of San Francisco, Southern Cal, and with the Buffalo Bills, where he broke just about every NCAA and NFL rushing record in existence. But OJ didn't pull himself up by his jockstrap alone, for he combines his prowess on the field with his personality at the microphone. In 1969 ABC signed him to a multi-year contract, which has now lapsed, leaving OJ to take his personality, packaging, and production over to NBC after a spirited bidding contest among the three networks.

Simpson's infectiousness overcomes his occasional lapses in syntax and semantics. But as one of his ex-colleagues at ABC said, "He's good and he's willing to learn. And anyway, I'm not antisemantic." Despite his habit of changing tenses faster than he can run a leg of the 440, Simpson has a style that injects any event he is covering with more than his mere presence.

One of Simpson's most unusual assignments for "Wide World" was to accompany McKay to Dublin, Ireland, in 1973 where he would serve as the expert commentator on an Irish football match and a hurling match, a twofer. (The artistic brutality of hurling was evidenced for several years by the vignette that appeared in the "Wide World's" opening and closing "billboards" of two hurlers simultaneously sandwiching an opponent, leaving him to slowly undulate to the ground like a wet noodle.)

Driving from Shannon Airport, the usually ebullient OJ was uncharacteristically silent for fifteen minutes. Finally, McKay broke the silence and leaned across Producer Doug Wilson to ask if anything was the matter. Simpson, who had been engrossed watching the people outside the car, finally responded, "Hey, I'll buy either one of you dinner if you can find me a brother." And while they did find one or two during their stay, they also found something just as unusual.

On this occasion, the "Wide World" visit to Dublin coincided with St. Patrick's Day. Celebrated with fanatical zeal by real and closet Irishmen alike in Boston, Chicago, and New York, St. Patrick's Day has always been just a religious holiday in Dublin. That is, until someone had the bright idea of attracting more tourists by initiating their own celebration—parade and all. And what band was brought over to help celebrate the occasion?

The Notre Dame band, of course.

As OJ walked down O'Connell Street, giving autographs to boys who followed in his wake, like the procession behind the Pied Piper, the Notre Dame band came into view playing their "Victory March." Simpson, who as an all-American halfback at USC, one of Notre Dame's rivals, had heard the fighting Irish band many times before and knew what was coming. Exhibiting all the moves he had shown the best eleven men Notre Dame could put on the field, he now single-handedly took on their band, 200 strong. Rushing to the curb, he put his hands to his mouth and called out, "*Boooo! Boooo! Give the bums the hook! Boooo! Boooo!*" As the Notre Dame band pulled abreast of the commotion, they turned as one to see who was giving them the Bronx cheer—in Dublin yet. Breaking their stride and falling all over themselves in the greatest exhibition of mass rubbernecking in history, the Irish band spent the next five minutes asking themselves and each other, "Isn't that OJ? What's he doing here?" It seemed that no one from Notre Dame was safe from OJ—anywhere!

That evening the ABC crew repaired to a local Irish pub to set the scene for the next day's events. There, among a group that seemed to have stepped right out of the pages of Liam O'Flaherty's *The Informer*, they found a little gardener who loved Irish sports and loved talking about them. He would make the perfect interview. After various shots of Irish pub games they sat the gardener in between McKay and Simpson in front of a coal fire for an ambience that couldn't have been more typically Irish. To enhance the scene, mugs of Harp's dark stout were placed in front of each of them as the cameras rolled. After quite a while, as the discussion and Harp's continued to flow, OJ stopped the conversation with a serious, "I've got to ask a question." It was his first big moment on camera.

"What is it, OJ?" asked McKay.

"Who's going to help me outta this place?" came back the somewhat subdued Simpson as he tottered to his feet. Naturally, everyone roared. The lot of the expert commentator is not an easy one.

* * *

It was on one of his many assignments in 1976 that Jim McKay found himself in South Bend, Indiana. It was a cold winter day with the first of a history-making 111 inches of snow falling around him.

The event that he and an entire ABC Sports crew had come to cover was to take place on the campus of Notre Dame University. Notre Dame at once a patch of ground and a state of emotion denotes something very special to most sports fans. It is still thought of as a university that can be spelled only one way—f-o-o-t-b-a-l-l. As McKay and the crew looked around the campus, they could easily conjure the everpresent tradition of football. It was there in the bronze likeness of Rev. William Corby, president of the university in the nineteenth century, who with his right hand upraised in a familiar stance, is known to the student body as "Fair Catch" Corby; in the massive mosaic of Jesus, rising thirteen stories high on the façade of the library and just overlooking the stadium scoreboard, and called by the students "Touchdown Jesus"; and even in the statue of Moses next to the library, with his arm raised and his index finger in the air, known to alumni as well as present-day students as "Number One Moses."

But on this particular evening, the names of Rockne, Gipp, Hart or Lujack would not be the ones to "shake down the thunder from the skies." Instead, they would be Olga Korbut, Nelli Kim, Ludmilla Tourischeva, and Nicolai Andrianov, for the event "Wide World" had come to tape was the touring USSR Gymnastics team. It would be the forty-fifth time gymnastics had been featured on "Wide World." This time the place is Notre Dame's 11,500-seat Athletic and Convocation Center, known affectionately to the students as "Hessburgh's Bra," because of its double configuration.

McKay and producer Doug Wilson saw this event in terms of a story line—with a beginning, a middle, and an end. The opening of the story, which would air some two months later in an abbreviated thirty-five-minute segment, showed an aerial pan of the campus of Notre Dame, with the Golden Dome and the stadium, while a backdrop of sound depicted Knute Rockne exhorting his team, "We're going inside 'em, we're going outside 'em. Inside 'em, outside 'em . . ." Then came a shot of the Russian Flag as the seventeen Soviet gymnasts were greeted by a warm reception on the floor. At last, Jim McKay described the incongruity of the scene. "George Gipp would be amazed at what's going on here on this occasion. First of all, an arena usually reserved for Notre Dame basketball just about filled to watch gymnastics. Why, even ten or fifteen years ago you couldn't have gotten more than five hundred people in here to watch the greatest gymnasts in the world. The other thing, well, I think they'd be very surprised to see the students of Notre Dame and the townspeople of South Bend gathered, ready to welcome some visiting Communists." This last observation prompted McKay to articulate a recurring theme of his that underscores the very title of the show, "But that points out something positive that we've seen in the world of sports since we started 'Wide World' fifteen years ago. . . . Almost everywhere in the world these days, sportsmen, whatever the political philosophy of their countries, are well received—whether it's Americans in China or Soviet kids right here in the United States."

With McKay was Gordon Maddux, the gymnastics expert in residence, who has spent half his life fighting to make gymnastics the major sport it has become today. He can vividly remember, "thumping the tubs and beating the bushes trying to organize events, all of which were losers," for "who gave a damn and showed up except mom and dad?" But now that small coterie of devotees, as if by magic, became 11,500 people. "It's a TV success story. Olga Korbut made the sport. When they write the gymnastic history books, chapters will be devoted to her," says Maddux as he looked out at the crowd still streaming into the arena. "And that's what those people are paying $12.50 a seat to see tonight. They're here to see Olga—no one else."

The program continued on the floor. To the tumultuous roar of the crowd, Olga, with a hair-do that looks like she finished it off with some of Ray Bolger's left-over straw, performed a tribute to Edith Piaf. Then it was Ludmilla Tourischeva in her tissue-thin leotard performing as she did at Munich and Montreal, although twenty pounds heavier than she was at Montreal. The crowd was extremely receptive. Then came Nelli

Kim, and the Russian pianist struck up the familiar strains of the "Notre Dame Victory March." Suddenly it sounded as if Adrian Dantley and Austin Carr had just scored another victory over UCLA. This time the "echoes" really "woke up".

* * *

Just as Rudy Vallee discovered Edgar Bergen and Fanny Brice started Danny Thomas on his rise to fame, so, too, has "Wide World of Sports" in its sixteen years on the air, discovered its own share of stars.

During the 1972 Olympics as Roone Arledge and the ABC crew considered showing a battle for third place in the team gymnastics exercises between Hungary, Czechoslovakia, and the United States, expert commentator Gordon Maddux chanced to look up at the Russians warming up on the floor. There he saw a little slip of a girl doing her exercises on the uneven bars. He hurriedly motioned to McKay, seated beside him to look up. "Jim, that little girl did something I've never seen before," said Maddux, pointing out what looked like a backward flip dismount on the uneven bars. They hurriedly referred to their program and to the ABC biographical "playbook," but there was nothing in there on the girl—a sixteen-year-old named Olga something-or-other. McKay read Maddux's feelings, and they tore up the script. Instead of following the two Hungarians on the balanced beam, Arledge, over some dismayed gasps and groans from those near him in the production control area, decided to follow the instinctive selection of McKay and Maddux. As they introduced the little girl who had merely been an alternative on the Soviet squad, Maddux could only utter something to the effect of, "Oh my, wow!" Olga Korbut, of course, went on to achieve much deserved stardom in the world of sports. And while it was her own winning talent that caused her to stamp her image on the world's consciousness, for Americans, at least, it was Gordon Maddux and ABC that had created the imprint.

Doug Wilson was the producer at the World Figure Skating Championships in Calgary, Alberta, Canada, in 1972. As producer he taped the performances of every entrant, including that of a fifteen-year-old skater who placed seventh in the overall competition behind Janet Lynn. After Dick Button pointed her out to him, Wilson had only to look at the long flowing hair, the captivating eyes, and the angelic face to remind him of "my first girl friend." But he also saw a future skating superstar in this young ingenue. "This girl is going to be 'it' someday," he predicted.

In putting on a program dedicated to the world champions, there is no possible way to insinuate a seventh place finisher, no matter how good she is nor how taken you are with her. Wilson called over the headphones to Bill Flemming, the announcer, that although they didn't have time for her then, they would be putting on another segment of the championships in another few weeks. Would he now cover with "two weeks ago we didn't have time to bring you this performer?"

Wilson brought that portion of the tape back to New York, and over the objections of others, he put on the seventh place finisher. And two weeks later the public saw Dorothy Hamill for the first time. If it hadn't aired, that historic performance would have been erased forever.

Wilson went on to produce most of Hamill's subsequent "Wide World" appearances—some three and one-half hours worth—and after she had won the gold medal in the 1976 Olympics, he called down on the headset to offer his heartfelt congratulations. "Hey, we're so proud of you," Wilson exclaimed. "I just want you to know how happy we are for you. . . . Congratulations!" But Wilson didn't know whether she even knew who he was nor whether he'd hear one of those classic, squeaky, "thank-you-very-much, I'm-so-excited-and-thrilled-to-be-here" pap lines that most young girls can barely muster.

What he heard instead was a heartwarming, "I just want you to know how much I appreciate everything you've done for me in the last four years. . . ." That, for Wilson, was worth everything; his own thrill of victory.

"Wide World" not only discovered but also developed a man who is writ large on the social history calendar of the seventies; a latter-day curiosity like Shipwreck Kelly. That man was Robert Craig "Evel" Knievel, a folk hero today, first shown on "Wide World" on March 25, 1967.

Knievel, who has been described as an accident on its way to a happening, was a last-minute added attraction to the "Wide World" event planned that day, National Tourist Trophy Motorcycle Championship. He had approached the promoter, J. C. Agajanian, offering to perform a jump over some cars.

Agajanian recalls, "I really didn't think I needed Knievel. But Knievel persisted, 'Listen, what attendance did you get the last time you ran this event? If I get more, then pay me a dollar for each head; if I don't get more, you owe me nothing!'

"I figured, what the hell. It was nearly a sellout the previous year, and I was getting anywhere from five to six dollars a head. So the more he talked, the better his deal sounded. Anyway, we had about 2,400 more people there and I wrote him a check for almost $3,000. Hell, I was making a lot more money because of him and could afford to be a little generous. But the next day Knievel came to see me and I thought, 'Oh-oh, he's gonna try to get more money from me.' But contrary to my suspicions, Knievel only said, 'Mr. Agajanian, you overpaid me by $600. If you want, I'll give you the money back.' I turned down the offer and asked him how he knew. Knievel replied, 'I had people counting heads at each gate.'"

That was the start of the legend known as Evel Knievel, a legend "Wide World of Sports" had a major part in building by featuring him no less than sixteen times. That exposure plus his propensity to be publicized not by his successes but by his failures made him an electronic curio piece. His first publicized failure took place on January 1, 1968. On that fateful day, Knievel, who was scheduled to jump the fountains in front of Caesar's Palace in Vegas, lost control of his 500-pound motorcycle as it touched down at the end of the 108-foot ramp. He was flung to the pavement, hitting it like a Raggedy Andy doll. He ripped his protective leather outfit in two and broke his back and his pelvis. That accident did more than merely mangle his body. It provided him with a daredevil image. Suddenly, crowds came to see him perform and possibly get hurt—or worse. His attraction, simply stated, was that each jump might be his last.

The indestructible performer who claimed, "I've broken every bone in my body, except my neck, at least once!" became a super hero who performed super heroics. In the public eye he held the same esteemed position that Tom Mix had forty years earlier—that of being able to conquer all and walk taller than ever despite the fact that he was one mass of broken bones and scar tissue from head to foot. (Tom Mix, unlike Knievel, even sold skeletal outlines of his body which showed twenty-six major injuries, including knife wounds, bullet scars, and broken bones.)

Forget that he failed more times than he succeeded: He was a happening. It was only fitting that "Wide World's" most popular show was the delayed telecast of his ill-fated Snake River jump; fitting for a television "first," since it was there that the inventor of the first television tube was born. Roone Arledge defended it to Frank Beerman of *Variety* as a "great event," one which was honest and was "show business."

That is what Evel Knievel is all about—nothing more, nothing less. Entertainment. His feats of derring-do are memorable. And even though "they ain't sports," it doesn't seem to matter. When Americans are asked to name the greatest racing driver of all time, they will, with a single voice, enunicate the name of Barney Oldfield, a publicity-conscious performer who barnstormed the small-town tracks and set one dubious "record" after another, always proclaiming himself to be the greatest. Knievel, of course, is not the only sportsman around today to have taken this tack. Like Ali, Knievel has found it successful. And like Ali, his success is clearly interwoven with the threads that make up "Wide World."

* * *

In 1963, when former National Basketball Association Commissioner Walter Kennedy was first interviewed for his job, the very first question the owners asked him was, "Do you think you can get us back on national TV?" A few months after Kennedy became commissioner, the President of ABC Television Tom Moore, an old friend of Kennedy's who had known him when he was the two-term mayor of Stamford, Connecticut, was in a meeting with Julie Barnathan and Roone

Arledge. The matter under discussion was "Wide World of Sports." The problem was that "Wide World," now planning its fourth year, was not quite sold out in the first quarter of 1965. The reason seemed to be the competition; CBS's "CBS Sports Spectacular," which had now moved to Saturdays, directly opposite "Wide World." Barnathan, the general manager of the network, mused, "If we could just get them down a few points . . ." Arledge interjected, "Why not put live sports—like basketball—opposite their taped events? Tom, you know Walter Kennedy, don't you?"

Thus a marriage was arranged with ABC hoping only "to get a five share." According to Tom Moore, "It would knock down CBS's programming and protect 'Wide World'." The contract between ABC and the NBA called for sixteen games to be telecast during the first quarter of 1965 for $600,000. If it was a major leap forward for the NBA, it was a slam dunk jump for ABC and "Wide World of Sports." And the "CBS Sports Spectacular," unable to defense its competition, soon fouled out.

* * *

NBA basketball was a "slow make," with ratings moving from a 6.0 in 1965 to an 8.2 in 1968 and an almost equivalent increment in share from a 20.2 to a 27.1. But the expected boom in basketball as the sport of the seventies wasn't realized. One advertising agency, Kenyon & Eckhardt, even theorized that because basketball was a simple street game nutured in the inner cities, it would fit perfectly with the new emerging activism. But such wasn't the case. The new buzzword among advertising executives was *demographics*, a word used to indicate an audience's profile. The very people it was said basketball should appeal to were not heavy users of products that appealed to, say, the football fan.

Although the NBA games enjoyed what even the most optimistic ABC sales brochure called "a steady growth" through the 1968–69 season, the figures started to plateau immediately after that. The 1970–71 season showed a 5 percent increase in total audience growth, compared with the 10 percent reflected by pro football. Arledge then added color commentator Bill Russell to the telecasts in order to add some devastatingly honest comments to Chris Schenkel's play-by-play description. (During a post-game wrap-up, he remarked, "I hate to say this, but the refs did a fairly good job today." Schenkel bubbled back, "I'm sure they'll be glad to hear that." And Russell, in the best tradition of W. C. Fields, then offered an aside. "In that case, I'm sorry I said it.")

Russell's custom-made ABC yellow blazer wasn't quite big enough to handle the king-sized job he was doing to liven up NBA basketball with perspicacious and witty remarks that were rarely heard from ex-jocks. The cognoscenti loved him, and ABC was sufficiently pleased with his performance and that of the NBA's to ante up $16.2 million for the rights to three more years.

But at the end of those three years, even with an option, the NBA took a new partner. CBS was more than willing to pay $27 million for the next three years, starting with the 1973–74 season. After nine years of nourishing along the NBA, ABC cried foul and took the contract to court. And even though they lost the court case, they won the ratings battle by counter-programming with a Sunday version of "Wide World of Sports" against CBS's telecasts of the NBA games.

The Sunday edition of "Wide World," by no means a kippered version of the Saturday show, premiered with several old standbys: the Hawaiian Masters Surfing Championship from the Banzai Pipeline; Ara Parseghian analyzing the classic confrontation between Notre Dame and Alabama for the national collegiate championship; and tossed in for good measure, that perennial favorite, the Harlem Globetrotters against "that other" basketball game on CBS.

After five weeks the Sunday "Wide World of Sports" series achieved twice the rating of the National Basketball Association games. Again they had clearly outmaneuvered CBS. To further add insult to injury, ABC double-teamed CBS and their new partners, the NBA, with another new show, "The Superstars." ABC had doubled the viewing pleasure as well as the ratings.

* * *

In the summer of 1975, a "Wide World" crew went up to the small community of Attica, New York, less than an hour's drive east of Buffalo, to tape an appearance of the Harlem Globetrotters at the scene of the most violent prison uprising in the history of the United States. But what started out as a basketball exhibition turned into a sociological documentary on penology—a documentary that would air six months later in January 1976.

Producer Don Ohlmeyer, Director Larry Kamm, and Associate Producer Norm Samet were the first to reach the Attica Correctional Facility. As they walked through the gate where the food and supplies were delivered to the prison, they were confronted by another set of steel doors, the first set clanking behind them, à la Maxwell Smart. There was a feeling of claustrophobia, even though they were outdoors. They walked through Times Square, the intersection of four corridor tunnels that quadrisected the prison yard, where the bloody riot of September 9, 1971 had occurred. The green-clad prisoners viewed them with a combination of curiosity and mistrust.

Director Larry Kamm remembers being in a hallway of one of the connecting passageways to cellblock A, near the source of the historic riot, taping a scene, when "the Black Muslims came through, on their way to church. They were in their prison garb, green khaki work pants and jackets and white shirts with little black bow ties. As they filed by in their orderly, regimental line, they called out 'make way' and *everybody* made way. Half an hour later, they came back from church, and again it was 'make way.'" As the other black inmates scurried out of their way, it became apparent to Kamm that they were more frightened of the Muslims than the whites were.

Two days later, the crew was joined by Howard Cosell, who was to do some preliminary taping, talking to the inmates in the yard prior to the basketball game. Even the normal brashness of Cosell seemed tempered by the environment. The session started in normal enough fashion with several of the inmates hollering, "Hey Howard Cosell, hey Howard Cosell." And Cosell, always a patsy for recognition and flattery, loosened up. The inmates started pressing in around the recognizable figure and Kamm placed a cameraman on the table behind him to electronically eavesdrop and catch the flavor of the rap session. The prisoners started questioning him; "You tell it like it is, but why don't you tell how bad it is in here?" Cosell responded, "Well, tell me what's bothering you."

Those in green suits started expressing their gripes, as prisoners often do, and Cosell answered them in his direct fashion. That is, until one highly activated man started yelling his gripes, which were related to his incarceration. Cosell, in an effort both to converse with him and to regain control of the unwieldy group, asked him, "All right, what are you in for?" When the prisoner answered matter-of-factly, "Murder," Cosell stopped dead. "The impact of standing there talking with someone who just told you he was in prison for murder brought Howard up short," related Kamm. "I've never seen that happen before." And then "Howard regained his composure and continued with the discussion."

The remainder of "Wide World's" stay at Attica was as normal as it could be, locked inside a prison. The game was an enormous success among the inmates, most of whom were blacks or Puerto Ricans. They openly showed their appreciation of the Globetrotters, who had "made it in a white world." On the other hand, after the game had concluded and Kamm and his camera crew went back for some fill-in shots, the inmates only viewed them hostilely. Kamm was moved to add an insight to the telecast: "They may feel they're in a cage, but they don't want to be viewed as animals in that cage. They want their privacy, too . . . and we were an intrusion."

* * *

In a world of success begets further success, "Wide World of Sports" has been used as a launching pad for other shows. That very first year, the third "Wide World" show, a PBA World Championship Bowling Tournament from Paramus, New Jersey, was actually a pilot within the show, the prototype of the "Professional Bowlers' Tour."

Paramus, New Jersey, might just be another landmark on the Garden State Parkway for bleary-eyed motorists, but for bowling fans, Paramus and the Paramus Bowl are the famous hallowed grounds where two of bowling's greatest television shows originated. When the Gillette "Friday Night Fights" came to ABC in 1960, Scherick recognized the need for a col-lapsible show after the fights to take up the time slack if the fight went less than the technical limit, which many did. In that constant flow of people who came through Scherick's small Sports Programs office like the waiting room at Grand Central Station, an old friend named Johnny Johnston came to visit one day. Johnston was not only the former husband of Kathryn Grayson and an actor in his own right, but also the son of a champion bowler. He was looking for a show, any show, that had something to do with bowling. Scherick, equal to the challenge, immediately thought of a show built around bowling to accordian in the programming schedule after the fights, whatever their length. The show was based upon mak-ing spares, to distinguish it from one then currently on the air, which had as its format the making of strikes ("Jackpot Bowl-ing" with Milton Berle) and even insured one difficult split for $10,000 with Lloyd's of London. The show, of course, was "Make That Spare"; the host was Johnny Johnston, naturally.

Later another old friend, Eddie Elias of Akron, Ohio, came to visit Scherick. He had a concept for a Professional Bowlers' Association and elicited Scherick's cooperation in making a pilot for a proposed series. Elias, Scherick, and Roone Arledge developed an elimination tournament, a sort of ten-pin king-of-the-hill, which went on from a pilot to become the longest *live* television show on ABC.

Everyone, including Arledge and Chris Schenkel, who has been the announcer since it started sixteen years ago, is amazed at the ten-strike success of the Professional Bowlers' Tour. "It just keeps rolling along and drawing terrific audiences," says Arledge. "The popularity of bowling on TV is a phenomenon that nobody seems to pay much attention to. I think sometimes even us at ABC take it for granted."

Schenkel offers a less complicated reason for its success: "You don't have to think when you're watching it."

There may be other reasons as well. Perhaps it's because $25,000 is given away every week or that the format is simple, or that in a recent Lou Harris poll it ranked fourth (behind the holy trinity of football, baseball, and basketball) as the sport most people follow. Whatever the reason, the show is followed by almost fourteen million fans every week—more than watch professional basketball. For ABC, it is, of course, one more success story.

* * *

Another show cloned from "Wide World of Sports" was "The American Sportsman." Both Tom Moore and Roone Arledge were avid outdoorsmen who loved to hunt and fish. They would accept invitations to go fishing with Joe Foss in South Dakota or hunting in Africa and thought that a show based on their mutual love affair—and that of some 60 million American fishermen, 25 million hunters, and 40 million boaters—might work. As Tom Moore recalls it, "We said goddamn it, there's a thing called 'Wide World of Sports,' why don't we see if we can't do a hunting and fishing show. We'll make a pilot on 'Wide World.'"

And so in January 1962 Arledge; Sportscaster Curt Gowdy, an acknowledged country boy from Wyoming who loves to hunt and fish; Joe Brooks, one of the legendary names in light-tackle angling; and a crew flew down to Buenos Aires and hauled tons of complex, highly advanced equipment inland 250 miles along bumpy roads to the shores of Lago General Paz near the Argentine-Chile border. There they set up a head-to-head trout fishing contest between Gowdy and Brooks and two Argentine fishing guides. Arledge served as the time-keeper and the official scorer, as the two teams were rewarded with points for the most fish caught, the biggest fish, etc. Gowdy and Brooks won in a close battle, and the show was aired in May 1963 to a more than respectable share of the TV audience. Plans were made for four more hour-long hunting and fishing segments, including tarpon fishing off the coast of Big Pine Key, Florida, and a live rattlesnake hunt in Okeene, Oklahoma. The results were similarly well received, and in January 1965, "The American Sportsman" went on the air in its own right as a "Wide World" spinoff.

The show was an attractive one as Roone Arledge provided his own specialized methods of placing the viewer as close to the action as possible—even to the point of putting microphones under dead zebras to pick up the slurping sounds of preying lions.

The philosophy behind the show was to approach a Robert Stack, Phil Harris, Bing Crosby, Peter Duchin, Jonathan Winters, Jimmy Dean, David Janssen, or any number of other outdoorsmen and ask them where they would like to go to fulfill their own Walter Mitty-esque fantasies. And regardless of whether they answered the Tanzanian Jungles or Kenya or Central America, "The American Sportsman" would pay their tabs as they set out to live their dreams, cameras trailing in their wake. It worked for the producers. They had nary a turn-down. And it worked for the sportsman at home, too, who tuned in in big numbers.

Although Tom Moore, concerned with the dangers inherent in a show that featured the hunting and killing of animals, engaged several consultants to provide direction, by 1970 the direction of the show changed in response to the ecology- conservation clamor. At first Arledge didn't know how to cope with the critics. It seemed that without the competitiveness of man versus beast, the show would be another casualty of the environmentalists. The promotion budget was cut, and promotion brochures sent to the agencies were made of artwork clipped from magazines and retouched so as to be unrecognizable. But that was before the success of the Marlin Perkins's No-Doz specials. They provided the impetus for a new tack, one concerned with the environment. The shows began to change from big game hunting in Kenya (which had been outlawed in the interim) to photographic safaris and programs featuring pure adventure, like Candice Bergen driving a Formula 1 racing car. The show again was back on the track; today over 10 million sportsmen—armchair and otherwise—at home during the winter months, vicariously live out their dreams each week.

* * *

"Wide World of Sports" has come a long way since that drizzling day at Franklin Field in April 1961. Through 1976 it had telecast eight hundred shows and over 1,200 hours of sports of every imaginable kind—dune buggying, track and field, football, baseball, mountain climbing, wrist wrestling, sumo wrestling, basketball, barrel jumping, parachuting, bicycling, volleyball, cricket, horse racing, snowmobiling, and demolition derbies among them. It has immortalized places that before had been known only to Mssrs. Rand and McNally: Snake River Canyon; Kinshasa, Zaire; Petaluma, California; Islip, New York; Le Mans, France; Pine Mountain, Georgia; and Hayward, Wisconsin.

Widely acclaimed by the critics as "the best show of its kind on the air," "Wide World" has won a total of twenty-six Emmys in eleven years—more than both of the other networks combined. And it has also won the George Foster Peabody Award for Television of Promotion of International Understanding.

But if "Wide World" is the backbone of ABC Sports, it is also their bread and butter and the anchor of Roone Arledge's fame. Today "Wide World" is a mammoth franchise, grossing over $20 million in commercial billings, a larger profit maker than Sports Illustrated.

As the second longest running show on television, it has become a tradition. And a whole generation has grown up listening to its slogan:

"Spanning the globe to bring you
the constant variety of sport:
The thrill of victory and the agony of defeat
the human drama of athletic competition.
This is ABC's Wide World of Sports."

5
If It's Saturday, It Must Be College Football

From that very first so-called football game—actually a mongrelized cross between rugby, soccer, and king-of-the-mountain—played between Rutgers and Princeton on Saturday, November 6, 1869, collegiate football was always a Saturday sport. It became so identified with the seventh day of the week that the National Collegiate Athletic Association emblazoned the words "Saturday IS College Football," like an ornamental coat of arms, on the nation's consciousness as well as on its brochures.

However, like Red Skelton's old line that "because the Monday meeting originally scheduled for a Tuesday this Wednesday has been postponed this Thursday and will be held on a Friday this Saturday because Sunday's a holiday," college football has been footballed around between the days of the week and can no longer be considered just a Saturday game. Games are now played on Mondays, Tuesdays, Wednesdays, any day of the week, but never on Sundays.

But one thing has remained constant—football's seasonality. No sport has colored a season more than college football; it is the embodiment of autumn, with banners, floats, cheerleaders, and brightly attired players and fans alike joining in what has become an American obsession. The preoccupation takes the form of myth-making, with heroes whose names are as colorful as the multihued trees of the season: "Red" Grange, "Brick" Muller, and Johnny Blood. And with numbers that count the teams like the days of autumn, down to a precious few: "The Seven Blocks of Granite," "The Four Horsemen," "The Touchdown Twins," and "The Top Ten." This, then, is college football, a sport that colors the sights, the sounds, and the smells of those playing, watching, and following it.

In fact, in the heartland of America, where there is no trace of a competitive endeavor known as professional football, there are those who not only follow college football, they mainline it, providing it with more than the mere trappings of a sport. To them, it is tradition, even life itself. It is the rivalries between Texas and Oklahoma, Michigan and Ohio State, Notre Dame and Southern Cal. It is effigies, bonfires, school cheers, and do-or-die for an institution that many of its followers identify with but many never attended.

At a recent game in Norman, Oklahoma, one is introduced to an alumnus who just had a serious heart attack. He waves off concern for his condition, replying "Ah cain't think of a better way of dyin' than at an OU game."

In Lincoln, Nebraska, where many followers of the University of Nebraska Cornhuskers dress in red and even furnish their homes in red, the colors of the school, one of the biggest sellers in the last few years has been a red radio in the form of a football, part radio and part toilet paper dispenser, which plays the "Nebraska Fight Song" as the paper is unrolled.

In Tuscaloosa, Alabama, the faithful dress in a similar reddish crimson in tribute to their favorite team, the Crimson Tide, and count their autumns not by the months but by the victories of 'Bama's team. At a recent reunion of the 1935 undefeated Rose Bowl champions, starting end Paul "Bear" Bryant got up to speak, welcoming all of those who could make it, including former teammates Don Hutson and Dixie Howell. He then offered to take the entire team to whatever bowl game Alabama would be playing in that year at his own expense. As he made his magnanimous offer, one of the co-captains of the team uneasily rose to his feet and as he steadied himself on the back of the chair, muttered, "Bair . . ."

and then stopped, choked with emotion. So he started again, "Bair. . . ." But again he had to stop, reeling both from his inner thoughts and the evening's hospitality. But then he started once more, and this time unable to finish it all, merely said, "Bair . . . you're som' bitch." As he slowly eased himself into his seat the room burst into wild enthusiastic applause. All of Alabama feels the same way.

* * *

The date was Monday, December 20, 1976. ABC's cameras were in Memphis, Tennessee, to televise the eighteenth annual Liberty Bowl football game—a game described in the program as "different because it doesn't honor a flower or a plant, a fruit or a dance, a bonnet or a cloth." What it did mark was the start of postseason play, the fitting climax to the long 1976 football season, which had started way back on Thursday, September 9, in a nationally televised game that saw UCLA beat Arizona State 28–10. It was just such a weeknight game that prompted a West Coast columnist to complain: "The colleges would do better to get rid of the nights and return to Saturday afternoon football the way God and Grantland Rice created it." This was to be the eighth consecutive year ABC had televised the Liberty Bowl, starting with the Colorado-Alabama game in 1969. Tonight it was to be "Bear" Bryant's Alabama team again, this time against the same UCLA Bruins, who were coached by Terry Donahue. It was the eighteenth consecutive year that Bryant had taken his Alabama team to a bowl game, starting with the very first Liberty Bowl game, which 'Bama lost to Penn State 7–0. Bryant, nicknamed "Bear" after he had attempted to wrestle a live bear at the age of thirteen, back in his old hometown of Fordyce, Arkansas, had won 261 games in his thirty-two seasons as head coach. He had taken his teams to twenty-two previous bowl games and had won four national championships and had been named national Coach of the Year a record three times. Donahue, on the other hand, was in his first year as head coach. And in that very first year, he had compiled a 9–1–1 record, taking UCLA to only its eighth bowl game, its first ever back-to-back, and also its first appearance in another bowl than the Rose Bowl. It was going to be, one of the Memphian supporters of the Liberty Bowl said, "one helluva shoot-out," between youngish 32-year-old Donahue, looking for all the world like the "Sundance Kid," and wily old Bear Bryant, an aging John Wayne, who had been coaching for exactly the same number of years—thirty-two.

* * *

The NCAA regular season football package for 1976 had consisted of forty-five games, thirteen national and the rest regional. The "majors," including UCLA, Alabama, Notre Dame, Ohio State, Michigan, Penn State, Texas, and Oklahoma, had been well represented in national exposure. In fact, over the last four years 10 schools had appeared seventy times. Sprinkled liberally throughout were teams such as St. John, St. Olaf's, East Carolina, Appalachian State, Hampden-Sydney, Mississippi Valley, Jackson State, and Alcorn State. More than 60 teams in all, including 9 that had not appeared the previous year. ABC had made a noble attempt to put as many of the 138 "majors" on the tube as possible. But they also had to balance that exposure with the "best" games for audience appeal. In the process, they found themselves in a damned-if-you-do-damned-if-you-don't dilemma.

The eastern college football fan—of whom there are more than it might be expected, although pro football is still king in those parts—was reawakening to the allure of its major gridiron powers such as Pitt and Penn State. But they also demanded Penn, Temple, Maryland, and even Cheney State. But when ABC put on an eastern game, showing Yale and Harvard, known thereabouts as "the Game" on thirteen northeastern affiliates, their switchboards were filled with those who now wanted the "A" game—Alabama and Notre Dame. It seems that although ABC announces its national games far in advance (most in March), as necessitated by the rules laid down by the NCAA's Television Committee, they only announce their regional games on the Monday beforehand. So it came as a great surprise and disappointment to many in the New England area to find that the regional game they were getting was not Notre Dame-Alabama but Harvard-Yale. None more so than the Notre Dame Club of Greater Boston, which had scheduled a bash for Irish alumni who thought they would be watching their alma mater fight it out with Alabama on a giant screen erected at the Boston Harbor Tennis Club for the occasion. The scheduling of Harvard and Yale fulfilled ABC's commitment to the Ivy League and no amount of phone calls could dissuade them. The president of the Notre Dame Club sorrowfully said, "I really don't know what to do. I guess we'll just show Harvard-Yale and hope their crowd will show up to help us make our bar commitment."

But it's not only Irish alumni clubs, real or subway variety, that complain. When ABC scheduled the Texas Tech–Houston game in the southwest region, a game that would decide the winner of the conference, irate phone calls from Houston inundated ABC's Avenue of the Americas headquarters demanding that the USC-UCLA game be shown. Most were from displaced alumni and alumni clubs of the two West Coast schools who had no allegiance whatsoever to the two schools of their adopted state and had already convened a Saturday afternoon get-together to whoop it up for their schools.

When the game between Mississippi Valley and Jackson State, two black schools, was televised in the deep South as one of the six regionals, editorials and letters rained complaining about having "black football forced down our throats" on the desks of ABC officials. A Louisiana civil rights group was simultaneously complaining to the FCC that ABC was discriminating against black schools by not showing them on TV. Although the FCC found no substance to the complaint, it merely pointed out ABC's dilemma. It was like the problem of the Arab sheik who was married to many wives; if he didn't make each one think she was the only one, there was hell to pay. So it was with ABC.

* * *

The NCAA and ABC had been an "item" ever since that March day in 1960 when ABC and its hired gun, Stan Frankel, had ambushed the on-going relationship between the NCAA and NBC.

ABC had once before held the rights to NCAA college football. Back in 1954, the same year ABC started their relationship with Walt Disney, they also initiated one with the NCAA. Robert O'Brien, a former Notre Dame football player and trustee who was financial vice-president and secretary of the American Broadcasting Company, made what Leonard Goldenson called "the deal with the NCAA." The "deal" was, according to Fred Silverman's master's thesis, the purchase of "the rights to the National Collegiate Athletic Association's schedule of thirteen football games for an estimated $2,500,000." ABC made "additional guarantees" to the NCAA, including the "telecasting of twenty-six weeks of Saturday afternoon winter and spring sporting events" and "at least seven radio and television programs." They had hoped that a national advertiser, most probably General Motors, which had purchased the package the year before on NBC, would buy the rights to the games. But General Motors was "not interested." But the president of the American Broadcasting Division of the corporation, Robert Kintner, according to Goldenson, did "not go out and sell the program," and ABC was reduced to offering the rights around on an individual game basis. This last-minute game-by-game sale, at a fraction of its estimated cost, wound up losing the network approximately $1,800,000. As the soft-spoken Goldenson noted, "they took a helluva lacing." In the wake of the debacle, ABC's entire sports department, in the words of one of the walking wounded, "crashed." ABC lost the rest of its two-year contract, which went back to NBC, and Kintner used its failure to get rid of O'Brien, the man he considered his intracompany rival. It also triggered Goldenson's search for someone to replace Kintner as head of the ABC network. Its ramifications were disastrous all the way around.

* * *

After ABC regained the rights to NCAA football in 1960 for $6.2 million, Scherick went out to hire the "talent." First he hired Roone Arledge, then the producer of local shows at WNBC–TV, to produce the games because his number one producer, Jack Lubell, was producing the ABC baseball "Game of the Week." Then, two months later, he added Chuck Howard as a production assistant (or PA).

Next, he sought broadcasters. The first one to come to mind was an announcer who was working with Mel Allen on the Yankee broadcasts, Curt Gowdy. Scherick remembered

Gowdy when he first came East in 1943 to play for the University of Wyoming's Cowboys against NYU in Madison Square Garden. Wyoming, then on its way to a 31–2 season and the NCAA championship, was led by Kenny Sailors, Milo Comminick, and Gowdy, and made nineteen out of nineteen foul shots to add NYU to their growing list of conquests.

After graduating, Gowdy went into broadcasting, earning his spurs first in Wyoming and later in Oklahoma with Bud Wilkinson. Gowdy was then hired by Trevor Adams, for whom Gowdy named his oldest son, as assistant to Mel Allen on the Yankee broadcasting team. As a Yankee announcer, he made a favorable impression on most of his audience, particularly Scherick. Scherick recommended Gowdy to Tom Moore for the NCAA announcing team, but Moore didn't think "Gowdy was good looking enough," preferring Jim Simpson instead. Scherick, taking issue with Moore, heatedly said, "Tom, we're not making a movie, we're just doing a game. . . . He's a good announcer." Scherick got his way, although Moore ultimately sent Simpson to Hollywood for a screen test.

Looking for that magic ingredient called chemistry in the broadcast industry, Scherick sought a color man who could work with Gowdy. He immediately thought of the late Paul Christman, whom he had heard doing the color for the Chicago Cardinal football games, a team he had led to two divisional titles and one world championship playing in the Cards' "million dollar" backfield. Scherick called Christman in Chicago, introduced himself, and asked if he'd be interested in doing the color on the NCAA games with Gowdy.

"Thanks a lot for calling, Mr. Scherick," Christman replied, "but you know I'm doing color on the Chicago Cardinals games. And you've got to remember something else, I played for the Cardinals. Also, I live here in Chicago."

Scherick answered each sally with "I'm aware of that" in what was beginning to sound like a rehearsed skit.

Christman continued, "and I'll tell you something, I'm in the paper box business here in Chicago and doing the Cardinals' color helps my paper box business and vice versa. I'm very happy here."

Scherick, waiting for an opening, now said, "Well, that's

very obvious to me. But tell me, how much are they paying you?"

Christman answered, "They're paying me $375 a game."

Scherick, warming to the hunt, shot back, "I'll double it."

Without missing a beat, Christman replied, "I'll take it."

Thus, he became the second member of the NCAA broadcasting team that is still remembered by many, including Roone Arledge, as "the greatest college broadcasting team."

The very first game on the 1960 schedule pitted the 1959 Southeastern Conference champion Georgia Bulldogs against Bryant's Alabama team. In postseason play to wrap up the 1959 season, Georgia had gone to the Orange Bowl and beaten Missouri, while Bryant had taken his Alabama team to the first Liberty Bowl and been beaten by Penn State. Georgia, with Francis Tarkenton returning for his senior year, was an easy touchdown favorite over the Tide.

Scherick had flown to Birmingham that Saturday morning. Upon his arrival at Legion Field he was met by Gowdy, who pulled him aside and said, "What's going on here?"

Scherick, somewhat surprised by the greeting he received, could only answer, "What's the matter?"

Gowdy launched into a whole dissertation: "I cannot tell you how mortified we all are. Last night my personal and good friend Bear Bryant extends an invitation to the entire ABC group to have dinner with him. I go out to dinner and we're all sitting there and I look up and some guy named Chuck Howard is having an argument with Bear Bryant."

The argument was over some esoteric point about football strategy. Scherick immediately called Howard over. "Let me tell you something, young man. For the next six months you will say nothing. Nothing, do you understand? Nothing, unless spoken to, and if spoken to, you will answer with 'yes sir' or 'no sir'. Is that clear to you?"

The young Howard, seeing his career pass before his eyes, could only gulp and say, "Yes sir."

And that was the end of the discussion. Scherick won his point, and Bryant won his game 21–6.

* * *

Gowdy and Christman had their moments, too. ABC once had the rights to a postseason game played in New York known as the Gotham Bowl. There were only two, and the last one was played during a newspaper strike on a cold, blustery day in December 1962.

Nebraska and Miami met before very few fans and almost as many ABC cameras. The telecast was to be taped, condensed, and shown later as a ninety-minute "Wide World" show. As the teams took the field, ABC experienced a technical problem, and the pregame show was jettisoned. Just five minutes before kickoff the engineers finally got things working, and Arledge instructed Gowdy and Christman to "do the scene set after the game is over."

The game itself was hardly a defensive battle; the opposing quarterbacks, George Mira of Miami and Dennis Claridge of Nebraska, took their teams to touchdown after touchdown over, under, and through the opposition's line, which resembles "The Seven Pats of Butter." Mira broke a Miami passing record, as he led Miami to a close 36–34 victory.

The game finally came to an end at 5:00. Gowdy and Christman had to catch the last plane out of New York to San Diego for an AFL game the next day, leaving only about ten minutes to theoretically set the stage for the game. With a copy of the statistics of the game in their hands, Gowdy and Christman went through the charade. "It's bitter cold here, windy and icy. Because of the climatic conditions, it's a terrible day to play a football game. There are hardly any people here. Paul, what do you look for?" wrapped up Gowdy.

Christman glanced down at his final stat sheets and started in, "Well, I think that either team to win this game will definitely have to score more than thirty points. I look for George Mira to have a big game, and I wouldn't be too surprised to see him break all the established Miami passing records." Scanning the Nebraska side of the sheet, he continued, "Now, you probably haven't heard much about Dennis Claridge. But this is an underrated quarterback. Big boy. He'll have a good day today. And I look for the tight end on Nebraska [who had caught eleven passes] to also have a big day."

Chuck Howard, who was in the studio editing the tape, merely groaned at Arledge, "It's a journalistic travesty."

But Arledge, able to conquer camera angles but not time or technical problems, merely shrugged and said, "Play the damn thing."

To this day there are those who think that Paul Christman was gifted with great foresight, citing his prognosis of the Gotham Bowl.

* * *

ABC's first concern upon winning the rights to NCAA football was to capture the sights, sounds, and smells that make college football unique. Tom Moore, called by Scherick "a very dynamic leader," gave direction to the coverage. He exhorted Scherick, and in turn Arledge, telling them that "it's got to be terrific." Moore's enthusiasm became infectious. When he said, "I want these telecasts to be better than anything that has ever been done before," Arledge prepared what has become a legendary thick notebook containing possible camera angles, innovative shots that would bring the viewers a look at college football they hadn't seen since NBC started televising it back in 1952, and an overall plan that would implement the motto of bringing the fans to the game instead of vice versa. But as imaginative as Arledge's plans were for NCAA coverage, it wasn't difficult to be "better than anything that . . . [was] ever done before." For NBC had but four cameras at the game, two on the twenty-yard lines and two on the fifty-yard line (a tight camera and a cover camera). In the words of Ed Scherick, "That was their idea of televising a game." It was like watching your Uncle Al's homemade movies of Lithuania.

From that standing start, Arledge devised plans to introduce hand-held cameras, bringing fans closer to the action, interview the coaches and players, utilize crane shots for panoramic views of the filled stadium, and even show the cheerleaders. For, as his notebook intimated, "When the fan goes to the game, what does he watch between plays? If you've seen one huddle, you've seen them all. The fan looks at the cheerleaders, other fans, anything that's going on around him." And so ABC, by merely understanding the game, brought a greater understanding—and enjoyment—to it.

* * *

The second game of the 1960 NCAA season was also Ed Scherick's last as an operative in the booth or in the truck. Admittedly "not known as a placid fellow at best," the excitable Scherick was given the job of serving as the stage manager in the booth for a game at the University of Pittsburgh. Nearing the end of the game in which everything had been going well, Gowdy prepared to sign off. There is an entire ritual to signing off, a whole set piece that contains all of the recognized cues for the cut-aways by the various stations, and must be read word for word. Every affiliate has a copy of the cues contained on the last page of the sheet in front of the announcers. Everyone, that is, except Curt Gowdy, who now turned to what was supposed to be the last page and found nothing. Scherick, desperately trying to be of assistance, ran over to the phones connecting the booth with the truck and yelled at Roone, "There's no last page in the booth."

Arledge said, "We'll read it to you," and proceeded with deliberation, "We'd like to thank the athletic publicity department. . . ."

Scherick ran back to Gowdy and whispered in his ear, "We'd like to thank the athletic publicity department. . . ."

As Scherick ran back for a second feeding of the information, Gowdy repeated the tag line to the affiliates, primarily, and the audience, secondarily, "We'd like to thank the athletic publicity department. . . ."

Scherick spent the next three minutes scurrying back and forth between the phone and Gowdy's right ear to bring the message and the telecast to a merciful close. Afterwards, he was dubbed "Quasimodo" for his crablike impression of the Hunchback of Notre Dame. He was also approached by a delegation consisting of Gowdy, Christman, and Arledge, who tactfully asked him, "Edgar, don't you think it would be better for everyone if next week you stayed home?"

The next week he stayed home. Coming to just one more game, the banished Scherick sought out a nearby campus building that had a television set. There he sat with his feet up on the desk watching the game being played just yards away, unaware that he was in the chancellor's office. The game now belonged to Arledge—and, ultimately, to his production assistant, Chuck Howard.

* * *

You can only ambush someone at the same pass once. When the NCAA two-year contract came up for renewal in 1962, ABC had no more Stanley Frankels or white rabbits to pull out of the hat. This time they lost it to CBS. After two years with CBS, the NCAA, like two-year locusts, reappeared at its third network in four years, NBC, for the 1964 and 1965 seasons.

But no longer was college football the only game in town. Both CBS and NBC had made major commitments to professional football; CBS to the NFL in 1964 and NBC to the AFL in 1965. Now Arledge, with Tom Moore's encouragement, made a direct pitch to Walter Byers, the executive director of the National Collegiate Athletic Association.

The thrust of Arledge's pitch was that ABC "was going to do a better show for them and by them than they could get anywhere else," recalls Tom Moore. But it was not that pledge that got Arledge into the Drake Hotel in Chicago to meet with the NCAA. It was his commitment that ABC, the only network without professional football after 1964, would not get in bed with pro football during the lifetime of the contract. And with no commitment to pro football, then or in the foreseeable future, Arledge could enter the contract with a clear conscience. "Walter Byers required that," says Moore. "It was the only way we got into the Drake Hotel to negotiate for the first time in the history of NCAA a unilateral deal." The pledge not to be led into temptation by pro football was described by Arledge as rendering unto the NCAA "some other things of value." And ABC had regained the rights for 1966 and 1967 at $15.5 million—$2.5 million more than NBC had paid for 1964 and 1965 telecast rights—with an option for two more after 1967.

Carl Lindemann, who had become vice-president in charge of NBC Sports in 1963, had fully expected the NCAA to continue its association with his network, an association that included ten of the previous fifteen years. Then suddenly, Lindemann received a two-line telegram informing him that the NCAA football package would be showing on ABC the next two years. Lindemann was beside himself. The man described by Moore as "not hard to run around in sports" had not only been run around, he had been bowled over. Now, in one of those long telegrams in the middle of the night that Lindemann was famous for, he accused the NCAA of everything but starting the Chicago Fire. They were guilty of "shoddy treatment," of an absence of "any spirit of fairness," and of being a "discredit to amateur athletics." Lindemann had not seen that NBC Sports's affiliation with the AFL had, in effect, ruled out any further association with the NCAA. The realization sent Lindemann crying to the rooftops—and the press.

Arledge could only delight in tweaking Lindeman's nose by commenting, "NBC makes a career out of hindsight and judging afterwards, and NBC, when they lost the rights to this screamed and yelled. I don't recall them screaming when they took the American Football League away from us, nor do I recall them claiming that anything was unfair about their negotiations for the Rose Bowl game or whatever other sports attractions they have." Arledge then went on to reinforce his point by facetiously saying: "Their management was quoted as saying that the only American way to award rights to something is by competitive bidding . . . . I don't think there's anything on the NBC network which they have gained through competitive bidding. So I just don't see what the screaming is about."

ABC was to have college football from that day on. Maybe that's what the screaming was all about.

* * *

Outside the tape truck, which is parked just inside the gate at Memphis' Liberty Bowl, men with improbable nicknames that even Chester Gould wouldn't give his villains—names like Sundial, the Hump, Barfy, Snootchy, Swazz, and Jaws—watch a tape recording of a presentation they put together for a party at the close of the regular NCAA season two weeks before. The party, titled, The First Annual Party of the Eleventh Season of NCAA Football Now in Its Thirteenth Year on ABC, had been a tribute to the team and to Producer Chuck Howard. It was more of a family sendoff than a party: The members of the NCAA team expressed a feeling that only comes through close association over the years. They had worked and partied together, in fact they had even played together.

Always feeling themselves to be competitive to "Monday Night Football," they challenged the "Monday Night" crew in 1972 to a game of football, naturally. The game was an outgrowth of the intramural rivalry between the two crews, engendered not only by the publicity and glamour the "Monday Night" crowd was getting in the papers, but also by the introduction of the engineers' names at the end of the NCAA telecasts. So both crews decided to flex their collective muscles in a game of two-hand touch. "Two-hand murder was more like it," remembers Frank Gifford.

Gifford called up the Yankee Stadium groundskeeper and got the use of Yankee Stadium for the afternoon. The "Monday Night" seven-man team was made up of Gifford, Director Chet Forte, Producer Don Ohlmeyer, Producer Dennis Lewin, and some of the other members of the production crew. The NCAA team was comprised of Chuck Howard, Director Andy Sidaris, and several masochistic members of the production crew. The final NCAA team member was Bud Wilkinson, the former Minnesota great, who flew in from Oklahoma at his own expense to play in his first game since he quarterbacked the College All-Stars to an upset win over the Green Bay Packers in 1937.

The NCAA team took the game seriously, printing up their own "NCAA Football" shirts and holding several secret practices. The "Monday Night Football" team, on the other hand, had sort of galvanized together in a grab-ass manner, saying, in the words of Chet Forte, "Hey, let's go down there and play them" and merely shown up.

With a small crowd of well-wishers and curiosity-seekers in the stands, including Ethel Kennedy, the two teams assumed their positions. The game started. "I couldn't believe the insanity. First play, somebody knocked me on my ass," Gifford recollected. It was almost as hard a hit as he took in the twelve years he performed at Yankee Stadium.

With referee Jack Fitzgerald, the ABC Sports comptroller, trying to keep some semblance of order amid the chaos, the air was filled with footballs, shouts, and bodies. The ankle of one of the NCAA crew was the first to go; then Dennis Lewin's shoulder went pop as he dove for a pass, and he had to be removed with a dislocated shoulder. Finally, with time and expendable bodies running out, Sidaris threw a "Hail Mary" pass to Wilkinson that was broken up and the "Monday Night Football" team limped away with a 24–16 win.

It was to be the only meeting of the two production teams in what had looked more like a slo-mo replay of the Seven Years War than a football game. And as the walking wounded of the two teams left the field, they all echoed Chet Forte's sentiments, "It was something I wouldn't want to do again."

.* * *

The scene at the Hyatt Regency, Memphis, the night before the Liberty Bowl was mass hysteria. In the middle of the fishbowl known as the lobby, UCLA was holding its pregame pep rally, with the entire lobby reverberating with the cheers and roars of 2,000 UCLA faithful who were getting their goodies off singing "Sons of Westwood" in unison. Off to the side, two of the Alabama adherents from the land of Billy Joes and Laurleen Lous, all dressed in red, looked up to see two of Alabama's black running backs walking through the lobby. "There go our Indians," they proudly proclaimed. Across the lobby, one of the 'Bama rooters held up his fingers in a V sign and shouted, "Bear don't walk on water, but he sure knows where the stumps are." Even the cocktail waitresses got into the act. They wore little "UCLA" patches on the left seat of their abbreviated blue jeans; the message was continued on the other cheek—"U Can't Lick Alabama."

While the fans partied, the ABC crew out at the stadium ran through their positions for the game. Andy Sidaris, the director, put seven cameramen through their paces as two extras stood in for the talent—Keith Jackson and Ara Parseghian.

The next morning, a production meeting commenced at 9:30 in the Tennessee Room of the Hyatt Regency. With everyone staring at their watches like the hare in *Alice in Wonderland,* it started promptly. Because of television's split second timing, no one in the room answers the time as "approximately 9:30." It's either 9:28:30 or 9:28:33. Watches are more important than ties, with only Ara Parseghian wearing one.

There are thirteen men surrounding the table. For this last meal, Producer Howard has laid out an elaborate spread: platter after platter of cheeses, melons, eggs, toasts, danishes, and urns of coffee. Director Andy Sidaris, replete in his cowboy hat and T-shirt emblazoned with "The Duke Kahanamouku Hawaiian Surfing Classic" (pronouned "Duke Caca" by Sidaris) looks at the platters. "No fuckin' fish," he grouses and returns to the table with a cup of coffee.

As everyone settles in his seat, Howard produces his game-plan, laid out on a sheet of paper, marked in reds, blues, and greens. The red marks are next to things he's going to video-tape; the greens, things on the field; and the blues, the live announcements. Accounting for every second, like a time-study man, he proceeds down the table, informing Bill Flemming, "Bill, you'll have forty-five seconds at the top to do a panaroma of billboards and set the pace." Everything is well delineated. It is far different than the production meetings that precede the Monday night games. There, all suggestions were listened to and some adhered to. Here, Howard alone chairs the meetings like a field general laying out a split second attack on an enemy's bunker position.

Howard ticks off those elements that will go into tonight's game—the scene set; the "Star Spangled Banner," sung by Marguerite Piazza, with fireworks going off just as the words "And the rockets' red glare" are sung; the halftime show produced by the Freedoms Foundation of Valley Forge; the Chevrolet Players-of-the-Year; and, finally, as a promise to the founder, Bud Dudley, the most valuable player award, time permitting. "And that's what it's all about, America," proclaims Keith Jackson.

Everyone at the table remembers when Parseghian retired.

ABC cut away at halftime for a special report direct from the studios of their affiliate in Duluth where he announced his resignation. Dudley and the Memphis writers took ABC to task for cutting away from their precious halftime spectacle. But not this year. This year they will stay with the halftime spectacle, promised by the Freedoms Foundation not to run over twenty minutes, including the bands.

Now that the timing, promos, obligations, and assignments have been covered, Howard mentions the other networks' programming. Finally he comes to the most important part of the meeting, the "escape"; the flight from the stadium.

The crew will stay in Memphis until the next morning, so Howard can only report, "We have a police escort to get us back here after the game. We'll be good enough to wait for you guys to come down from the booth before we leave." Bill Flemming immediately shows interest and interrupts, "I have never, never knowingly stolen anybody's escort . . . ," but the rest of his sentence is drowned out by roars.

* * *

Most college games are played in small towns from State College, Pennsylvania, to College Station, Texas, that are little more than a zip code. Almost impossible to get to from most major cities without connecting flights, and long car rides, they also require split-second timing. It is almost quicker to go by plane from New York to Los Angeles than from New York to Fayetteville, Arkansas. Compounding this problem is the fact that the college football game ends just moments before the last plane on a Saturday leaves. So the necessity for an "Escape."

If one man can be singled out to give meaning to the word *escape* it is Flemming. Flemming, so renowned for his escapes that he is the brunt of an in-house epitaph that reads: "Bill Flemming will crash in his own private plane on the field during the fourth quarter of a game he was announcing," is a grandmaster at effecting many.

But there have been escapes, and then there have been "escapes" worthy of the name. Some have been well-executed drills; others have been harrowing or hilarious. Just last year, after a game at Ohio State ended at 3:50, with the last plane out at 4:10, the crew was given a police escort six blocks to one of Ohio State's tall campus buildings, where they got into an elevator, went to the top of the building, and boarded an Army helicopter whose blades were already turning in preparation for its human cargo. From there the helicopter took them to the airport, landing next to the last jet from Columbus to New York, just twelve minutes after the closing credits signed off the game.

Once after a game at Stanford, a PA devised a scheme in which he conscripted motorcyclists to whisk the broadcasters to San Francisco. As all of the production team mounted the reverberating motorcycles, which formed a long line, Bud Wilkinson took his place on the back of the last one in line. Just as they were ready to take off in formation, Wilkinson, with his legs astraddle and his arms hugging the driver, shouted, "Are you sure you know the way?"

The motorcyclist, a perfect make for Chino, in The Wild One, half turned around to Wilkinson, and showing red eyes under his goggles, wheezed, "Man, I don't know . . . I'm so strung out today." Before Wilkinson could mouth a reply, he took off with a roar down the road, Wilkinson hanging on for his life.

* * *

The last order of business, after the escape plan, was the "pool." Thirteen experts on college football now sat down with slips of paper in front of them to mark down the probable winner and the point spread. Then, each folded-up paper is pushed to the center of the table accompanied by the bowl game ante of ten dollars, up from the five dollars a week on the regular season games. Researcher Jerry Klein tabulates the early voter returns, and if these men were as expert in their jobs as in their prognostications, there would be no game that night. All thirteen had selected UCLA, from Chuck Howard's minimum of four points to Keith Jackson's sixteen, Flemming's seventeen, and Associate Director Rick LaCivita's seventeen. All were sure they had the winner. Only Howard, who had consciously "shaved" the number of points to inch towards the Alabama side was now heard from. "What happens if Alabama wins?" he asked, a thought which had apparently not occurred to any of the other experts. "I should win the entire pool if Alabama wins or it's a tie."

"Vote! vote!" the voices at the table cried in unison.

Howard was voted down, 6–6, with one abstention. If Alabama won, the pool would hold over to the Sugar Bowl, the next time this same group would be together.

Jackson noted that winning a pool isn't a total blessing, but something like making a hole in one and having to treat the entire bar at the country club to free drinks. Jackson had won the last $5 pool with a total of $65 in it from the thirteen men. After treating everyone in the group to drinks at the bar in a classic belly-up-to-the-bar setting, he wound up paying $130; losing only $65 on the pool he had won.

* * *

Roone Arledge had served as Producer of NCAA football for two years—1960 and 1961. During that time he introduced America to the instant replay, first used during the Texas-Texas A&M game in 1961, and to the variations inherent within isolated shots, which had been used before, but never with such virtuosity. He invariably found the underlying story line to the game above and beyond the results.

But not all of Arledge's attempts to bring the fan to the game had been successful. There had been the time he sought to introduce the fan to that sanctuary, the team's dressing room at halftime. As Curt Gowdy conspiratorially intoned, "Now we go to the Utah State locker room as Utah State coach John Ralston talks to his players. Let's listen in . . .," the cameras came alive at the Utes' intermission meeting. The microphone was placed close to Ralston, who let the entire audience in on his innermost thoughts: "Hello everybody. Hope you're enjoying the game."

By 1966, when ABC reacquired the rights to NCAA football, it was to be another ballgame. Arledge had become executive producer and left the ball in the capable hands of Chuck Howard, his former assistant, and the man Tom Moore called "Roone's secret weapon."

Howard started as a production assistant, the lowest rung on the production totem pole. Every week for the first two years he had traveled the country with Arledge, Christman, Gowdy, Bob Neale, a director, Bill Bennington, who was not only from Hollywood, he was Hollywood, complete with cigarette holder and ascot, and Associate Director Marvin Schlenker. Howard would sometimes be physically divorced from the rest of the ABC Sports team: When the crew went to Northwestern, he stayed in Evanston, while the rest of them stayed in downtown Chicago, or when they went to the University of Kansas, he was in Lawrence while the others lodged in Kansas City. He was not there to see the sights; instead he was there to see that the nuts and bolts got done—the bags taken to the airport, the dignitaries met with a car upon their arrival—generally things beneath the dignity of those on the starting team, but so essential to the split second timing of a telecast.

Howard had definitely proved his worth. Now the post-pubescent-looking producer, still the embodiment of a college student himself, was to place his mark on the college games. A Duke grad, class of '55, Howard is a sports fanatic, having broadcast the Blue Devils' home baseball and basketball games and edited the sports section of the paper. He "immerses himself" in whatever he's doing, and according to those who work with him, "he has remarkable recall," and impresses those around him with his "capacity to bring up facts and comparisons" quickly as well as relevantly. Others feel his strongest point as a producer is helping his crew—both engineers and announcers—with facts, "not just facts, but specific facts." Very often during the course of the game, Howard will be subtly coaxing Jackson, "Keith, doesn't this remind you of Terry Miller's game when he ran for 228 yards earlier this year?"

Ed Scherick hired Howard in August 1960 direct from the Chase Manhattan. After serving as the production assistant on NCAA football and "Wide World" in 1960 and 1961, Arledge promoted him to a full-fledged producer of "Wide World" in 1962.

Every college football telecast from that day—or actually

from 1966—bears the sole imprimatur of this forty-two-year-old stickler for detail. And now he has become vice-president in charge of Program Productions and runs the entire NCAA show in his own style. The only times Arledge has shown up since Howard's ascension have been either because the game was a "biggie" or by mistake. The first time was the 1969 Texas-Arkansas game—the game of the year, if not, in the Southwest, "the game of the century." He left his then wife, Joan, in Hawaii on a planned vacation trip to join thousands of football-crazed fans in Fayetteville, including President Nixon. The other time he ended up unannounced for a game in Boulder, Colorado, when he accompanied his close friend Bob Beattie to the airport so that Beattie could get a plane back to his home in Colorado Springs. Arledge got so caught up in Beattie's persuasive and animated argument for the telecast of a skiing tournament Beattie was staging that he found himself unconsciously buying a ticket and boarding the plane with Beattie. Later that afternoon he joined the surprised crew at the Colorado game just a few miles down the road. Other than those times, it has been Howard's ball game.

* * *

Being wrong is an occupational hazard in most fields. It's endemic in sports. Newspaper pundits and television prognosticators alike had selected the Baltimore Colts to beat the New York Jets, Sonny Liston to thrash Cassius Clay, and now UCLA to beat Alabama. When the symbolic cannon in the Super Bowl IV halftime pageant backfired, someone hollered, "They've just shot Jimmy 'the Greek,'" the man who professionally handicaps games and who had made the losing Minnesota Vikings heavy favorites over the victorious Kansas City Chiefs.

In 1976 ABC had had its share of miscalculations as well; one of which was moving that year's Texas-Arkansas game from October 16 to December 4, so that they could televise it as the season's finale. They gambled that it would be another one of those traditional shoot-outs in the long and bitter rivalry between the Longhorns and the Razorbacks that more often than not decide the Southwest Conference Champions and Cotton Bowl hosts. Instead, it had a meaningless game of also-rans played for fifth place in the SWC.

Such isn't always the case. More times than not ABC is correct in its selection of a game, as it was in having Penn State reschedule its home game against Pitt at Three Rivers Stadium on Thanksgiving Friday that same year, a game that showcased Tony Dorsett's talents. The bait? Penn State Coach Joe Paterno said it all when he said, "We couldn't turn down the quarter of a million dollars they [ABC] were offering for the TV game." A quarter of a million dollars buys a lot of facilities, such as lights at Tennessee's Neyland Stadium, TV facilities at Washington's Husky Stadium, and several other goodies for college campuses West, North, and South—and occasionally in the East. Its attraction is so large that even a stalwart like "Bear" Bryant is not immune to it. "If they want to start a TV game at 6:00 that's okay with me," he said. What he left unsaid was that Alabama would be sharing in the television moneys generated by an appearance on TV, whether that appearance was at 3 P.M. or 6 P.M. or 9 P.M., Saturday or any other day of the week.

The "bread" paid by ABC consists of $250,000 to each team for a national TV appearance and $190,000 for a regional appearance. After the NCAA takes its 6 percent off the top, the remainder is split with those schools in its conference—seven others in the Big Eight, nine others in the Big Ten, etc. Independents like Penn State and Pitt keep it all. In this day of deficit financing for almost every college in the country, the entertainment dollar is one way for them to get money without having to go to the alumni and the trustees with hat in hand. That's the inducement to change schedules for TV.

But even then, some schools rebel at changing dates. When ABC approached the University of California to change the date of the Stanford game, known in those parts as "The Big Game," from November 20 to November 25, Thanksgiving Friday, and from Berkeley's Memorial Stadium to Candlestick Park, the athletic director turned the network down. "I told ABC it wasn't feasible because a change creates problems ticket-wise and the trade-off [ABC money versus gate sales] was not even close," said California Athletic Director Dave Maggard. Again, the consideration was the same—money.

This prescheduling and rearrangement was but a small problem considering the fact that ABC could now go after a game they considered key on short notice—a so-called wild card game. It wasn't always thus.

Every two years after they first formed their alliance in 1966, Arledge would renew ABC's contract with the NCAA who would up the price without throwing anything in the pot. One newspaper wag described the relationship thusly: "Byers is to Arledge as a dog is to a tree."

In 1970, although ABC had lost $4.5 million the previous year (not having sold all of its advertising spots) the NCAA still exacted an additional $1 million. This was due in part to the fact that there were several ABC affiliates who didn't care a fig for the newly announced NFL package, but wanted to keep the undiluted 150-plays-a-game bottled in bond pure college stuff and partly because ABC was no longer the only network without pro football. All three networks had pro coverage and NBC was back in the bidding.

By the end of 1971, it had become evident to everyone that the NCAA–ABC marriage was a one-sided affair and that something had to give. One writer was even prompted to write, "NCAA Chief Walter Byers should get down on his knees and salaam toward the Hall of Fame at Rutgers every time he sees the network's initials."

ABC, which had lost money the past two years, now came forward with a plan for a Poll Bowl—a game between the two leading teams in the country at the end of the year, which would be determined by the wire service polls. But the NCAA was hamstrung by the powerful Bowl lobby and turned them down. Instead they sweetened the pot by giving ABC more leeway in deciding what games they would cover. As an alternative to announcing their schedule six months in advance, living and dying with their preset games as the teams selected either lived or died, the NCAA allowed ABC to select the last nine dates of the schedule just twelve days ahead of kickoff. Moreover, they gave a dispensation to those teams playing on what they called "exception dates." No longer would the games played on holidays or days other than Saturdays be counted against a school's quota of television appearances over a two-year period. Added to the holiday and non-Saturday specials was an additional game, the eleventh on many of the teams' schedules. And finally, to alleviate the financial hardships ABC had suffered by televising NCAA football, the thirteen-man NCAA Television Committee allowed ABC to add a nineteenth commercial minute to each game, to pass $60,000 on to advertisers, still less than the twenty minutes on pro games. The NCAA had finally been brought struggling into the twentieth century of network TV.

* * *

As the Liberty Bowl production meeting broke up and everyone headed out to the stadium for the pretaping of the Chevrolet Players-of-the-Year Awards, publicity man Donn Bernstein was beset with requests for additional tickets. Ordinarily, Bernstein resembles a man who has just taken a four-way cold tablet and has to run three more ways to catch up with it. He spends his time handing out favors and little "ABC" pins, earning him the name the Candy Man. Now, in answer to several requests for tickets "for a friend" and even a "friend of a friend," Bernstein answers, "Yes, and get six credentials for Jewish relief," and runs into the hall, drawing neither a breath nor an answer.

* * *

In the rarified atmosphere of Madison Avenue, words take on a different complexion and hue than those recognizable on-the-field signals. The word *hut*, no longer has anything to do with the snap of the ball, but more importantly, it's the number of Homes Using TV. Added to these are such arcane phrases as *CPM, ratings, share,* and *AA homes.* But make no mistakes about it, these signals are as important to the ultimate success of a televised football game as the more recognizable signals of *red dog* and *blitz.* For they are the signals that those men who pay the freight, the advertisers, study more than the game stats to find out whether they won or lost. To them, the cost-per-thousand (CPM), share of viewers watching, ratings, and average audience (AA homes) are *their* game stats. It's not whether they won or lost, but how they sold their product that counts.

One of the biggest advertisers of NCAA football is, and almost always has been, General Motors. They were there in 1954, when ABC hoped they would come along with the package when they outbid NBC, and they were there, through their Chevrolet Division, in 1976.

And to reinforce that relationship and establish a close affinity with college football, Bob Lund, former general manager of Chevrolet, devised an award to be given to the outstanding offensive and defensive players of each of the games televised—nationally and regionally. During the six years of the promotion, Chevrolet has not only fully aligned itself with college football as well as generated favorable publicity, but had donated over half-a-million dollars in scholarships to the colleges in the names of the winners. Ironically, most of these scholarships go to nonfootball related areas, and the athlete who is selected as the winner merely gets a letter telling him of his selection—no plaque, no trophy, just a letter.

Sometime just before the conclusion of the game, the three announcers—in the case of the "A" game, Jackson, Parseghian, and Flemming—get on the headphones and decide on the winners. Usually there is little difficulty in selecting the outstanding players. But every now and then, Chuck Howard, a college football maven who understands the game and those in it and one who has seen every aspect of the game on the thirty-two monitors in front of him might inject a little prompting: "Hey, wait a minute, don't forget. . . ." But according to one of the three announcers, "We've never had an argument where one of the three absolutely refuses to give in." But he added, "That's not saying we won't!"

Like most advertisers, Chevrolet is extremely conscious of not only their public image, but also of mentioning the competition. They are not alone in this concern, which is almost a phobia. Chrysler, one of sports' biggest advertisers, was once instrumental in having the Goodyear blimp banned from NBC, although most Chrysler cars use Goodyear tires as part of their standard equipment. As the major sponsor of the 1967 Rose Bowl, they had become incensed when the Southern Cal

Marching Band had struck up "See the USA in Your Chevrolet" and every camera shot seemed to pick up banners reading: "Take the Mustang Pledge." Finally, when Lindsay Nelson mentioned the "shot from the Goodyear Blimp" for the second time, one of the Chrysler account executives leaned over and asked him, "How much are they paying for that mention?" When told the painful fact that it was nothing, he hit the proverbial roof. He complained to the powers-that-be at NBC, and NBC quietly kept the Goodyear blimp off their airwaves for ten years.

Chevrolet had never resorted to such direct tactics. However it was hinted that they had once gotten the ABC announcers to change the nickname of an entire football team to avoid mentioning the competition. It was the first game of the 1967 season, between Southern Methodist University and Texas A&M, a 20–17 win for Texas A&M in what Chuck Howard called "one of the ten best games on ABC." Somehow, during the course of the afternoon, Chris Schenkel continually referred to the SMU team as "Ponies" rather than "Mustangs." Many newspapermen questioned the use of that sobriquet the next day.

Chris Schenkel, then the "Voice of NCAA Football," had been the only broadcaster to properly pronounce Erich Barnes's name when the defensive back reported to the New York Giants in 1961 from Schenkel's alma mater, Purdue. He pronounced it as "E-rich" as a result of directly approaching Barnes and asking him how his mother pronounced it. For the game between SMU and Texas A&M, he again went to a source, Andy Sidaris, the director of NCAA football and an SMU alumnus. Sidaris told him that the name "Ponies" was one of "endearment." And so it was, as Schenkel continually called them the Ponies. But even today the SMU athletic department answers the phone "Mustang Football," as they always have, and Bob Condron, the sports information director at SMU says that "while it sounds plausible, it doesn't really work." In fact, says Condron, some of the coaches have even complained that the occasional "reference in the papers to the Ponies makes them sound slight, 'cause Ponies are little bitty horses." However, he does admit that one can substitute

"Ponies" when "Mustangs" is overused, like "Vols" for the Tennessee Volunteers and "Horns" for the Texas Longhorns. As for it's being used as a term of endearment, Condron could only fittingly say, "Horseplop." And there the matter rests.

Chevrolet has now risen above having to resort to such an out-and-out subterfuge. They stand behind their creation, the offensive and defensive players of the week—even if the winners are Mustangs from SMU, Falcons from the Air Force Academy, or Cougars from Brigham Young.

* * *

The temperature had dropped precipitously, down from the sixty-one degrees of just the day before to just over thirty degrees, with a windchill factor to match. It has become a Liberty Bowl tradition that the weather drops to freezing on the day of the game no matter how balmy it was beforehand. Those roaming around the field setting up the cameras for the mid-afternoon presentation of the Defensive and Offensive Players-of-the-Year Awards by Chevrolet are hopping up and down on the artificial turf, attempting to stay warm. It was no mean feat.

The two winners this year of the awards, which mean $5,000 in scholarship moneys to their respective schools, are Tony Dorsett of Pitt and Greg Morton of Michigan. Dorsett, who bears a striking resemblance to Flip Wilson—so much so that one of the Chevrolet welcoming committee who met him at the airport swore loudly, "Jesus, they didn't send Dorsett, they sent Flip Wilson"—stares at everything and everyone with doleful eyes, shrinking down inside the regulation wear of all athletes, the leather coat. Greg Morton, a friendly giant who raises beans as a hobby and downs opposing ballcarriers as a pursuit, was talking animatedly at everyone around him. He, too, wore a leather coat, albeit somewhat longer than Dorsett's.

On the sidelines Bob Cook, the general manager of the Chevrolet Division, did a last-second rehearsal with cue cards held by one of his advertising agency execs and spoke with Bill Flemming, who would serve as interlocutor. Finally, it was time to roll the tape, and Dorsett, who has only recently come to pronounce his name "Door-sett," a revelation to his mother, who is still Mrs. "Door-sit," advanced to the prescribed area, where he was flanked by Flemming and Cook. As Cook started to deliver his prepared speech—"On a slippery field against Penn State, and it was a memorable game . . ."—the man holding the cards fell woefully behind. But Cook, almost lapping the cue cards, knew his prepared speech well enough to substitute "symbolic" for "emblematic," not being distracted by what seemed to be a scene that was strangely out of synch. Next it was Morton's turn, and he took Dorsett's place in front of the camera on a high-rise platform. The entire scene was repeated again, tardy cue cards and all.

As the presentation awards came to a close, Chuck Howard demanded that they be supered "Recorded Earlier" to explain why the viewer of that night's game would see a presentation in daylight. Flemming accompanied Morton to his car to take him back to the airport for his immediate return to Pasadena and the upcoming Rose Bowl game. The Michigan coach, Bo Schembechler, had called his good friend Flemming and told him that he was leaving it in Flemming's hands to get Morton back on a plane. Now Flemming, the consummate Michigan man, was going to acquit himself.

* * *

Bill Flemming is the perpetual undergrad turned announcer. A University of Michigan premed graduate who won a campus oratorical contest with a speech "The Body, Why Not the Mind"—a forensic discussion of nothing more risque than psychiatry—he had gone into broadcasting immediately after graduation. First he broadcast the Michigan games over the local campus station, then he had gone to Detroit, and finally to New York to sub for Jack Lescoulie on the "Today Show." After teaming up with Dave Garroway and Frank Blair for a few months, NBC asked him if he would "work NCAA football with Mel Allen in the fall of '57," launching Flemming's career as a network sports announcer. Then Bill Reed, commissioner of the Big Ten, recommended him to Ed Scherick as a possible spokesman for Big Ten basketball, and Flemming became an employee of Sports Programs, Inc. Later Sports Programs hired him to do the very first "Wide World" show from Des Moines, where he did the Drake Relays to McKay's Penn Relays.

Today Flemming does the scores and halftime highlights for the NCAA football "A" game of the week, golf events, and the Sunday afternoon NCAA highlights. It was during one of those Sunday wrap-up shows that his old school loyalties, if not chauvinism, surfaced. The music selected for a scene of the Rutgers-Colgate game was to have been "Men of Rutgers." But Flemming recognized it as "an absolute infringment" on Michigan's *Varsity* and refused to play it. The engineer brought the record out to where Bill was seated and showed him the label. It read "One of Rutgers most loved fight songs written by Joe Glutz, class of '23 ." Flemming once again roared in a tone almost as round as he is, "an absolute fraud."And Michigan's honor was saved for another day. Flemming, whose lovely French baronial house in Bloomfield Hills is done in early Michigan memorabilia, is also as demanding of the correct spelling of his last name—with two "M's"—although the current chancellor of the University of Michigan is Fleming, spelled with one.

* * *

The temperature had dropped even further, down to twenty-nine degrees with a windchill factor under ten, as 52,737 hardly if not foolhardy fans paraded into the stadium, almost every one waving a little American flag given out free at the entrances. Memphians believed the purpose of the game, in the words of the program, was "to call attention to our most precious gift, to honor what so many Americans have fought and died for." You began to wonder why the two teams even bothered to show up.

The two trucks, the control truck and the videotape truck—collectively called Phase V—stand just inside the chain link fence. It's a cliché to recount the number of machines, the amount of money involved in sending out remote units, and the number of men involved in the production of an event. Suffice it to note that there, parked beside the stadium, was a complete television studio on wheels, in two separate units. In one, the control or "hot" truck, the producer, director, and technical director, or TD, sit side by side, instructing everyone within earshot what they're going to do next: what the TD is going to "punch up," what they want to cover, and when they're going to break. The other truck, the tape truck, has all of the facilities necessary to provide the dimension that television in general, and ABC specifically, are noted for: slo-mo machines, videotape recorders, and graphics. There is also one other item found in the tape truck that is probably found in no other unit anywhere else in the world—and as such is not a cliché. It's a sign that reads: "For your outstanding performance you are awarded one Attaboy. Fourteen hundred Attaboys qualifies you to be a leader of men, to explain simple problems to bosses, to pick your nose in public, to work overtime with a smile, and to be looked upon as a local hero. P.S. One "Awshit" wipes the record clean and you have to start all over again!"

Associate Director Rick LaCivita is in the tape truck building an opening tease. He is alternating heads of players who will be pivotal in the game with action shots of those same players: Wendell Tyler and Theotis Brown of UCLA, Jeff Rutledge and Ozzie Newsome of Alabama. Howard has allotted him one minute and twenty seconds. LaCivita needs one minute and thirty-two seconds. Howard begrudgingly gives in, now down twelve seconds to his self-imposed time clock before the game begins.

Jim Lampley, an added starter to the NCAA team only three years ago, comes into the control truck. "Looks like I don't have too much on these two teams," he says to Howard, holding out his notes.

Howard looks at him and asks, "The NCAA just suspended Kentucky today; why don't you talk on that?"

Lampley tells him that he has former Tennessee Coach Bill Battles standing by and that he "promised we'd get Pepper Rogers on."

Howard feigns a look at the heavens, actually the top of the truck just a foot and a half over his head, and rolling his eyes replies, "You couldn't keep him off with a bazooka."

Lampley has been the sidelines man for three years, an attempt by Arledge to enhance the feeling of college football by having an announcer close to college age provide the color and in-depth material from the sidelines. He sought a youngish, rah-rah type of announcer. That announcer was to be Lampley, who auditioned while still an undergraduate at the University of North Carolina. He was assigned to interview George Mira, then the quarterback of the now-defunct Birmingham Americans of the old WFL. Unbeknown to ABC, Mira was a high school idol of Lampley, from his hometown of Miami. He got the job.

Lampley's first game had been UCLA and Tennessee, not far from the site tonight. It was an inauspicious start, as a relief cameraman just in from Hollywood was directed by Sidaris to "get Lampley down on the sidelines." The cameraman scanned the field and shouted back over his headset, "What number is he?"

But Lampley earned his spurs, getting most of the coaches at halftime—with the notable exceptions of Woody Hayes, Bo Schembechler, and Tom Osborne—as well as coming up with in-depth pieces that added a collegiate flavor to the game.

* * *

Just before the talent, Keith Jackson and Ara Parseghian, make their way up to the announce booth, Tony Azzelino, the lightman is up in the booth studying the lights that illuminate the field. Last night during rehearsal he thought he noticed something. Now he's sure. The candle power had been reduced from 150 last year to 110 this. "GE or somebody sold them a bill of goods," he mutters over his headset as he directs the lenses to be opened wider to compensate for the inadequacy and not lose depth on the field.

Every man is at his battle station. The time is 7:00 P.M. and counting: One hour to go until kickoff. Keith Jackson comes into the booth, somewhat tulip-shaped in his smartly tailored brown overcoat. He takes his place next to the monitor and puts his notes on the gerrymandered, plank desk. Realizing that something's different, he looks up to see a window shielding him from the elements and the crowd. Wanting to be as much a part of the game as those in the stands and also to get the feel of the crowd, he props the window open. A gust of wind immediately rewards his efforts, rearranging his notes.

The window is closed to the discomfort of Jackson, now en-
cased in a hothouse atmosphere. He is joined by the second
member of the broadcasting team, Ara Parseghian, the former
Notre Dame coach, who will be doing the color on the game
tonight. While Jackson studies the monitor, watching the one
minute and thirty-two seconds LaCivita put together earlier in
the evening and making notes, which will become the basis of
his narration, Parseghian studies the crowd below him—somewhat removed by the window pane.

Jackson looks up and says, "I know it's UCLA by the air
horns."

* * *

Keith Jackson is the principal voice of NCAA Football, having replaced Chris Schenkel on the primary game in 1974,
partly because Roone Arledge wanted "to make it up to him"
for being summarily dismissed from "Monday Night Football"
and partially because, as Howard Cosell recalls, "the NCAA
preferred Keith to Chris."

Jackson's dulcet voice, bearing a slight tinge of his native
Georgia, and professional manner have won him the award of
National Sportscaster of the Year five times and the Peabody
award, His philosophy of sportscasting is simply: "You am-
plify, you clarify, and you punctuate and then you stay out of
the way, because it is a visual medium. This is not my show,
this is not my platform. It belongs to the kids—the athletes on
the field. It's not my place to inject any personal message or to
interfere with the game." Of his desire to enhance rather than
detract from the action, he says, "All I simply want to do is
help the people; I want to help the truck driver in Talladega
who went out and spent $800 for a color TV set as a primary
source of his entertainment to get his money's worth."

And Jackson has been amplifying, clarifying, and punctuat-
ing in pear-shaped tones, which somehow fit his manly phy-
sique, for twenty-five years now. This good-looking, mucho-
macho man is a cross between a filled-out and rugged-looking
Chester Morris and ex-Marine, which he is. He wears a slight
southern accent well; one he doesn't "even try to cover up anymore." Born and raised on a farm just down the road apiece
from Carrollton, Georgia, Jackson left that little western

Georgia cotton center just after World War II to join the Marines, where he played football, boxed, played baseball, and served in the air wing. "But when you can't hit, can't throw, and can't run, you better go do something else," he said. That something else was broadcasting. After a four-year tour of duty at Washington State University, where he studied political science, policing methodology, and also worked his way through college by driving a garbage truck for $1.75 an hour, he took a job with KOMO–TV, the ABC affiliate in Seattle. For ten years he served as everything from production director to news editor to announcing special events to chief cook and bottle washer. He also had been the play-by-play announcer for several AFL games and the Washington State football games.

In 1958, while he was with KOMO–TV, he announced the very first live radio broadcast of a sports event from Russia. He just decided that if the University of Washington could send their crew to Moscow, he could go, too, and paid for his trip out of his own pocket. Arriving with an engineer, he asked a bystander for directions to the United States Embassy. The bystander, part of a mob, told him to "follow us," and Jackson arrived just in time to see "spontaneous demonstrations" by the Russians against the American Embassy for landing in Lebanon.

After one week of cutting through red tape he finally arranged to cover the race. But when he arrived at the gates to the reservoir where the race was held, he couldn't get in unless he exhibited something with a notary stamp on it. After rummaging through his briefcase, Jackson found a Seattle police and fire card that had such a stamp on it. The gates opened as if he had said "open sesame," and he broadcast the first live direct feed from Moscow as the Washington crew beat five Russian teams.

It wasn't until 1962, however, that Jackson came to the attention of the network. Tom Moore, head of programming, had gone out to Seattle to witness the Gold Cup Hydroplaning Championships, being taped for "Wide World." His father-in-law, George Stirrat, suggested he "look at this sports announcer," who just happened to be Keith Jackson. "Although," remembers Moore, "he weighed about thirty pounds less at the time."

Moore came back to ABC to recommend him to Arledge. "Roone, this guy's pretty confident and he's got good looks."

Arledge looked at the tape Moore had brought back and liked what he saw. The next time there was an event in Seattle, the National Skydiving Championships in November of 1963, Arledge used Jackson and has been using him ever since.

* * *

The man he replaced, Chris Schenkel, is still the announcer on the back-up NCAA game. But his fall from grace was what one of his colleagues called "sudden" and "embarrassing."

Schenkel came out of Bippus, Indiana, and Purdue University to go on to a broadcasting career. But first he was a race caller at Narragansett Park in Rhode Island for six years, finally coming to New York to broadcast the New York Giants games in 1952. His was the great voice of early television, the golden sound of broadcasting. And it was one of the nicest sounds, too, with a "gee-whiz" quality that he imparted to his listeners.

But just as the geographic center of the country has moved from the banks of the Wabash, so too had the popularity of one of Indiana's favorite sons. The man described by everyone, everywhere as "a love," "one of my favorites," and by Howard Cosell, who spews out few accolades, as "one of the two extraordinary gentlemen in our business—the other is Jack Whitaker," has become a victim of broadcast fatigue and the critics. For in an industry that eats its young and devours its talent, it seems that Chris Schenkel's overexposure finally caught up with him. His Pollyanna approach, seen and heard since he started doing "Monday Night Boxing" fifty weeks a year back in the early fifties, has become too familiar and has bred contempt among his critics. His great voice—of the old school where broadcasters were cheerleaders—is now just a "grating" voice to many.

Schenkel's quality of innocence and continual use of adjectives have taken their toll. Once Arledge had enough of his sugar coating and screamed over the headset, "Shut up, Chris." And it was his enthusiasm that made his "Look at that jig!" reference to Elmo Wright of Houston, once doing his theater of the end-zone dance on his knees, so much more damaging than if he had meant it.

The man described as "virtue being its own reward" might have suffered at the hands of his chosen profession, but he has brought it much. This thin, wiry son of Indiana was the first announcer to gain a long-term network contract as well as the first to be nominated for an Emmy. In this Age of Aquarius, it is unfortunate that there is no place for an announcer who can make an abatoir in August sound like fun. No matter how great his voice.

* * *

It's 7:55, 8:55 EST, and the teams have now come on the field. Donahue leads the blue and gold of UCLA, and then it's the red of Alabama surfacing out of the runway entrance. Bear Bryant, looking almost naked without his traditional skinny-brimmed plaid hat that he manufactures in association with Sonny Werblin, has donned instead a bright red ski mask that works in reverse to outline his face, in deference to the cold and the wind.

At 8:02:15, just as the opening tease is finishing, the UCLA Marching Band enters the stadium from out of one of the vomitoriums, as the public-address announcer intones: "ladies and gentlemen, the 'Solid Gold Sound of 1976!' . . ." Three more songs, including "Sons of Westwood," and Marguerite Piazza comes to midfield to sing the "Star Spangled Banner," complete with rockets' red glare.

Then the coin toss by "dawn's early light" and Alabama elects to take the wind at their back and kickoff. The game starts at 8:11:59, two-and-a-half minutes later than Howard wanted it to.

The game itself is less a shoot-out than a blow-out. In wham-bam-thank-you-ma'am fashion, Alabama scores a touchdown, kicks a field goal, and scores two more as the first half ends 24–0, leaving Chuck Howard on the headset trying to pull out of Parseghian an answer to his question, "How could this happen? How could UCLA, which has looked so good against Arizona State and Ohio State and seemingly has better personnel, suddenly be behind 24–0?"

Ara Parseghian has been having trouble all night pronouncing the multisyllabic UCLA defensive tackle's name, Manu Tuiasosopo. "If it had an 'ian" at the end of it, it would help," said the French-Armenian coach who had won ninety-five games in his eleven-year coaching career at Notre Dame, including the 24–23 victory in the Sugar Bowl over Alabama for the national title. Jackson, who had had to study every night at the Olympics and familiarize himself with 2,300 athletes' names from every part of the globe, helped him through it, 'Two-E-eye-so-so-po." But the man who had had difficulty in conveying how his own name, Parseghian, was pronounced continued to fumble it.

A favorite Ara Parseghian banquet story and one he chances to tell at the sight of half a grapefruit goes something like this: "I was once at a banquet and had a nervous toastmaster who was having difficulty with my name. So he kept asking me how I pronounced it. I kept telling him and enunciating every syllable very clearly—'Par-see-G-yen.' Of course, coaching is a transference of information and I wasn't getting this message across. So the next time he asked me, I was challenged and told him, 'I've got a very difficult name. I'm going to break it down into three syllables and when I get through with it, you're never going to forget it. Now the first syllable is "par," like in golf. You understand the game of golf, don't you?' And he said, 'That's my favorite game, coach.' I continued, 'The next syllable is "see" and then a hard "G," like in Seagram's. You know, the whiskey.' And he said, 'Coach, that's my favorite brand.' And I concluded, 'The third syllable is "Yen," as in Japanese money, "Par-see-G-yen." ' And he said, 'Jesus, coach, that's the finest job I ever heard of anybody ever explaining anything.' So he got up to introduce me in a very confident manner and I could hardly wait for him to introduce me, because I felt I'd really communicated with him. He said, 'Ladies and gentlemen, I'd like to present . . . ,' and he began to rustle his papers, and I thought, 'Oh, my God!' And he continued, 'Coach . . . well, anyway folks, here he is . . . a drunken Japanese golfer . . . that's what he is!' "

* * *

Some years before ABC had tried an experiment with different head coaches serving as the color commentators on a week-to-week basis. It didn't work. Besides the fact that many of them were as entertaining as a test pattern, some were unintelligible, including Bear Bryant, whose southern drawl needed consecutive interpretation. Moreover, ABC was besieged by coaches who wanted to go on. And just as importantly, very few of those in the head coaches' closed fraternity would second guess their brethren; it got to the point where their comments were meaningless.

Another disappointment had been Duffy Daugherty, the affable former coach of Michigan State, whose talent for dropping bon mots, like "a tie is like kissing your sister," was storied. When hired by ABC, he had been given much the same pep talk that Fanny Brice had given Danny Thomas when she first hired him and he came up to her and told her how grateful he was for his start in show business; she had replied, "Cut the shit, kid, just go out there and be funny." But Duffy wasn't, and he was ultimately phased out.

And now it was Ara Parseghian and Bud Wilkinson alone. Both were capable and competent analysts, but both were still ex-members of that same fraternity and would occasionally come out with a line like Wilkinson's at that year's Michigan-Minnesota game when he referred to a Michigan field goal that had made it 31–0 as "a lot more important to Michigan than people realize."

Parseghian had growing pains fitting into the slot as well. During his first game, the Notre Dame–Pitt game, as he watched his former team losing 31–10 to a team he had once beaten 69–13 (for the most "away" points scored by an Irish team in their history), he saw a ray of hope in a Notre Dame fumble recovery of a loose ball. "That's a big break for us," he said in a voice that has the whisper of a small frog in it and keeps us on the edge of our seats waiting for it to be cleared. Jackson had to correct him at the next commercial break, "It's not us anymore, Ara."

With the score Alabama 24, UCLA 0, a complete reversal of the expected results, Chuck Howard was anxious to pry something more revealing out of Parseghian to explain the potential blow-out. How was Alabama able to push UCLA all over the field? Should they take a saliva test? Or was it just Bear Bryant? Parseghian offered no analysis.

* * *

It was now halftime and the Freedoms Foundation of Valley Forge was "privileged"—or so it said in the program—to present a pageant entitled, *Family Time, a Revolutionary Old Idea.* ABC had promised the powers that be at the Liberty Bowl that they would not cut away from the show, and in return, had elicited a promise that it would be twenty minutes. No more! But from the very start the program was getting caught up in its underwear. First of all, the bands were off late. UCLA had four numbers, including the "Bugs Bunny Theme," and during all of them, an Alabama fan danced madly around the band, distracting its members. Finally, the band director, Kelly James, came down from the bandstand and held up a threatening fist in the face of the booster, screaming, "If you ever do that again when my band is on, I'll beat the hell out of you," a comment hardly calculated to speed up a halftime show. With the score 24–0, all those sounds in the eastern time zones are not crickets, but the clicks of sets as viewers turn them off and go to bed.

Then the Freedoms Foundation show starts, a show that has cost them $25,000 to stage. Four geodetic domes, resembling the pods from the "Invasion of the Body Snatchers," are carried out to the center of the field. The bands strike up "Zip-de-doo-dah," the lights go out, and Bill Flemming, made available by ABC, comes over the public-address system and tries to explain the theme: "Families are an integral part of free society . . ." As Director Andy Sidaris looks at the monitors up on the wall and holds his head in his hands. "Jesus, I can't put that on . . . silly . . . that looks ridiculous."

As if prompted to outdo themselves, the Freedoms Foundation program continues and continues and continues, way after it should have been "gonged;" twenty-three and a half minutes in all, a whole prime time show of indistinguishable figures doing indecipherable things to unfathomable music. Chuck Howard was livid. A master of condensing halftime to get the game back on, he was losing control of it and there was nothing he could do. The halftime lobby had won out again. But this time they had won with a vengeance.

At best Chuck Howard is embarrassed. At worst he is beside himself. Plotting and planning an entire game down to the nanosecond had come to a lot of little domes opening up and spewing out people all over the field—and eight minutes over their alloted time as well. "It's like trying to put twenty pounds into a five-pound bag," he remarks as he looks at the time again.

In a game that promises to be the most one-sided affair in the history of the Liberty Bowl and the twelfth largest runaway in major bowl history, consisting of over 240 games, it would be hard enough holding the audience without this!

* * *

More often than not, during a game Howard not only knows how to plot the time, he also knows what plays are upcoming. This is because he knows the ins and outs of the teams, and because he has sometimes been tipped off by the coaches as to what to watch for. Once when Wilkinson was coaching Oklahoma, he told Howard to "watch out on your cameras" for his hurry-up offense. One time, he told them, "We're not going to huddle," and Howard took this to mean that he should warn his cameramen not "to be cocking around and shooting broads" when Oklahoma had the ball.

But Howard, one of the dedicated students of the game, has also figured out in advance what is going to transpire on his own. One time he was producing a Tennessee-Auburn game, when it became obvious to him that Tennessee was going to be covering Terry Beasley, Pat Sullivan's favorite target, and that the tight end was going to be able to get free. And sure enough, they isolated on him and he caught no less than eight passes that day, mostly, in a third-and-long situation.

Rick LaCivita, Howard's associate director, finds him to be "very logical and a very quick thinker. But he becomes infuriated more quickly than any person I've ever met when things don't go off as planned." Keith Jackson has called the USC-UCLA game an "exciting" one, which begins "when that horse comes galloping out on that field and 90,000 people start stomping their feet." To catch that excitement Howard has even taken to "cuing" the horse. He has a PA standing by, next to the horse, and wants to have the horse bolting down the track coming out of a commercial. But not five seconds after hollering "Go," LaCivita says Howard is "all over the field hollering,'Where's the horse?' He doesn't allow for the PA to direct the rider, Tommy Trojan, and the rider to say 'giddyup.' "

But Howard is not alone. During the first year he produced the NCAA games, Roone Arledge wanted to go down on the field and strangle the University of Michigan band leader, William Revelli, for not coming in on cue. Producing an event, particularly a college football event, and trying to capture the spirit and the electricity that make it unique is not an easy lot.

Even with preparation, there are sure to be mix-ups. One of the more legendary ones occurred at the Coaches All-America game held that year in Atlanta, Georgia. The PA on that occasion was, naturally enough, Joe Aceti. It was his job to stand next to the band director for the Morris Brown University Marching Band, members of which march over two hundred steps a minute, and cue the director when they came out of a commercial. Aceti had explained to the director, Cleopis Johnson, the band's part in the entire program; coming out of the commercial, he would tell him "when," and Johnson could signal his band, which was standing some 70 yards away in the entranceway to the field. They had been standing on the field for the first ten minutes of the halftime activities, waiting for the big moment—Joe Aceti with his headset and Cleopis Johnson with his purple uniform and white gloves. Going into the final commercial, Aceti hears the count down "60 . . . 45 . . . 30. . . ." He turns to Johnson. "Are you sure they're all right?"

Johnson says, "No problem."

Aceti looked down the field and could barely discern the figures in purple uniforms. "Are you sure they can see you?" he asked.

"No problem," replied Moore, "all I have to do if I want the band to start is flip my wrist like this and they go. . . ." And with his demonstration flip of the wrist, in comes the Morris Brown Marching Band, high stepping their way into the stadium, with twenty seconds left in the commercial. Chet Forte, who was producing the game, is on the headphones screaming, "What did you do? You cued the band too early." But Aceti is rolling on the ground, doubled up with laughter. Finally, he composes himself and tells Johnson, "Please stop them." Johnson, on his way to join his brigade, only says, "I can only start them. There ain't no way to stop 'em!"

* * *

If Howard could figure out football formations and prognosticate plays, he was not having any of the same luck deciphering what "the hell was going on down on the field" as the halftime show became chained to Morpheus's slow carriage.

Seated next to Howard and watching the nonsense is Andy Sidaris, the director of NCAA Football games since 1966 and Howard's "eyes." Sidaris is a craftsman who likes close-up, tight shots. Tonight he has no tight shots to "punch up" as he just sits there disbelieving what he is witnessing.

Andy Sidaris's fame rests with the show business values he has brought to the game, most notably "honey" shots. It has been said that if there are any beauties in the stands, he will find them like a Fellini. Actually, he says some of the credit should go to one of his cameramen, Sal Falinio, who does nothing but look for girls, both on the sidelines and in the stands. "Sal's an Italian and really loves it," adds Sidaris somewhat gratuitously. Falinio not only looks for gals in the stands, but meets the cheerleaders and talks to them, in effect rehearsing them for their shot on national or regional TV.

The first time he went to girl shots was in 1960. Sidaris was an SMU graduate, who had stayed in Dallas and produced and directed on WFAA, an NBC affiliate which later became an ABC affiliate. He became the youngest director in network history when he directed his first game, a "Wide, Wide World of Entertainment" segment just two weeks before his twentieth birthday. He later directed at ABC, including "Confession," did "The Magic Land of Ali Kazam" for CBS and ABC, and emigrated to the West Coast in 1959. He was called by Arledge to direct the very first "Wide World of Sports" show from Drake in 1961 and since then has been under contract to ABC for NCAA football and other events. Sidaris also directs other shows, including segments of "Kojak" and "The Gemini Man" and had a cameo part in "Two Minutes Warning" as the television director. But it's not the shows he's directed nor the ones he's "starred" in that have brought him the most satisfaction and fame—it's NCAA football and his honey shots.

Sometimes during the first AFL games—"we had more people in the huddle than in the stands—" he chose to roam around the stadium and see what, if anything, he could pick up. "But once we started with the NCAA in 1960, we did little of that. And when we got it back in 1966, we tried to pick up the flavor of college football. And in doing so our cameramen would start singling out individual girls, and we said, 'Hey, that's great.' "

The man who has contributed almost as much to college football as Walter Camp was not usually as despondent as he now appeared to be. Sidaris is usually an upbeat, ebullient character, who imparts that feeling to his cameramen. When one of his cameramen took a fake and missed a 99-yard touchdown play, Sidaris told the cameraman, "Look in your viewfinder. You might see a jockstrap there!"

Every director on NCAA football wants to do his best, whether it's the "A" unit or the "B" or all the way down the line to the sixth game of the day. Sometimes they'll be given two or three or four cameras and want to use some of the extra cameras in the remote truck to improve the quality of their coverage, regardless of whether it's in the budget or not. Sidaris doesn't have to worry about that—he has a full complement of eight—including crane or blimp, two on *Luv* machines along the sidelines, three on the press side, one in the booth, plus a hand-held. Sidaris also has something else, an intangible. The same basic crew has worked with him year in and year out, with a few minor exceptions or fill-ins. As such, each man is assigned to the same camera and same position, and they know just what they have to cover. When

Sidaris needs a certain shot at a certain juncture of the game, he knows that all he has to do is ask for it—"Take 1" or "Give me Johnny's camera," or "Give me the end zone"—and he's got it. Sidaris and Howard run a tight ship. Their propinquity to each other is an asset. As Howard tells Sidaris what he wants, his voice is heard over Sidaris's headset by the cameramen, obviating any necessity of having it repeated.

One of those cameramen Sidaris has in his stable is Mike Freedman. A lookalike for Yul Brynner, down to his shaved pate, Freedman often is stopped on the streets of New York for "his" autograph—which he dutifully renders, scrawling "Yul Brynner" on scraps of paper. But Freedman is less known for his looks than the looks of his shots. Part cameraman, part daredevil, and all guts, he has positioned himself in several unusual places attempting to get the one shot that best captures the flavor of the event he is covering. He has gone underwater, climbed into a pit beneath a raging brahmin bull, shot from a helicopter high above a stadium, and come dangerously close to Ohio State coach Woody Hayes. And it has not been without incident, as his proximity to danger has won him several purple heart clusters: the helicopter he was flying in over the Hula Bowl Stadium went down in nearby Kailua Bay, killing the pilot; the emotionally-charged University of Pittsburgh team stampeded the crouching figure of Freedman into the ground; and Hayes took exception to Freedman's capturing his frustration and tears on a hand-held camera from twenty feet away after his team fumbled away the ball (and the game) deep inside Michigan territory. But Freedman took Hayes's flying right-hand shot in stride, remarking only, "I caught him with his hair down. They pay me handsomely not to get the backs of guys' heads."

* * *

As the halftime show stumbles off the field, the two teams reemerge. Jackson looks at the monitor to his left to synchronize his words with the picture going out over the air waves. While listening to three cross-discussions going on at once over his headset, he says with a sigh, "And now for second half action. . . ."

Seated between Jackson and Parseghian is Jim Ritts, a young graduate student who had been graduated from the University of Texas and now attends Northwestern Business School. After starting as a go-fer, he had risen to the exalted position of statistician, a position once held by Jerry Kapstein before he went on to become an agent deluxe. Ritts spends the entire game, all 150 plays, making little marks on the paper in front of him, marks that take on a meaning of time of possession, yards gained, first downs, and other esoterica that Jackson makes ample use of during the course of the game. Weeks before Ritts's little pencil, tabulating time of possession, indicated that Arkansas and Texas had shortchanged themselves three minutes in the first quarter. And even though the officials disputed it at first, they finally agreed that the scoreboard, when it registered three points for a field goal, had somehow discounted three minutes from the time clock. But it was too late to readjust the clock when they realized the mistake sometime during the second quarter. Others have lost three minutes in a game before, most notably the Mizlou network when they produced the Blue-Gray game. That was to avoid overtime Telco line charges. But it had never happened on an ABC-televised NCAA game. Until Ritts caught it, that is.

Ritts's start as a go-fer is encouragement to that coterie of college kids who congregate around every remote to help out. These men-boys are the Regimental Beasties of the unit. In reality, they are the assistants to the assistants to the producers or the ones who help the PA's. In days of yore they followed the circus. Now they follow the electronic circus—television. They're given no per diem, no transportation pay, merely a room and twenty-five dollars a day. And yet they're there, hoping to be recognized, utilized, and ultimately synthesized into the organization. The unsung heroes know that Jim Ritts, Terry Jastrow, Don Ohlmeyer, and others in the ABC Sports organization once were just like them, and that knowledge fires their hopes that someday, some way, somehow, they may also become members of ABC Sports on a full-time basis.

* * *

Slowly the game winds down to a charitable close, Alabama winning by the largest score in Liberty Bowl history, 36–6, in a game that was not as close as the score would indicate. Off the air at 11:04 CST, without the most valuable player selection or the flag waving part of the show, the crew makes its quick escape through the 52,000 fans who still cling to their little American flags. The eighteenth Liberty Bowl is now history.

* * *

Despite the rout and the halftime nonfestivities, the game posted a 16.3 rating and a 27 share, according to the Nielsen spinal tap, making it the sixth most viewed bowl game of the postseason. However, it was the only bowl game ABC televised that actually lost numbers from the previous year, in what was to become one of ABC's best all around college football seasons.

The comparatively poor showing of the Liberty Bowl, however, was more than made up for by the viewers picked up by the three other bowls ABC televised and its bullish NCAA year, a year in which they increased the number of viewers by almost 1.5 million on an average Saturday. And just as important, no longer did they have to resort to selling NCAA commercials as part of a package with "Monday Night Football." They now sold by themselves.

ABC had now made NCAA college football a part of Saturday, as well as other days and nights of the week. ABC's success and commitment—and money, $105 million—prompted the NCAA to extend their relationship through 1981, giving them a contract longer than two years for the first time in the quarter-century history of televised college football. It was rumored that the NCAA had "whip-sawed" ABC by threatening a two-network TV contract, an inevitable step. But whatever the reason for the signing, ABC, like Alabama, had won their game.

6
Boxing: And in This Corner ... ABC

They had descended on San Francisco in a tactical pincer movement that would have brought tears of joy to the eyes of Robert E. Lee: Coordinating Producer Dennis Lewin from Seattle, where he had taped an Evel Knievel jump for inclusion in a later "Wide World of Sports" telecast; Director Chet Forte from New York, where he had made a pit stop between "Monday Night Football" assignments; Howard Cosell from New York, on his way to Los Angeles to do the voice layover for "The Battle of the Network Stars"; George Foreman, from his training camp-cum-home in Marshall, Texas; and the crew from Los Angeles, New York, and all points east. The event that had brought all of them to "Baghdad by the Bay" for only the seventh time in the sixteen-year history of "Wide World" was the Jimmy Young–Ron Lyle heavyweight fight, a classic confrontation between the third and fourth ranked heavyweight contenders. Boxer versus puncher.

* * *

Walter "Pete" Riley, a marketing executive, has left his Orinda home a little before noon to drive down to San Francisco's Civic Auditorium for the fight, which is scheduled to start at 3:00 PCT to accommodate the "Wide World" viewers on the East Coast. As he makes his way into the arena, he passes two large trucks that look like oversized refrigeration units but which are clearly marked "ABC-The Network of the Olympics" and are connected to the auditorium by an umbilical cord of cables and wires. Continually spilling down the makeshift stairs is an army of technicians, hurrying back and forth to the arena. Entering the partially filled arena, he begins mentally to pick out those familiar and unfamiliar faces which are to play a part in this afternoon's fight: Don King, the fight promoter with the Elsa Lanchester electrified hairdo, hailing everyone in sight as "My Main Man"; George Foreman, former heavyweight champion of the world, who has only recently signed a package deal with ABC to appear as a color commentator on boxing shows and a few "American Sportsman" and "Good Morning America" shows plus on a few boxing matches of his own; a heavyset man who had introduced himself to one and all as "Mr. Hayward Moore," George Foreman's advisor, who has been a promoter on the "Chitlin' Circuit" (a black entertainment circuit) years before and is greeting everyone with a closed-fist-bang-knuckles greeting; Howard Cosell, the blow-by-blow announcer; Dennis Lewin, coordinating producer of "Wide World" and producer of this segment, who is talking to Cosell; and Chet Forte, the director of this remote event, who is checking the cameras before going back inside the truck.

Forte has supervised the placement of five cameras and eight microphones throughout the arena. The five cameras include two on a platform on what might be considered the fifty-yard line of the ring, dead center (one framing the fighter from head to toe, the other for tighter shots); two at ringside (one on a pedestal and the other a roving hand-held that could look in under the ropes or capture the crowd, à la *Rocky*); and a fifth camera to render a reverse angle to shoot into the corners between rounds. Eight microphones, including the corner mikes (two for the overall crowd effect and one wired into a public address system), are seeded throughout the auditorium.

Lewin has calibrated the timing to the microsecond. The "Wide World" show is to start at the conclusion of the Florida-Georgia game, which now seems interminable as Georgia runs touchdown after touchdown in the second half. There will be a tease at the top of the show, 2:30 PCT, and then, after the postgame scoreboard, "Wide World" will return to the San Francisco Civic Auditorium for interviews with both fighters in their dressing rooms. From that point on, the interviews will alternate with a pretaped National Drag Racing Championship being fed out of the New York studios. Then at 3:05, the fight will go on. Lewin has even taken into consideration the fact that the fight could end early and has a contingency plan that calls for another fight, which must begin before 3:38 to get in the decision before they're off at 3:58:39.

As Lewin goes through his last-minute instructions with Cosell for the prefight interviews and Forte gets ready in the control truck, making sure all of the monitors, cameras, and microphones are ready when he raises his baton, John McCleary and his son are sitting down in front of their television set in Westchester County, New York. What makes John McCleary different from most other televiewers this afternoon is that his TV set is wired into a special AT&T line, for McCleary is one of that small sample of viewers whose opinions dictate the success or failure of any television show. And this afternoon he is going to watch the boxing bout, as he always does, having been an amateur boxer in his native Oklahoma. McCleary, a program administrator at IBM, has designed programs for several companies, including, ironically, ABC as well as CBS.

The time is now 3:02 and the fighters are coming into the ring. The National Drag Racing Championship has been mercifully concluded, and after a commercial break, the "Wide World" studio in New York will transfer the show to Chet Forte in San Francisco for the scene set. Forte sits ready: on his left, his technical director, who faces a keyboard with more than 100 keys which he switches with all the dexterity of a Carmen Cavallero, and Producer Dennis Lewin on his right. Next to Lewin is a red phone, which only Executive Producer Roone Arledge knows the number to, known as the Roone Phone.

As the scene set, taped earlier showing the Lyle-Foreman fight with both fighters going up and down like bouncing balls in what has been called "the most two-sided fight in history," runs through to conclusion, Cosell puts in his earpiece containing the IFB (interrupted feedback), which connects him to the truck, and prepares to take over. Foreman is spared that tie-line to the truck in his first job as a color commentator because of its tendency to confuse all but the most experienced broadcaster. And now it's back live and the fighters are being introduced.

For twelve rounds Jimmy Young dominates the action and the fight, a throw-back to the Tippy Larkin school of finesse and movement.

And by 3:58:39, the most blessed words, outside of "good job," are heard in the control truck: "You're away." The doors fly open to disgorge the men who have made the event happen outside the ring. John McCleary turns off his set to wash up for dinner.

* * *

Back in the fifties boxing suffered a black eye when the Kefauver Committee disclosed widespread corruption in boxing. The underworld had planted a general air of mal- fragrance, essence of Frankie Carbo and Blinky Palermo. The networks, gun-shy after the quiz-show revelations, dumped it as a sport. It has taken boxing twenty years to come back after having been "used" by television. And twenty years later, boxing has finally figured out a way of getting even—and "using" television.

* * *

"Wide World of Sports" had been slow to discover boxing or what has been called the Sweet Science. This was in part caused by the existence of Gillette's "Fight of the Week," which had started on Friday nights in 1960 with the scheduled championship bout between Sugar Ray Robinson and Gene Fullmer and ended on Saturday, September 11, 1964, with a middleweight fight between Dick Tiger and Gene's younger brother, Don. Then the "Fight of the Week," which by then was suffering ratings of the "weak," packed in its stool and bucket and dropped off the airwaves.

Throughout its first four years, "Wide World" only devoted a portion of one show to boxing: the delayed telecast of the first Clay-Liston championship bout on its 139th show. The next year, 1965, saw three delayed telecasts of other championship fights. A live fight wasn't shown on "Wide World" until the Cassius Clay–Henry Cooper bout, live from London in 1966. It was the first live heavyweight title fight on home TV since Patterson-London in 1959.

But slow as they were to discover boxing, they have now clutched it fully to their programming sternum, dedicating segments in no less than 157 "Wide World" shows to boxing and making it the second most popular sport on the show— just behind the perennial winner, auto racing. The reason, quite simply stated, is that it is a ratings winner, which, according to a study by the advertising agency McCann-Erickson, "delivered high ratings and showed significant viewing interest among young men." In fact, the second highest rated "Wide World" show of all time was the January 5, 1975, showing of the previous October's Ali-Foreman fight.

From its earliest days, predating the merger in 1953, ABC had depended on a boxing connection to supply it with inexpensive programming. When Paramount merged with ABC in 1953, they found prime time a veritable gymnasium, with Monday night fights from Eastern Parkway Arena, Tuesdays from Willow Grove, and Saturday nights from up and down the eastern seaboard. Every small boxing club was a ready-made television studio. They soon added a Wednesday night program, sponsored by Pabst Blue Ribbon Beer. As their between-rounds spokesman, Bill "the Bartender" Nimo, filled glasses with Pabst week after week and James D. Norris and his International Boxing Club filled the airwaves with the likes of Ralph "Tiger" Jones, Chico Vejar, and Chuck Davey every week, it seemed that we were being served these fighters more on Wednesday than fish on Fridays. And with the addition of the Gillette Friday night package in 1960, ABC carried boxing on prime time every night of the week—but never on Sundays.

ABC, radio, too, had seen the potential drawing power of boxing. They had broadcast the second Louis-Conn fight to a record audience and continued to score their share of ratings knockouts by acquiring the rights to heavyweight championship bouts, including the second Patterson-Johansson fight in 1960, heard by an audience of over 61 million listeners—at that time the largest audience in the history of advertising.

* * *

The color announcer on the Patterson-Johansson fight, as he had been on every ABC radio fightcast since the Patterson-Moore fight in 1956, was Howard Cosell, who did not so much bring color to the bouts as put them under siege with a bombardment of words and phrases never heard by sports fans before. For eleven years he had acted as the color commentator for the likes of Les Keiter, Steve Ellis, Don Dunphy and others on both radio and on closed-circuit telecasts from 1956 through the Ali-Patterson fight in 1965.

* * *

Reams of copy have been written about Howard Cosell, including the best-selling books by the man himself. And yet, despite all the words devoted to capturing this most singular of men, he still remains elusive, incapable of being reduced to type. He is the Rashomon of broadcasting, described differently by every observer—friend, acquaintance, and detractor alike.

Many things to many people, Howard Cosell, depending upon whom you talk to, is (A) a warm and responsive human being; (B) an acerbic, abrasive man whose real talent lies in provoking people; (C) a man who will take anybody's position if there's a buck or a break in it for him; (D) a real celebrity; (E) a journalist who "tells it like it is"; (F) a vainglorious man, intent upon gaining universal adulation; (G) a stargazer, who collects the friendship of stars the way some collect baseball cards; (H) a man who doesn't know what he's talking about and can't stop talking about it; (I) the catalyst at an event to make something happen; (J) a past-master of the put-down and the put-on; (I) a brilliant man with total recall, but sometimes full of bullshit; and/or (L) the workhorse of ABC Sports. The list goes on and on. You can check all of the above or none, for Howard Cosell is all of these and none of these. He is one of the most complex human beings to come upon the American scene in decades and one of the most unusual.

From the time he first awakened the consciousness of a nation comfortable with sportscast after sportscast where never was heard a discouraging word, Cosell has had an enlivening effect on broadcasting. While others became merely sterile voiceover announcers to the pictures being shown, Cosell became an event unto himself. And while others asked don't-rock-the-boat questions ("When did you think you had the game won?") or didn't ask questions at all, Cosell asked all the wrong questions and got the right answers.

Howard Cosell has always been Howard Cosell, even when his name was Howard Cohen. Art Paley, a high school friend, remembers a clause in his fraternity's by-laws that said, "Howie Cohen cannot be a member of this fraternity," because he was then as he is now opinionated and outspoken. Trained to be a lawyer ("I never wanted to be a lawyer, but my dad went to the bank every three months to renew a loan. It was his dream and my mother's to have a son who would be a lawyer or a doctor"), he instead became my-son-the-broadcaster.

Clawing his way hand-over-raw-knuckle up the ladder, Cosell at first suffered the worst sort of humiliation imaginable—he was ignored. But then as his style and his voice became uniquely recognizable, he was discovered in turn by the ABC Radio network and Roone Arledge. He was on his way. "He was Howard Cosell for years before I even knew who he was," recalls Ira Topping, another high school friend. But New Yorkers were beginning to recognize him, and by 1965 the man with the staccato nasal twang was making close to $200,000 a year doing what he does best, being himself.

It became fairly obvious that Cosell's face was not just another of those pretty faces one is accustomed to seeing on TV. As a police sketch it would have been used to identify a suspicious lookout at a break-in. As a political sketch, it would be a duplicate of Charles de Gaulle. It is a ferret's with a little bit of hangdog thrown in, punctuated by larger than large ears and an outsized nose. But still it retains charm in the unlikeliest of places, his toupée. Not only do you know he wears one but he knows that you know and has even occasionally referred to it as well as taken delight in others doing so. Comedian Pat Henry on one occasion was heard to say, "I'm getting stoned just sniffing the glue on his hairpiece." Cosell loved it!

Instead, it was his voice, the most imitated in the world, that was to serve as his passport to fame. (It was a "make" for Lloyd Nolan's with more of a sense of urgency and an edge to it, delivered in the manner of a public prosecutor trying to nail a defendant for jaywalking to a life term.) In fact, its unique quality was so indigenous to the overall character of Cosell, that if you were to awaken him at two in the morning, unlike the proverbial Englishman with the affected accent who would talk straight, you were certain to hear vintage Cosell.

Coupled with his voice was his use of the English language. Nothing merely "happens," it "eventuates." No one "speaks," they "articulate." And events "continue apace." He also ascribes exotic and alliterative names to the participants—"Big Bu Bulash" and "Zook 'em Zooker." No one had ever used words and "word-toids" like that before. If there were a Nobel Prize for cumulative work in enunciating polysyllabic words, it would go to Cosell, words down. Many of the colorful and bombastic pronunciamentos delivered with near arrogance have begun to form a parody of himself; much like W. C. Fields's "Flower Belle, what a euphonious appellation," and "suffering sciatica." Had the time reference been reversed and Fields come after Cosell, Fields would sound like he was parodying Cosell.

But it took one other master stroke to perfect his artform; an artform he excelled in. That was his seeming intellectual grasp of every subject he chose to consider. He had "a completely retentive memory" remembers Paley, one which allowed him to "know what page something was on and be able to recite it word for word."

The proof of the impact of his voice, use of words, and what Sherlock Holmes called "his little brain attic" was the volume of criticism his utterances begot. As his fame and platform grew, so, too, did the crescendo of criticism. His voice became the voice that launched a thousand "shits." As he harangued from the front of the bus, his critics were kneejerking themselves off the back. He became the embodiment of everything many of them, viewers and newspapermen alike, ever disliked, and besides calling him everything from Mr. Jaws to the Most Powerful Irritant Since Itching Powder, they took to tearing patches off his hide in public. But even they missed his presence when he absented himself from boxing matches and football games because of scheduling conflicts. Their lightning conductor had disappeared and so, too, had their interest.

It would seem that a man in the public eye who has been accused of everything from "insufferable comments" to "sounding like a man complaining that Creation should have been accomplished in four days" would not be sensitive to much of the criticism his remarks engender, especially since he sets himself up in a vulnerable position. But Howard Cosell is sensitive. And therein lies the other part of the man, obscured by the millions who detest him for real or imagined reasons. Not only does Cosell react to everything written about him in the papers, reading and devouring them daily, but he can spit it back, chapter and verse days, even weeks, afterward. He becomes traumatized by everything—from what he calls "carefully calculated campaigns" to "smart-ass throwaway lines" by reporters he respects—admitting he has "gone through hell at the hands of the press."

Cosell's sensitivity doesn't end with his critics for he is not only extremely responsive to the attitudes of others, but to their friendship and needs as well. He often contributes his time, effort, and money to charitable causes. He has also responded to the pedagogical needs of students. But perhaps the best indicia of his sensitivity is his happy homelife, a rare occurrence in show business. Many afternoons he breaks away from his office to play with his grandchildren and join his wife Emmy—the only Emmy he has ever won.

Added to Cosell's sensitivity is a faint trace of insecurity. You can see it when he looks around for visual or verbal approval after he has delivered a bon mot in the announcing booth or when he walks over to a colleague or reporter to ask, after delivering a speech, "How did I do?" You can also see it as he signs an autograph for a little boy in front of the Century Plaza Hotel in Los Angeles and turns around to columnist Kay Gardella to say, "See that, you thought nobody knew me."

Both sensitivity and insecurity are readily identifiable traits of a show business superstar. And there can be no doubt that Howard Cosell is that. He himself first recognized it when he returned from Munich in 1972 and saw his picture on the cover of *Newsweek*. For the next few years he had to adjust to "being Howard Cosell," as one of his colleagues says.

But now, like most performers, he delights in performing for crowds. While one of his critics has likened "ten minutes of Howard Cosell with spending twenty-four hours with Idi Amin," Cosell possesses an enormous charm, which he can turn on and off at will. He is a consummate performer—able to turn complete audiences, which have come to prey, into hero-worshippers. And, at ABC affiliate meetings, he is the most popular and sought-after personage around, more so than a Henry Winkler or a Gabe Kaplan, particularly among the women in attendance. He walks up to elevator operators and tries to get them to play out their options and sign with the New York Jets; announces to the publicity director of college football, "Donn, baby, if you had me on the college game, you'd be number one"; and as Woody Allen says, "announces his dinner."

He loves repartee and will cackle when Don Klosterman hails somebody over to "help me listen to Cosell." Sometimes he can even be bested, as when he shouted across a restaurant at columnist Frank Boormann, who had damned with faint praise ABC's coverage of the Kentucky Derby when track announcer Chick Anderson announced the wrong winner: "I know every winner of the first 100 Derbies." Beermann yelled back, "Fine, but I still don't know the winner of this year's."

But perhaps the most telling retort is one Cosell responded with when Doug Wilson gave him a backhanded compliment that he'd like to stand in his shadow. Sounding like Fields sounding like Cosell, he said, "You can't stand in my shadow, because I cast none."

* * *

Cosell's partner for the Patterson-Johansson fight was Steve Ellis, a boxing manager, and broadcaster for the Wednesday night fights. Ellis, who managed many of the boxers whose matches he announced, often peppered his commentary with "there's a left to the body, another left to the head, another to jaw . . . c'mon, Chico . . . you got him." An example of objective reporting he was not!

Ellis was also famous for his interviewing techniques. In a manner that would have done justice to Howard Cosell's caricature of himself in the Woody Allen film "Bananas," Ellis went in the ring after the first Liston-Patterson fight to interview the winner. "We're not going to disturb Floyd Patterson," he cried as poor Patterson lay on the floor trying to regain his senses. "Now, Sonny, what are your plans?"

"I want to go home to my lovely wife," answered the new champ.

"He wants to go home to his lovely wife," repeated Ellis. "Sonny is really breaking me up here!"

Cosell had already earned his veteran's stripes. His interviews often led to the interviewee-victim trying to gnaw his own leg off in an effort to escape the trap. In an inquisitorial Tomas de Torquemada-fashion, he would ask questions that somehow sounded like "when did you stop beating your wife?" His doomsday voice made his questions sound more like statements awaiting Perry Mason-esque confessions.

Sonny Liston chewed up reporters and spat them out regularly. When one reporter doubted his age before the first Clay fight, he roared at the cowering reporter, "My mammy says I'm thirty-four. Are you calling my mammy a fuckin' liar?" It was this less-than-willing subject—one Cosell had called "a congenital thug"—that Cosell approached before the first Patterson fight for an interview. Liston was livid—even though he had been arrested over twenty times, was a union goon who cracked heads with the same frequency that a short-order cook fries eggs, and had even answered the Kefauver Committee as to why he was in constant trouble: "I keep finding things before they get lost." When Cosell came to see him, he merely glowered at the man and boomed out, "You ain't my friend." Cosell was neither running for prom king nor from Liston. "Sonny, you're a professional and I'm a professional. So cut it out!" Liston roared. His bluff had been called. Later, as they walked along a beach together, Liston answered questions about his gangster past and present connections. Cosell had made one of his first boxing conquests. There would be many more.

Cosell then moved to the television side to take part in "Wide World's" first live fight, the Ali-Cooper heavyweight championship bout. There he joined veteran boxing announcer Chris Schenkel, who had been the voice of the long-running Monday night boxing series from Eastern Parkway and St. Nicholas arenas, and Rocky Marciano, who had served as a color commentator with Cosell on several radio fightcasts. The bout, held in London's Arsenal Soccer Stadium, was Britain's first heavyweight championship fight since 1908, when Tommy Burns knocked out another British battler, who had assumed the legendary position assumed by so many English fighters throughout history—supine. After fifty-eight years, a heavyweight championship was once again being fought in the cradle of boxing—England—and chauvinistically being called "The Fight of the Century."

As for the fight itself, Ali, called Clay by the proper Britishers, made use of the larger-than-normal ring to circle away from "Our Enery's" vaunted left 'ammer' for the first five rounds. But when he opened up with his combinations in the sixth, so did Cooper's eye, which spouted blood like a grotesque geyser. The referee mercifully stopped the bloodbath at 1:38 of the sixth round. But the real Battle of Britain was ABC's, and that won't be found in any record book.

Prior to the start of the title bout, ABC came on the air with an entire production number scored to Roger Miller's then-popular number "England Swings Like a Pendulum Do," containing shots of Ali strolling down the boulevards of London in his formal cutaway, top hat, and cane, doing a black-face impersonation of Fred Astaire, intercut with hordes of adoring Londoners. This plus scenes of the two fighters in their training camps was to take at least thirty minutes and lead up to the fight itself. But Jimmy Ellis, fighting a heavyweight by the name of Lewene Waqa from Fiji, obviously had not been in on the production meeting and took matters into his own hands by tap dancing on Waqa's chest midway through the first round of the fight that preceded the Ali-Cooper bout. The British boxing officials made their way to the dressing room to notify the boxers in the next bout, the heavyweight title fight, that, according to the rules of the commission, they were to be on in two minutes. Cosell sprang into action. He made his way to Ali's dressing room and implored both Ali and his manager, Herbert Muhammad, to save the beginning thirty minutes of the show: "Muhammad, remember that great footage we shot of you walking around London? Well, they're not going to be able to see it in the United States . . . if you go out there now." That's all Ali had to hear. He stood there for eighteen minutes, while a crowd that had been there since a little after six in the evening now fidgeted in their seats after four hours of prelims.

The scene after the fight was not pretty. There were what Ali described as "a few little title fights outside the ring," but they were worse. Immediately after the fight was signaled to a halt by referee George Smith, several groups of Teddy Boys jumped over benches and stormed the ring, screaming "Dirty nigger!" One of them climbed over the press seats and stepped on Chris Schenkel's hand as he was trying to wrap up the fight, prior to "sending" it to Howard Cosell in the ring for the postfight interview. Schenkel, absorbed with concluding remarks, swatted one heavy-booted interloper away with his right elbow. The hoodlum was having none of this byplay and stepped heavily on Schenkel's left hand, cracking two of his knuckles.

Jimmy Brown, in London for the filming of *The Dirty Dozen,* leapt onto the ring apron to provide some protection for Ali, but he wasn't foolhardy enough to go into the ring. Only Cosell was, along with Production Assistant Joe Aceti. With microphone and monitor, Aceti climbed through the ropes first so that Cosell could watch the replay, and then he helped Cosell into the ring. Almost immediately Aceti became involved in a couple of skirmishes with English bobbies, who didn't recognize Cosell. In fact, one of the eager bobbies started to swing at Cosell with a stick, and Aceti grabbed at him and pulled him off.

Ali just looked out at the rebellious crowd, after being cuffed by one of those who made it into the ring, and said to Cosell, "I thought it was just someone offering me congratulations."

Cosell's next assignment was for the Muhammed Ali—Brian London fiasco three months later, also live on "Wide World." Again there was some thought given to the same type of scene setting as producer Chet Forte had developed for the Ali-Cooper fight. This time he gave the assignment to a young associate director, Doug Wilson. The first song that came to Wilson's mind was "A Foggy Day in London Town." But what the hell did that have to do with boxing, he asked himself. What indeed. He would turn it into a parody. He then went about building a group of insert shots for lines like, "I met the morning with much alarm," which had him doing roadwork with Jimmy Ellis; "How long I wondered could this thing possibly last,"—a serious musing shot at Ali, etc. But the *piéce de rèsistance* was to be one insert of Brian London over the line "for suddenly I saw you there." For that shot and an interview, Cosell and Production Assistant Aceti flew up to Brian London's training camp in Blackpool. The scene was reminiscent of an old John Garfield movie—discarded newspapers wafting around the desolate looking camp, blown by the wind, which whistled through almost abandoned facilities. When they finally found London, they plunked him down on a bench that Aceti set down in the middle of the old ring, next to Cosell. Cosell put his arm around London in an obvious attempt to establish rapport, and then, on cue, launched into his typical interview: "Brian, they say you're a patsy, a dirty fighter; that you have no class; that you're just in there for the ride and fast payday; and that you have no chance against Ali. Now what do you say to that?"

London, who knew neither Cosell nor his technique of always attempting to provoke the subject by attributing outrageous views to third parties, screamed back, "Go fuck yourself!"

"No, no, no," shouted Aceti, as he hurried forward. "You see," he explained, "those really weren't Howard's descriptions of you—they were the opinions of others."

"Oh, I see," said the somewhat-confused London. But he didn't. The question-statement was repeated, and London flared back, "Whoever said that can go fuck themselves." Scrub the second take.

Once again Aceti came forward and explained to London that this was meant for American "telly" and that no matter how much you wanted to, you simply couldn't express yourself in those terms. London said he understood. Third take. Same question. Now London wet his lips slowly, and then he spoke; "Well, then, the people who said that—not you, but the people who said that—can *all* go to hell!" So much for the interview.

Now for the one insert shot of London for the "Foggy Day" sequence. Aceti lined him up in the corner of the ring and instructed him, "Turn around to the center of the ring slowly, gulp once, and throw your best right at the camera. Do not hit the lens, merely throw your best punch at the camera and pull up short."

English cameraman Dick Carruthers took his position, and they started filming. London turned, gulped, and threw a right hand, possibly the best he had ever thrown. But they had counted on his timing too much. He didn't pull up short, but instead smashed his hand into the lens, knocking down and cutting Carruthers, whose eye had been hard against the eyepiece of the camera.

That was the only punch thrown by London that was seen on television. The man Ingemar Johansson claimed "couldn't beat up my sister" and whose manager boasted "might be a bum, but he's a good bum" went down under Ali's barrage of punches in the third round. The bout was one of the most humiliatingly one-sided fights in recent years.

Producer Chet Forte, who had planned an entire "Wide World" show around the fight, hollered over the production line to Aceti as London hit the canvas, "Does he look like he's going to get up?" Aceti took one look at the inert form lying just above him and hollered back, "Well, his tongue's out of his mouth and he's drooling and his eyes are white. But other than that, he's all right."

After a postfight interview in which Cosell cut Ali's meandering eulogies to his teacher Elijah Muhammad with an "awright, we've been through all that before," "Wide World" went back to New York to fill out the remainder of their time with a repeat of a previously run Figure Eight Stock Car Championship from Islip.

By the next boxing bout, September 10 in Frankfurt, Germany, against the man Ali called Karl Milton-berger, Cosell, in the words of Chris Schenkel, had "grabbed boxing."

* * *

It was not, however. until Ali, aka selective service number 15–47–42–127, refused to take one symbolic step forward at the army induction center in Houston on April 28, 1967, that Cosell and "Wide World of Sports" grabbed headlines as well.

As boxing commission after boxing commission did the popular thing and stripped the heavyweight crown from Ali's brow within mere hours after his refusal to accept induction into the armed forces, few stood up to be counted in his defense. One did—Howard Cosell. Trained as an attorney and a liberal with a capital *L*, Cosell saw him being deprived not only of his livelihood but of the constitutional protection of two amendments.

Whether it was planned or not, Cosell's step was also a masterful public relations coup for ABC and "Wide World." As Ali was consigned by public opinion and the press to the musty old archives former heavyweight champs are supposed to occupy, his name was kept alive in an almost total absence of exposure by Cosell and "Wide World." Cosell's championing of his cause allowed ABC to monopolize an already popular athlete and provided ABC with its first step toward realizing their present claim, "the recognized leader in sports programming," a claim they had not established by 1967.

The Cosell and Ali duo went down more roads than Hope and Crosby. It was a throwback to the early days of vaudeville, and no one would have been surprised if they had set up an annunciator on stage to proclaim, "For your viewing pleasure, the successors to Smith and Dale—Ali and Cosell." Some of the fans loved the new team and seemed to be especially partial to Ali's taunting Cosell with lines like, "You ain't as dumb as you look," or "I got this way fighting. What's your excuse?" It was pure ecstasy, too, when Ali alluded to Cosell in his poetry: "When I'm finished and at the bell, I'll jump over the ropes and take on Howard Cosell." Cosell was able to bask in Ali's limelight, and "Wide World" basked right along with him.

While the affiliation charmed many, the majority of fans were incensed by Cosell's support of Ali. Letters poured into Cosell's office that started with endearing saluations such as "You nigger-loving Jew bastard" and went downhill from there. Newspapers castigated Cosell in editorials and on the sports pages, one even called him a "White Muslim."

Muhammed Ali's defiance of the government in refusing his draft induction caused many Americans to reconsider painfully their own thoughts on the many issues tearing at the fiber of America in the turbulent 1960s. Ali had a different notion of patriotism ("I ain't got nothin' against them Cong"), a different religion, and a different view of himself as a black man. He was not "a credit to his race" as was Joe Louis. He was a proud black man who renounced his so-called slave name. When Cosell respected him for his views and for what he was —not what white people wanted him to be—the latent bigotry of viewers reared its ugly head.

Arledge had found that bigotry was a negotiable commodity that begat ratings and press attention. And because of it, or maybe in spite of it, the Cosell-Ali show carried on, faster than a speeding insult, hurdling large protests in a single bounce.

During Ali's enforced absence, "Wide World" and Cosell not only championed Ali's right to fight and his title, but were also in the embarrassing position of televising a World Boxing Association (WBA) elimination contest to crown his successor. Very few saw the irony in this as 36 percent of all TV households and almost 30 million tuned in to ABC's first prime time boxing special to see Ali's former sparring partner, Jimmy

Ellis, crowned his successor on the very network that had supported the deposed champ.

Throughout the intervening seven years, "Wide World" continued to telecast, both live and on a delayed basis, most of the major boxing bouts around the world. Their cameras went to Las Vegas, Monaco, Madison Square Garden, San Juan, Buenos Aires, the Astrodome, and Paris. They even introduced the weigh-in as a full-fledged event in much the same manner as P. T. Barnum charged admission to witness the auction of prized tickets for Jenny Lind concerts.

* * *

"Wide World" continued to bring high drama and low burlesque to the viewers in the name of boxing. Mixed among their many notable fights was a notable nonfight, the 1975 exhibition that saw George Foreman take on five different boxers in one afternoon. The "match" had all the trappings of a masquerade party with has-beens, never-wases, wrestlers, and even a "Kissing Bandit" parading around the ring as boxers. It was such a low blow to boxing's somewhat shaky reputation that even host Jim McKay, after the conclusion of the George Foreman and the five dwarfs episode, felt compelled to apologize to the audience.

* * *

The stakes had risen. Back in 1964 when "Wide World" had started telecasting fights, they had been the only game in town. Now, with interest in boxing rekindled by the successes of the movie *Rocky* and the American entrants in the Olympics, both CBS and NBC had thrown their hats into the ring and were prepared to slug it out with big bucks.

NBC had Madison Square Garden in their corner. Having formed a working partnership with the citadel of boxing, they obtained the rights to a number of fights, including the shortest main event in the history of the Garden when Duane Bobick's parachute opened in just fifty-eight seconds in his bout against Ken Norton. CBS had taken a route similar to the one Japanese TV networks took years ago to insure themselves of continual boxing fare. They had signed several of the Olympians to exclusive contracts, thus forming their own stable of fighters: These included the Spinks Brothers, John Tate, and Howard Davis. Davis's contract, representative of all of them, called for him to fight six fights over the next year and eight months, receiving $40,000 for a six-rounder, $50,000 for an eight-rounder, and $200,000 for a ten-rounder, with him supplying the opponent—or $165,000 for a ten-rounder, if CBS had to dig up a suitable victim.

ABC, the longtime champ, was forced into a proverbial corner in their attempt to maintain their supremacy in the field. First they signed George Foreman to a package deal that not only included his doing the color commentary on boxing shows and some entertainment shows, but also gave them the right of first refusal on his future TV bouts. Then ABC effectively blocked CBS's total monopolization of all the Olympic champions by signing Sugar Ray Leonard to a contract on the threshold of his signing with CBS. In fact, had not one of the members of Leonard's group of advisors called Howard Cosell the very day they were planning to come to New York to sign, ABC would have never known about the pending deal with CBS nor would they have been able to meet it—$500,000 for three guaranteed television fights a year.

But ABC's main event wasn't a fighter, it was an entire tournament. With boxing interest the highest it had been in years, it was only natural that somebody would attempt to exploit that newfound audience—especially when there was only one American champion in the eight recognized divisions—Muhammad Ali.

That "somebody" was Don King, a flamboyant high roller who looked as if he had stepped right out of the black version of Damon Runyon's *Guys and Dolls,* complete with a head of hair unseen since *Bride of Frankenstein.* His style of speech was a cross between a state-of-the-union pronunciamento and an evangelist's sermon at a prayer meeting, filled with potholes that contained malaprops, references to Shakespeare, and adverb piled atop adverb.

King exploded on the boxing scene, right out of the Marion Correctional Institution, in Ohio, where he had been No. 125734, up on murder one. Upon his release in 1973, the former kingpin of the Cleveland numbers racket emerged in a new arena—boxing. He was a black man making it in a white man's world and was as different from his predecessors in the Byzantine world of boxing as the color of his skin to theirs. Not only had he insinuated rather than intimidated his way to the top, but he had continually used his own blackness as a device for appealing to other blacks. "He speaks from the soul," his onetime partner and now archenemy Hank Schwartz once said.

King had started as a manager, taking Earnie Shavers and Jeff Merritt just about as far as he could, then stepping over their prone bodies into the promotional end of boxing. He had somehow jive-talked Muhammad Ali and George Foreman into the same ring in Zaire and sweet-talked President Mobuto into grubstaking him to $5 million to stage the "Rumble in the Jungle." But just as quickly as he had risen, King seemed to fall from grace. The mercurial Ali was now available to other promoters as well. And to support his $85,000-a-year habit—the rent on his penthouse high atop the same Rockefeller Center building where ABC had started—he "hustled" fights, fighters, and now a tournament called the United States Boxing Tournament of Champions.

Most of Don King's promotions were with ABC. But like many wedded partners, he flirted around a bit. At one point he took the tournament of champions idea to Barry Frank at CBS. But with a roar that could be heard within a ten-block radius, he broke off negotiations with CBS, telling everyone, "I don't trust that man. He was going behind my back to my fighters." Then he walked across the street to ABC.

The basic concept seemed sound to ABC. It was a way to reestablish its credentials as the leader in televised boxing—except that in a sport renowned for its lack of governmental structure, this seemed to have even less than usual. By what standards would the competitors in each of the eight classes to be picked? How was the tournament to be given credibility? Without the proper administrative and logistical safeguards, it had all the makings of a nightmare.

King, who had once tried to buy *Ring* magazine for

$500,000, went out and enlisted the magazine's participation in the tournament. For a fee of $70,000 they would lend both their name and their rankings. As the so-called Bible of Boxing, their name gave the project the seal of approval; and their universally accepted rankings became the standard for the selection of the fighters. For one-seventh the amount he had offered for the entire magazine, King had bought their credibility and lent it to the tournament. ABC, now assured of the trustworthiness of the tourney, committed $1.5 million, naïvely unaware of the intricacies—or "trickerations," as King calls them—of the sport.

Later, King added New York State Boxing Commissioner James Farley, Jr., who would become the director of the tournament's Rules Committee, to add even more credibility. Now there seemed to be a governmental structure to it. And, finally, King hired two matchmakers, Al Braverman and Paddy Flood, who had worked with him before and kept offices in his penthouse. All was ready.

And so, in September 1976, the tournament was announced in New York. ABC had bought the television rights to the United States Boxing Tournament of Champions for sixteen weeks at the price of $1.5 million. It was hailed as a godsend for eighty-eight young fighters, particularly those in the lighter categories—most of whom had never had the opportunity to fight on television nor in their entire careers seen the $5,000 per fight that they were to get in the first round. *Sports Illustrated* heralded it as a "boxing revival," and Don King, with a puffed-up chest and a sense of his own accomplishment, called it a "monumental, historic moment."

Over the next three months Braverman and Flood started to round up the fighters. Some they found were beholden to others. Some they eschewed. Finally, by December they had signed most of the eighty-eight who were to be entered in the tournament, which was scheduled to start on January 16, 1977. King's office released the names.

Even as the call to arms and fists was going on, two boxing aficionados were becoming concerned with the quality of the fighters involved. One was Alex Wallau, the production associate producer for the fights, who saw some soft spots and felt uncomfortable with the overall choices. Wallau, a boxing maven for years, wasn't thrilled with those named, believing that several weren't worthy of being champions of anything and that several others who weren't enrolled in the tournament deserved to be. He conveyed his doubts about the quality of fighters to others at ABC, and they questioned King as to why he couldn't come up with everybody promised in *Ring*'s Top Ten Ratings of Contenders.

The other individual who was distressed by the names of the fighters mentioned was Malcolm "Flash" Gordon, something of an antihero to the boxing cognoscenti. Flash is a small man-boy in his twenties who has been publishing and selling a mimeographed program-newsletter from a suitcase outside all arenas in the New York area since, according to one of his followers, "his mother gave him a mimeograph machine for his bar mitzvah." Called everything from a journalistic mugger to a Diogenes, Gordon first released his misgivings about the quality of fighters in one of his December sheets, pointing out that some hadn't fought in up to four years. And it seemed that many—too many—were contractually associated with Don King or one of his inner circle.

But if Wallau and Gordon were legitimately concerned with the very fabric of the tournament, they were not alone. Or so it seemed. Internecine warfare is a way of life in boxing, with struggles unseen since the early power wars between Italian feudal states, and it is not to be taken too seriously. Don King's roar that "Teddy Brenner is the undertaker of boxing" would be met with charges and counter-charges. Some of these charges were brought directly to the attention of ABC prior to the start of the first televised bouts on January 16, 1977, including that of Marvin Haggler, manager of one boxer who was excluded. He wrote ABC directly, complaining that his fighter was left out. The Armstrong Report, issued by an independent investigator, Michael Armstrong, after the cancellation of the tournament, said, "It appears as of late December, 1976, with the first telecast of the tournament being less than a month away and affiliates being already on line, ABC was unprepared to terminate the agreement without specific evidence of improprieties that were not purely subjective." To assuage their misgivings and to provide peace of mind—while also, possibly, protecting ABC from future claims of wrong-doing, ABC got King and *Ring* to sign affidavits before the first bell of the first round attesting to the credibility of the tournament. King's affidavit averred that the fighter and the manager listed were legitimate, without any kickbacks being paid to get in, and that there weren't any "house" fighters—the "house" being King's. *Ring* confirmed that they had rated the United States boxers accurately, using the same methods by which they determined their world rankings.

Just seconds after ABC had received its affidavits swearing that the tournament was more on the level than the rolling ship where the first round of the tournament was to take place, Chet Forte counted down to Howard Cosell, who started the show with all the doomsday nasal twang he could get into his intonation: "Most of the good fighters aren't here. But still—all in all—this tournament, as a concept, has a chance." It was an uncharacteristic understatement, hardly the well-oiled sound of a shill. King continued to trumpet from on high, telling everyone who would listen, "The mothers are waiting for us to blow this one. But ain't no way it's going to happen." All seemed shipshape for the moment.

By the second round, held February 13 at the Naval Academy in Annapolis, the tournament had sprung a leak. It was a small thing at the time, or so it seemed, when the overriding consideration was the species of the boxer, not the degree of his quality. Biff Cline, one of the light-heavyweight entrants, was credited with a perfect record in the press releases handed out by Don King Productions. But Wallau knew differently. He had already read a report of Cline's loss to Johnny Blaine in Providence and had phoned the Rhode Island Boxing Commission to verify his belief. And so the superimposed mat on the screen reflected twelve wins and one loss, rather than the 13–0 record that the King organization insisted on crediting to the fighter. It was an isolated instance, later to take on a greater importance.

But Cline's record was well-hidden compared to what hap-pened in the next fight, the Scott LeDoux–Johnny Boudreaux bout. Both Cosell and Foreman, in announcing the fight, believed that going into the eighth and final round Boudreaux "needed a knockout to win." Understanding that most com-mentators are not as adept at scoring a fight as the so-called officials, still it seemed to the audience that such was the case, Boudreaux already having gone to the canvas once and the ropes several times. But the three officials thought otherwise and gave Boudreaux a unanimous decision. LeDoux was at first stunned, then enraged. While the "winner" was standing at ringside being interviewed, LeDoux rushed over to the ring apron and started shouting at Boudreaux, Cosell, and Fore-man. When Boudreaux called LeDoux a "chump," LeDoux screamed back "Who's a chump?" and emphasized his point with a well-placed drop-kick to Boudreaux's back.

In the aftermath of the LeDoux to-do, Foreman stepped bet-ween them, admonishing both not to fight: "You ain't gonna prove anything here; do your fighting in the ring." A cup filled with ice hit Cosell, knocking his toupee askew. General confu-sion reigned. Everything was to be askew from that moment on.

As Cosell tried to wrap up the show and restore some semblance of order to the chaos that was taking place around him, the special "U.S. Boxing Champions" program was signing off the air, with the regularly scheduled "Wide World" show to follow at 4:30 EST. But just at that moment, Roone Arledge, using the phone in his apartment to the red Roone phone in the remote unit in Annapolis, instructed Chet Forte to "get back there. Get the rest of the story." Within minutes, Cosell was back on the air, patting his hairpiece into place and talk-ing to a somewhat subdued LeDoux, who apologized for his conduct but made a charge: "I was told before the fight I couldn't win. Don King, Paddy Flood, and Al Braverman con-trol all the fighters in this tournament. We're the only out-siders." And for good measure he threw in the accusation of a "fix." Cosell cautioned him that "making charges is one thing, but it's another thing to prove them at law." Cosell then pursued the matter with referee Joe Bunsa, who thought the charges of a fix were ridiculous, that it was a "dull" fight that might have been different "if it was a point system," rather than the round system used. But over and above the "I-wuz-robbed" postfight interview seen by fight fans over and over again, Cosell now sought to journalistically clarify the one point that had been unspoken before Annapolis—that the tournament was made up of controlled fighters. He went to the King-fish himself to question him on the charge made by LeDoux that all fighters were en famille, controlled by members of his own company. King's answer was a milestone in ambiguity. Adroitly fuffumping as if he had been asked about 18½ minutes of missing tape, he referred only to LeDoux's being "wounded by the decision."

"Okay!" Cosell politely but firmly cut him short and bore in. "What about the controlled fighters?"

More unresponsive nonsense, delivered with impressive gravity and concluded with an impressive apple pie declaration that the tournament was "good for America."

Cosell then closed out the reprised segment by saying, "This has not been, rather obviously, a very pretty situation. You can judge for yourselves; we have held nothing back." But Don King had. And the viewer was left with an empty feeling that there was more—much more—and that Cosell had failed to elicit the answers he and the viewing public were seeking. He had let King off the hook—momentarily.

No longer was ABC worried about ethereal rumors. They were now concerned with the entire underpinning of the tournament and were seeking answers that King was obviously not giving them—or anyone else for that matter. The following Tuesday, Arledge heard that "someone" down on the sixteenth floor had "misgivings" about the structure of the tournament, and he sent down for Wallau. The self-described "wooly-headed kid" told Arledge what he thought about the quality of the fighters in the tournament and the dramatis personae of those running it. The fix cry was merely the tip of the iceberg. And although the U.S. Attorney's Office in Maryland later investigated LeDoux's charge—an accusation he was later to recant—ABC was now investigating the other just as serious charge of "house" fighters under King's control, which, if true, was illegal in several states, including New York as a conflict of interest between a matchmaker and a manager.

Perhaps the "house" charge was true, but perhaps it had stemmed from the braggadocio of the men surrounding King. Four months earlier, when Al Braverman had heard about another group planning a similar tourney, he had boasted, "Whatever fighter they reach out for—they will find Don King already has his arms around him." Was this just bragging, or was it really so? Whatever the case, it bore further investigation by ABC, now suspicious all was not above board.

To counteract the possibility that the fighters were those favored by King to the exclusion of others, in a takeoff on the old John L. Sullivan "I-can-lick-any-man-in-the-house" pronouncement, Arledge issued an invitation that would *let* any man in the house. "Any fighter who feels he should be in and is not, only has to contact me directly." His office would examine inquires from interested parties concerning the conduct of the tournament. He was determined to have an open tournament that honored its basic premise—that the best boxers in the United States would be fighting for the U.S. Championships. That was the very heart of the tourney, and ABC intended to keep it that way, regardless of Don King.

The rumors continued to fly. Now reinforced by the LeDoux to-do, they began to take on substance. In the February 23, 1977, edition of the *Chicago Daily News* John Schulian came up with the same findings that Wallau had the week before, that at least one of the fighter's records was less than accurate. Under the headline "BOXING BETTER DEAD THEN LED BY KING," he wrote that King was "stealing boxers from the people who really deserve to make a buck along with them." This was the first mention in a paper, outside of Flash Gordon's mimeographed sheet, that the fighters resembled all the King's men.

The third round of fights was held March 6 at Don King's alma mater, the Marion Correctional Institution. King was there in a tux, sporting a mink bow tie. Someone also was there as well. Roone Arledge had personally headed up an ABC task force to investigate the worsening situation and the rumors. Now understandably worried over the credibility of the entire tournament, Arledge and Vice-President of Sports Planning Jim Spence attained signed affidavits from every fighter and manager attesting to the fact that those held out to be the managers of the fighters really were their managers. The tournament that Cosell had said at the top of the first round of fights had "a chance" was quickly dissipating that opportunity. What had originally looked like a programming dream was fast becoming a nightmare. If the tournament was worth saving, Arledge would make all efforts to do so; if not, it would be TKO'd.

On March 8, two days after the Marion show, while most writers concentrated on the possibility of rigged fights, another voice was heard. Gary Deeb, TV-radio critic of the *Chicago Tribune*, wrote an article that repeated several of the still unconfirmed rumors and added a new one: "*Ring* magazine had falsified fighters' records." The massive headline over his article read: "PROMOTER KING AND ABC ARE GIVING BOXING A BLACK EYE." It was the first time anyone had associated ABC with the ever-widening mess. Not since the bearer of the bad news in ancient Greece had the carrier been subjected to such abuse. The article read, "The stench gets stronger by the week. The outraged cries of injustice grow louder. And yet, ABC, the undisputed worldwide champion of television sports, seems oblivious to the cruel charade being perpetrated."

When the *Tribune* hit his desk, Arledge saw red and called the editor of the paper, threatening to sue. Instead, he was given rebuttal space the following Thursday and answered that "the tournament was beyond reproach because of the 'controls' instigated by ABC."

ABC had begun to instigate those additional controls after they found out that the King had none. Arledge and his Programming Vice-President Jim Spence, once delighted with their purchase of the TV rights to the United States Boxing Championships, now sensed it was made up of many wrongs. They attempted to institute controls where those that theoretically existed before were inadequate or nonexistent.

With the fourth and last round of the quarter-finals scheduled for April 2 at Randolph Air Force Base, the cutoff time for new entrants was fast approaching. In response to both the time limit in which he could get a fighter into the tournament and Arledge's open invitation, Arledge's assistant Jeff Ruhe received a phone call from a Texas fight manager named Doug Lord—one of the many received by ABC since Arledge had thrown open his doors to all ranked fighters. Most complaints had come from managers and fighters who did not understand why they were not in the tournament. But Lord, while making the same protest, sounded different. Lord said he couldn't "understand it. My fighter's supposed to be in it. But he's not. Kenny Weldon and Jerry Kornele are. My guy is ranked." So far Ruhe thought that nothing more explosive than the possibility that a ranked fighter who should have qualified had been frozen out by King. But then Lord dropped the bomb: "Besides, Weldon paid off some guy $2,500 to get in."

ABC, which had been defending its tourney against unsubstantiated charges and innuendos, now had something concrete to go on—the charge of a kickback. Ruhe immediately tracked down featherweight Kenny Weldon in Houston and got him to sign an affidavit averring that he had paid George Kanter, a boxing manager and booking agent, $2,500 to get Jerry Kornele (who was managed by his wife) into the tournament. Later, when asked to sign a contract, Weldon found that Kanter was listed as his manager.

On March 22, ABC turned the charges of improper conduct over to Jim Farley, Jr., director of the U.S. Boxing Championships Rules Committee, and Don King. They were, at best, charges of improper conduct in the boxer-manager relationship; at worst, they were charges of a kickback or extortion, or both. The supporting affidavit named George Kanter as the person who had extorted the money from Weldon on the premise that "if you're ranked, you're in." This was the same George Kanter whom Don King had once called "my foreign representative." He went on to say, "I want to rule the world, and I figure with George I've got a shot at Europe." It was yet another example of all the King's men controlling the tournament.

But even after ABC publicist Irv Brodsky released the information to Bert Rosenthal of the Associated Press—without mentioning the fighter's name, which was subsequently uncovered by Dave Brady of the *Washington Post*—the newspapers continued to reign body blow after blow on everyone, especially ABC, with headlines such as: "SCANDAL BREAKS AROUND ABC."

Jeff Ruhe soon got a second phone call. This one was from a Houston fighter named Ike Fluellen, who had been approached by a Washington, D.C. manager named Chris Cline, asking him if he "wanted to be in the boxing tournament." Cline told Fluellen that he would get him into *Ring's* top ten Junior Middleweights, although he had not fought in a year and a half. ABC had Fluellen sign an affidavit stating that "Cline informed me that the 1977 edition of *The Ring Record Book* would list two fights on my record which took place in 1976 in Mexico. I did not fight in 1976."

This was the first documented evidence of what Gary Deeb had alluded to and what Flash Gordon and Alex Wallau had sensed—falsified records in *Ring* magazine, the basis for the inclusion of all fighters in the tournament. But until the publication of the 1977 *Ring Record Book* with the 1976 records, nothing could be documented.

Then on Monday, April 11, the newly published *1977 Ring Record Book* was issued to the public. Alex Wallau went down to the offices of *Ring* magazine and personally picked up several copies of both the 1976 and 1977 record books for distribution around the ABC offices. There it was for all to see. No less than eleven fighters in the tournament had thirty fights that never took place in the *1976 Ring Record Book* but were reflected in the 1977 version. In the olden days you had to fix fights for your fighter to move up in the rankings; now in this computerized age all you needed to do was fix the results of nonexistent fights and get them included in the greatest work of fiction since *Gone With the Wind*—the *Ring Record Book*. That did it. ABC threw in the towel. In a meeting that lasted until five o'clock in the morning of the day of the scheduled semifinal bouts from Convention Center in Miami, ABC Sports, together with their outside counsel Hawkins, Delafield, and Wood, sculpted the proper language to announce that ABC had "suspended its telecasts of the U.S. Boxing Championships pending the outcome of a full-scale investigation."

The tournament that had had "a chance" blew it. The "historic, monumental moment" that Don King had envisioned had evaporated, done in like so many pieces of Humpty Dumpty that couldn't be put back together again. It was partially because King himself, so intent on controlling the rights to the eight United States champions, hadn't thoroughly considered the possibility of cupidity by those around him—while he was concentrating on the big theft, he hadn't taken into account the possibility of minor chicanery by those around him. And it was partially because *Ring* magazine, which had sold itself out for $70,000, was suspected of juggling the books and the ratings of the fighters—the very premise upon which the tournament was founded. And, it was partly because ABC had assumed they were buying the television rights to a creditable sporting event with proper safeguards. It wasn't.

It was what Paddy Flood, one of King's "consultants" called "the most treacherous, dirtiest, most vicious, cheatingest game in the world. . . . That's the nature of the business. It's a terrible business!" But it wasn't a business at all—it was boxing!

After the suspension of the United States Boxing Championships, a group calling itself the National Newspaper Publishers Association, and representing the black press of America, met at the Pierre Hotel in New York, ostensibly to support King. They read a statement that said, "The daily press has virtually totally ignored a statement by the attorney general of Maryland made a week ago that Don King is clean and has been found innocent of any wrongdoing." Furthermore, they went on, King had been given "a bum rap by white newspapers" for the purpose of returning the fight game to "white promoters." But the so-called statement by the attorney general of Maryland was as nonexistent as the many fights listed in *Ring* magazine which led to the KO of the tournament by ABC. Anyway, it wasn't the Maryland attorney general who was investigating the tournament and King; it was the United States attorney for the district of Maryland. And, to add insult to the bogus quote came the revelation that the entire lunch had been paid for by none other than Don King!

* * *

After the recent hearings conducted by the House Committee on Interstate and Foreign Commerce's Subcommittee on Communications into the U.S. Boxing Championships, a conveniently "leaked" staff memorandum issued by counsel was sent forward to Chairman Lionel Van Deerlin. The memo was severely critical of Howard Cosell's part in the tourney, not only finding that "ABC's sportscaster Howard Cosell apparently played a key role . . . in the business decision to move forward with the telecasts," but that in contacting Angelo Dundee, the manager of no less than four fighters in the tournament, his conduct bordered on a "conflict of interest . . . for a journalist." Perhaps counsel's most damning allegation was that "as the sole representative of ABC to the viewing public" Cosell's "tepid disclaimers would put few people on notice about ABC's reservations." But to his credit Cosell had said at the top of the very first show that "the tournament has a chance." Now all he said, in answer to the memo by the subcommittee counsel, was "rubbish." But even more to the point, Chairman Van Deerlin said:

"The subcommittee staff memo on our recent network sports inquiry is just that, and no more—an accounting by staff employees to members of congress culminating four months of investigation and public hearings.

"Any and all recommendations in the document carry no official weight, and are not intended to.

"I might add that I disagree emphatically with some of these recommendations, yet I believe in a full and free exchange of ideas."

* * *

Jim Spence, whose pockets were picked at the Ali-Norton fight, should have been forewarned that it was not the last time he was to suffer at the hands of those in boxing.

And ABC, which endured the banquet for the malicious that followed the demise of the tournament, did the only thing possible in the television industry when the ratings go bad. It cancelled the show.

7
The Five-Ring Olympic Circus

The Olympics is a telling phrase with multiple meanings. It is talismanic. It is the Olympic flag with its five intertwined rings denoting the participating continents. It is the Olympic oath pledging fidelity to true sportsmanship "for the honor of our country and for the glory of sport" and the Olympic motto, *Citius, Altius, Fortius,* calling on the athletes to move even faster, soar even higher, and be even stronger in each quadrennial competition. It is the Olympic Village, where athletes from the nations of the world congregate in one heterogeneous community of friendship and understanding. It is the Olympic awards ceremony with nationalistic anthems and flags attesting to the achievements of the winners. And it is the Olympic pomp and pageantry, from the lighting of the torch and the release of the pigeons at the opening ceremonies to the extinguishing of the torch and the relaxation of the competitors at the closing ceremonies.

But the real spirit of the Olympics cannot be found in any of those highly recognizable symbols. Instead, it is best celebrated by the thirteenth letter of the alphabet—the letter m. There are only twelve cities in the world starting with the letter m having a population of over one million. Four of them have hosted the last four Summer Olympics, and five of the last seven—Melbourne, Mexico City, Munich, Montreal, and

Moscow. And the letter *m*, not coincidentally, is used as the symbol for *million* and *medium*. Today, the Olympics are better represented by the millions spent in fierce competition by the medium television than by the more obvious symbols of pomp, pageantry, and pigeons associated with it since the start of the modern Olympics in 1896.

* * *

The first Olympic games were held in 776 B.C. in the town of Olympia on the coast of the southern peninsula of Greece. The games did not, however, derive their name from the town, but from the fact that they were a tribute to the greatest of all Greek gods, Zeus, who dwelt on Mount Olympus.

At first the games consisted of one event—the 200-yard footrace or "straight race." Later on additional events were added: wrestling, javelin throwing, boxing, jumping, weight lifting, and the aristocratic chariot races. There was also an event known as the pancratium, involving both boxing and wrestling, in which no holds were barred except for biting and gouging—but strangling was a necessary skill.

Held every four years, an olympiad, the games soon became part of the religious rites of the early Greeks. Kings and commoners alike competed; the winner was awarded a sprig of olive and treated as a demigod. The games themselves became so important that all fighting between Greek villages and states was suspended for three months preceding them, as the Olympics dominated thought and action.

The games were eventually banned by Emperor Theodosius in 394 A.D. because the athletes were demanding money and corrupting the events and because the Roman emperor viewed them as a pagan carnival. For almost 1,500 years thereafter the Olympics were but a historic footnote. Then the French government commissioned Baron Pierre de Coubertin to study physical culture. Convinced that athletics combined with education could improve international understanding, in 1894 de Coubertin presented his idea to revive the ancient Olympic games. His recommendation led to the first modern Olympics, held in Athens in 1896, near the famed plain of Olympia.

The Olympic Games are still held every four years, but are far different than de Coubertin ever envisioned. They lack the religious significance of the ancient games, replacing it instead with a political significance that manifests itself in nationalistic pettiness and international squabbling. Other changes have also taken place: Whereas once wars were stopped for the games, now the games are stopped for wars, as they were in 1916, 1940, and 1944. But perhaps the greatest change of all occurred in 1924, when the smaller countries, which favored winter sports, successfully petitioned organizers of the Olympics to put on a separate meet, first held at Chamonix in the French Alps.

* * *

But all of the Olympics that took place before 1960, including the 1896 Summer Olympics and the 1924 Winter Olympics, are as ancient as the games held in 776 B.C. And all of the superstars from each and every one of those games are now heroes of a day long gone—heroes like Johnny Weissmuller, Paavo Nurmi, Jim Thorpe, Babe Didrikson, Jesse Owens, Fanny Blankers-Koen, Bob Richards, Harrison Dillard, Ellery Clark, Sonja Henie, Charlie Paddock, and hundreds more. That all took place B.C. —Before Cathode tubes—before the electronic revolution, before television.

From that first day the cathode camel stuck its nose under the five-ringed tent, the Olympics have become almost an ideal made-for-television event. If they hadn't existed, television would undoubtedly have invented them.

TV "found" the Olympics when CBS News paid $50,000 for the rights to televise the 1960 Winter Olympics from Squaw Valley, California, and then $660,000 for the rights plus some production "gimmes" to the Summer Olympics from Rome, both anchored by Walter Cronkite. Suddenly the American ice hockey team, skaters David Jenkins and Carol Heiss, boxers Cassius Clay and Nino Benvenuti, sprinter Wilma Rudolph, distance runners Peter Snell, Herb Elliott, and Abebe Bikila, and swimmers Murray Rose and Dawn Fraser were seen by more people than had witnessed the previous twenty games combined. They were instant stars and television had an ideal quadrennial program.

By 1964, the two other networks had entered the Olympics arena. NBC paid more than $1 million for the exclusive TV rights to the Summer Games in Tokyo and ABC $200,000 for the Winter Games in Innsbruck. Although new to the Olympics, ABC was no stranger to the coverage of sports like skiing, bobsledding, figure skating, speed skating, and ski jumping, having telecast all these events during their first three years of "Wide World." In fact, they had mastered their artistry by going to the continent no less than nineteen times; three of those times being the World Two-Man and Four-Man Bobsled Championships in Innsbruck the previous year and the International Ski Jumping Championships earlier that year. They were ready. Roone Arledge felt that "from a television standpoint the Winter Olympics from Innsbruck gave us the opportunity to utilize the techniques we have developed on 'Wide World of Sports' during the previous three years and put them all into effect at one time."

But there was a basic difference between the Squaw Valley games and the Innsbruck games. While the Squaw Valley games had been telecast live, the six-hour time difference between New York and Innsbruck plus the still-experimental state of the circling satellite necessitated ABC airing their Olympic coverage on a delayed tape basis. "There's just no comparison in the built-in excitement and tension of an event that is live, no matter who wins, because you don't know what's going to happen," Arledge said. "If the results are known, as they were in most all of our telecasts from Innsbruck, then showmanship and creative ability is much more important than it is in a live show."

"The logistical challenge as well as the creative challenge was very exciting." Arledge later noted. "Challenging" hell! "Ball-breaking" better lends itself to describing how ABC was able to air thirteen programs, many on the same evening they occurred in Innsbruck. With a logistical battle plan that could have gotten Phineas Fogg around the world in eighty minutes, they made the impossible possible. Figuring the time difference down to the microsecond, they could complete the editing of a day's taping by four in the morning in Innsbruck—doing in one day what had usually taken a week for a "Wide World" show—and have it in New York in finished program form that night. Their preparations included having the edited master driven to Munich, where a dub was played back on the air to Frankfort and put on a plane from Frankfort to New York. The master was then put on Pan Am's "Around-the-World" flight which left at 9:00 A.M. Munich time, 3:00 A.M. New York time. After stopping over in London, it arrived in New York at 1:00 P.M. EST. That gave New York six hours until the scheduled 7:00 P.M. air time, the first prime time telecast of an Olympics in history. Also calculating the accuracy of Murphy's Law, "Anything that can go wrong will go wrong," they had set up emergency plans in case the Munich flight was delayed. In which case either the dub from Frankfort was to be used or a mobile unit standing by at Kennedy Airport would air the tape directly, rather than entrusting it to a courier to wage battle with New York City's unforgiving rush hour traffic.

ABC also had the potential use of something that would revolutionize all of television, just as videotape had done six years earlier—the communications satellite. They made a complete schedule of its passes, usually thirty to forty a day, ranging from twelve to fifty minutes at a time. They worked out the infinite possibilities fed to them by NASA via ABC News in New York and were prepared to use it if the United States won any gold medals. But instead of the average of three captured by American athletes since the start of the Winter Olympics, including the three at Squaw Valley, the United States won only one, that by 500-meter speed skater Terry McDermott—and ABC was able to accommodate his award ceremony without the use of the satellite. However, they did use it to transmit fifteen minutes of the opening ceremony as Jim McKay described the four hundred athletes representing thirty-eight countries parading through the huge 50,000-seat stadium in the Bergisel mountains. As the signal beamed his opening remarks from Bergisel Stadium to Bethesda split-levels and Billings singles bars, ABC began its milestone Olympic coverage.

* * *

The art of negotiating for Olympic rights is an Olympian feat in itself, somewhat akin to the art of keeping a mad dog at bay until you have time to pick up a big rock. Nobody understands the strategy better than Roone Arledge. But then, nobody understands the lineup and the ground rules that govern Olympic bidding more than Arledge. In the whole of sports negotiations those ground rules are by far the most complicated to follow without a program.

That lineup includes the International Olympics Committee (IOC), a committee constructed to represent all participating nations in the Olympics. Situated physically in Lausanne, Switzerland, the IOC is governed by a thirty-member executive board. Lord Killanin of Ireland serves as president of the IOC, superseding the late, unlamented Avery Brundage, who ran the Olympic Games for the preceding twenty years with a dictatorial hand and a ramrod straight position—both physically and mentally. But the real power behind the IOC is Monique Berlioux, officially the executive director of the International Olympics Committee and generally conceded to run the thirty-member board. She is the administrative head of the organization, who not only answers the letters, but makes deals on merchandising rights and many other matters. The IOC has the power to select the sites of future Olympic Games, parceling them out as if they were Colonel Saunders franchises, and then only within the framework of their flexible rules: There cannot be two successive games on the same continent; there cannot be more than two out of five games in the same country; etc. The Winter and the Summer games operate severally under the rules, so Montreal can have the Summer games and Lake Placid the Winter ones.

The second body in the lineup—but first in the hearts of the network—is the Olympics Organizing Committee, representing the city where the Olympics will be held. The committee is independent of the country's Olympic Committee, being made up of people who might best be characterized as local Chamber of Commerce "booster" types, such as local politicos, real estate dealers, and the like. (At least, this categorization held true until the Moscow Olympics.) After incorporating, they seek to acquire $10,000 to $15,000 in local credits as well as some sort of governmental participation, usually in the form of adding some national Olympic committee personnel or the local mayor or others with clout on their board of directors.

And then they, like several other similarly structured groups, will go to Lausanne to pitch the IOC on the benefits of their city to host the Olympics. It's a full dog-and-pony show, with brochures, graphs, and pictures embodying the basic sales message: "Here's why you should bring the Summer Games to . . . ." The stated benefits being: "We have the facilities to house the guests," "We have running water," "We have a real, functioning organization," or just "We've never hosted an Olympics before." These groups usually make their presentations anywhere from six to eight years in advance of the leap year in which they seek to host the Olympics, Los Angeles making its winning bid seven years before the 1984 summer games.

Now for the ground rules. Immediately following the completion of the preceding games, the Organizing Committee has the authority to sell those rights that are negotiable, most notably the worldwide television rights. Usually the television rights for the United States are the first olive out of the jar since their price sets a benchmark for the rest of the world, representing well over 60 percent of the total dollars obtained for such rights. The United States is unique in the civilized world, having the only television system run by entrepreneurs who seek financial support directly from advertisers. Almost everywhere else in the world the Organizing Committee is dealing with national broadcasting entities, such as BBC (England), CBC (Canada), EBU (European Broadcasting Union), ORTF (Austria), Nippon Hosu Kyokai, the Soviet Television Ministry, and others who are offended by the thought of paying big communication dollars for the events.

The IOC then shares in the moneys generated by the Olympic Organizing Committee to the tune of a little more than one-third of the rights payment. However, here the formula starts to resemble the enactment of the family will. In recent years, the total price paid by the winning television network has consisted of a rights payment and a payment for such intangibles as "production facilities," moneys the IOC does not share. And so in the tradition of Dr. Doolittle's "Push-Me-Pull-You," it is to the IOC's benefit to claim that all of the money is for rights and thus one-third apportionable to them; and for the Organizing Committee to contend that almost all of it was for "other than" rights, with little going to the IOC.

No deal is made until it is approved by the IOC, with any agreement between an Organizing Committee and a network being strictly provisional until it attains the imprimatur of the IOC in Lausanne and its attorneys in Geneva. Then, and only then, is it a deal.

In 1968 ABC hit the giant quinella, winning the rights to both the Grenoble, France, Winter Games and the Mexico City Summer Games, but not without some spirited bidding against NBC. NBC has always been proud of its escutcheon, "The leader in live sports TV." The self-serving motto was one that they appropriated partly because of their historical presentation of several sports exclusives, including the World Series every year since 1947, the Super Bowl on an alternate basis with CBS, and the Rose and Orange bowls since 1948. And, in part, from the fact that they had carried these events live as opposed to the tape-delayed telecasts of the majority of events on ABC's "Wide World." At the final presentations to the Grenoble Olympic Organizing Committee in 1965, the NBC team, in the Peacock multicolored trucks headed by their Vice-President of Sports Carl Lindemann, put on an extravagant "new business" presentation in the best tradition of Busby Berkeley. With slides, films, flip charts, and narration, they recounted their numerous accomplishments in chapter and verse.

ABC followed with their own pitch, concentrating on their critically acclaimed coverage of the 1964 Winter Games and their globe-trotting experience with "Wide World," particularly their telecast of four events from France, including the World Skiing Championships from Chamonix, the site of the very first Winter Games in 1924.

Their presentation, plus a bid of $2 million, won the day and the television rights to the 1968 Winter Games. After accepting the Organizing Committee's decision to award the upcoming games to ABC, Arledge felt a tug at his sleeve. It was the chairman of the Grenoble Organizing Committee. "I want to offer my congratulations and please could you also help me? I want to know why NBC kept talking of their 'Bowel Games.' It was in very questionable taste."

* * *

The acquisition of the rights to the 1968 Summer Games depended not so much on a misunderstanding as on what many suggested was instead an "understanding." Mexico City was selected as the site of the XIX Summer Games by the IOC long before the Tokyo Olympics. But even with an Organizing Committee duly constituted to administer to such things as the awarding of television rights, the entire situation was as rife with intrigue as Rick's Café Americaine in *Casablanca*.

ABC let it be known that they were in the bidding for the 1968 Mexico City games. Anxious to add their very first Summer Games to their ever-growing charm bracelet of Olympics, they were prepared to investigate every opportunity, but even they weren't prepared for this. They soon began to receive phone calls—over a hundred a week. The message was always the same, delivered by an unctuous Latin, who could be pictured in another pose somewhere on the streets of Tijuana, leering at his prey and whispering, "Psst. Hey Buddee. You like my seester?" The message he imparted to Arledge or anyone he could reach on the twenty-eighth floor of the ABC Building was "the televeesion rights for the Olympeecs are available . . . and I can deeleever them for you, Señor."

NBC was receiving its share of calls as well. William Johnson, senior editor at *Sports Illustrated*, suggested, "Many of these calls, it was assumed, came from a phone booth in Grand Central Terminal and lacked any mark of officialdom." Still, Johnson wrote, "No one knew for sure who would be the real influential force on the Mexican committee, so nearly every contact had to be taken seriously." In a cloak-and-dagger atmosphere, NBC set up its own secret operative to follow up the furtive callers and ferret out the right pressure point. But the right pressure point was one that ABC had found months before.

In 1960, James Hagerty, press secretary for President Eisenhower, had been hired as vice-president in charge of news, replacing John Daly. One of his unannounced jobs was the maintenance of goodwill, and no goodwill meant more than that of the Mexican government as the Mexico City games approached. In 1962, he had made a trip to Mexico, ostensibly on a fact-finding tour, but in large part to rekindle the friendship of Eisenhower's close Mexico friends, including the former president of Mexico. Arledge himself was to take several trips South of the Border, this time not to bring Acapulco cliff divers down from $100,000 to $10 a dive, but to bring the Olympics back to ABC.

Each network was finally called to Mexico City to make their presentations to the Olympic Organizing Committee. NBC opened the bidding with $2.2 million. Then, after ABC had made its presentation, along with a bid of $4.5 million, NBC sent a telegram to the International Olympics Committee that they "would top any figure submitted by ABC," regardless of how outrageous ABC's bid was. What price tag glory when you're going for an Olympics? But the local Organizing Committee awarded the 1968 Summer Games to ABC, never getting back to NBC for their counter offer.

The winner of the TV rights to the Mexico City games, Roone Arledge, indicated he thought the reason he won the gold ring was because "after watching us covering past Olympics, they just assumed we could do it best." But the loser, Carl Lindemann of NBC, thought other reasons concerning gold had something to do with it. He told Johnson that "maybe ABC had given Colonel What's-his-name, the Mexican chairman of the Olympic committee, a $15,000 Maserati."

And although the sour grapes quote gained wide circulation—and some mild acceptance—it was something Arledge neither had to do nor was reduced to doing. For ABC had won the Mexico City games on their past merit; nothing as meretricious as the bribe laid at their doorstep by Lindemann.

* * *

To the six sports and thirty-five events at Grenoble, a small city in southeast France was added yet another—television.

And the biggest team at the X Winter Games was ABC's, with over 250 engineering and production personnel on hand to telecast the games. Theirs was an Olympian effort, worthy of the games themselves. In order to lay a forty-mile web of cables throughout the mountains and slopes that surrounded Grenoble, they moved their fifty tons of equipment by hand, helicopter, and heavy snowmobiles with the help of a detachment from the French Army to positions along the treacherous terrain and precipices.

The cameramen, technicians, and engineers—as opposed to the "production" people—are by and large as fearless as any group of counterespionage agents in the world. They hang from scaffolding and cranes high above the earth, position themselves in front of action that no sane man would, and generally rank as second only to stuntmen in assumption of risks. But the inevitable happened at Grenoble. As the crew was setting up its web of cables, skittering around the mountains like snowy spiders, one of the engineers, who was up on the mountainside connecting the points on the cables to see if the cameras "fired," literally froze in his tracks. The crew at a particular cross connect point up on the downhill slope hadn't finished until late in the day. By that time the ski lift had ceased operating, so the rest of the crew took off their heavy, weatherproofed, blue ABC jackets, made them into sleds, and came down the icy "Piste" on their rumps. The hill was no longer just snow covered, but a sheet of ice, watered down by the soldiers. But no amount of talking could get this one engineer to take off his jacket and slide down the hill. He was petrified. And no amount of persuasion on the walkie talkies could budge him either. Finally, two French troopers on skis walked up the hill and walked him down, step by step. One more of the hazards of being an engineer at the Olympics.

The twenty-seven-hour television feast served up by Arledge's army included course after course: beauty shots of gold medalist Peggy Fleming, dramatic shots of three-time gold medal winner Jean-Claude Killy, slo-mo shots of American skiing hope Billy Kidd falling skis-over-teakettle down the 2-mile Casserousse run, breathtaking shots of skiers coming down the

1½-mile downhill course at 70 miles-per-hour, and fearsome shots of a Canadian bobsledder being dragged along the bob-sled course after a spill on one of the turns. The old Arledge touch of placing the microphones in the place best calculated to bring the event into the living room had mikes imbedded everywhere. They were near the very edge of the 90-meter ski jump so that each airborne skiier's frightening "huuuh" could be heard at the precise second of takeoff. A second micro-phone, near their landing spot, caught their deep inhalation, "ooomph," as they landed. And a third, at the bottom of the run, the "sssssss-s" of their skis as they skidded to a final stop. It was all great theater, great entertainment.

But it also was a dry run for the Summer Olympics, to be telecast that very October from Mexico City. There the 250 men mushroomed to 450 and the forty cameras to fifty. The coverage also increased from twenty-seven to forty-four hours, most of it prime time. ABC's first Summer Olympics would be the standard by which all future ones would be judged.

And it was here that the hand of Roone Arledge was most evident. The generalissimo of all that surrounded him, he grafted his technical skills onto the spectacle and made it as much a part of the Olympics as the athletic competition itself. Arledge became the *A* to de Coubertin's *D*; by their own indi-vidual efforts these two men brought the Olympic age from B.C. to A.D.

"To me, Roone's talent is being the producer in the control room," says Jim McKay, who has worked with him for seven-teen years. But to say Roone Arledge is only a producer is to say that Cellini was only a sculptor. For sitting in that middle chair in the main control room—known throughout the industry as The Chair—facing a board containing thirty-two monitors with an equal number of images, assaulting him, Arledge is at his best. "It's in the Olympic Games that Roone Arledge shows what a brilliant mind he is because he becomes a line pro-ducer," says another of his famous disciples, Howard Cosell. "He's looking at a bank of thirty-two monitors, evaluating each one contemporaneously and making a judgment: 'OK, go to Howard with the boxing . . .' 'Howard throw it to Beattie,

The ABC team at the 1972 Munich Olympics—the third largest group represented at the games.

Chuck Howard (left), producer, and Roone Arledge, executive producer, watch a battery of monitors from every venue at the 1972 Munich games.

The Munich tragedy unfolds on ABC television.

Julie Barnathan.

Keith Jackson interviews seven-time gold medal winner Mark Spitz at the 1972 Munich Olympics. Spitz has now joined ABC's "Wide World of Sports" stable of color announcers.

Don Ohlmeyer, director, and Roone Arledge, executive producer, listen to Howard Cosell before the start of the telecast of the 1976 Olympic games. Larry Kamm watches the monitors.

An ABC cameraman stationed at a strategic position to catch a crucial part of the action at the 1976 Innsbruck Olympics.

there's a record coming up in weight lifting. . . .' Whatever. And it all meshes!" he adds incredulously. But perhaps the man who best understands the technical wizardry that allows Arledge to orchestrate men, machines, and monitors into one total show is Julie Barnathan, the vice-president in charge of broadcast operations and of engineering for ABC and the true unsung hero of the Olympics. "He is great under fire—in The Chair. And I have seen more events than anybody I can imagine. I have never seen a man operate under conditions in such a cool way. Cool, clear, explicit, incredible under fire. There's no one like that." Barnathan recalls one incident where, in the middle of a station break, they turned to Arledge and said, "Alright, Roone, where are we going?" And Barnathan remembers Arledge answering, "I don't know yet."

Somehow, unlike Humpty Dumpty, he always manages to put the pieces together again, cutting from live coverage of one event to a tape of another and then back again for another live shot. And so it was in Mexico City, as Arledge choreographed a shot from a cameraman hanging 225 feet above the stadium to a tight shot of the Olympic torch, accompanied by a "whoosh" of the flame at the moment of ignition, which was picked up by a tiny microphone . He caught it all, the results of hundreds of human competitions to incisive moments that only TV could bring us. Everything from Tommie Smith and John Carlos raising their black-gloved fists and lowering their heads during the playing of the "American National Anthem" to a Czech gymnast turning away her head during the playing of the "Soviet Anthem." And when he didn't quite catch it, he would send his reporters after it, directing Cosell to get Smith for an interview or even sending him onto the track to get an interview with Jimmie Hines who had just broken the Olympic record in winning the 100-meter championship. As we all watched the incongrous sight of an athlete in a tight-fitting track suit being chased by a middle-aged athlete-that-never-was seeking an interview, in spite of the Mexican's ban on interviews, we knew what we were watching was the best in sports journalism.

Nothing seemed to stand in Arledge's way: not the construction of a twenty-foot-tall camera tower, built by the Mexicans, that obstructed ABC's view of some of the track and field events, which he got removed by his persuasiveness; nor the failure of power in a stadium control room, which went dead after one live show and which, upon investigation, was found by technicians to have been caused by tiny particles of dirt in the Mexico diesel oil clogging the generator, a recurrency of which he averted by having the generator cleaned before the countdown for every show.

Roone Arledge had seemed to reduce all the chaos to order, all problems to solutions, all competitions to something deeper, and the Olympics to a permanent place on ABC's quadriennial schedule.

* * *

The 1972 Olympics were the most socially significant since the 1936 Berlin Olympics. For the first time two defeated countries were to take their place in the world community by hosting the two Olympic Games—Japan the Winter Games and Germany the Summer Games.

NBC, which had last telecast the 1964 Summer Games from Tokyo, won the rights to the 1972 Winter Games from Sapporo, purchasing them from the worldwide owner, Nippon Hoso Kyokai (NHK), the government-owned Japanese broadcasting system. Failing to negotiate unilateral coverage in 1964, leaving that entirely in the hands of the Japanese, NBC compounded their felony in 1972. This time they also neglected to obtain the rights to cover the events themselves with their own cameras and interviewers. Jim Simpson, Curt Gowdy, and several expert analysts were back in a studio, but interviews with the winners would have to wait until they came to the studio. It was treated as a news event of what *had* happened, not what *was* happening. Those in the studio might just as well have been back in New York sitting in front of a chroma-key of Sapporo in the background. And even what was shown needed subtitles, with the American audience treated to performer after performer, including the last sixty skiers in the downhill—all of them downhill Kamikaze pilots—from every country in the world, with virtually no chances of winning. In the words of one benumbed NBC executive, "They showed every goddamned one of them on American television." With thirty-six hours scheduled, including the last half hour of the "Today Show" for a week and nine "Johnny Carson Shows," it was an artistic disaster and a commercial debacle. No wonder NBC was wary about putting any future Olympics on prime time television.

* * *

ABC's road to the 1972 Munich games was less complicated but as difficult as their acquisition of the '68 Mexico City games. Once again they found themselves locked in a bidding war with that hardy quadrennial, NBC. The German Organizing Committee had mentioned a figure of $30 million as their opening gambit, almost seven times higher than the rights for the 1968 games. Arledge, who had made an "ABC closer" bid of $6.5 million for the games, was flabbergasted. He had never been off by $23 million before. But as gambit turned to ploy and push turned to shove, the Germans' expectations came tumbling down and the networks' bids went skyrocketing up. NBC upped its opening $9.5 million to over $11. The stakes were building and nobody was dropping out of the bidding, even though the sales departments of both networks had assessed the bottom-line dollar amounts and recommended that after the rights payment got above the rarified atmosphere of $10 million the games would no longer be a profitable venture. But no network was in this for love or money alone. The prestige the Olympics brought to a network, as well as the open forum in the summer for "promo-ing" and "hype-ing" the fall package of new shows can't be found on any balance sheet. And, as one of those in ABC's financial division says, "Profit and loss is all a function of how you keep the books."

ABC had learned from experience. The Olympics were great entertainment, particularly in the summertime against throwaway and rerun competition on the other networks. And so, in an internal meeting on the fortieth floor of ABC, it was decided to take a crap-shoot: devote a full sixty-seven hours to the Summer Olympics, forty-seven of them in prime time. By passing on the costs to advertisers for prime time commercials, ABC had figured out a way of offsetting both the rights and production costs. They would charge $48,000 a minute for almost five hundred commercial minutes they expected to run during the sixty-seven hours of coverage passing almost $24 million on to advertisers. Arledge's mandate was to "get the Olympics," at almost any cost. Almost!

Finally, a series of meetings were held in April 1969 that had all the appearance of those in Frankfort to sign the final treaty ending the Franco-Prussian War. Once again the Germans were in the position to demand what they wanted, almost 100 years since the last time they had the upper hand in international bargaining. Arledge brought scrapbooks filled with enthusiastic reviews of ABC's coverage of the 1968 Summer Games and a letter from the United States Olympic Committee attesting to the network's "excellent" work at Mexico City. But ABC was vulnerable on one very important point, the network's overall financial position. The previous year they had lost over $20 million as a network, and NBC was playing the tune of the network's dire financial straits in a Johnny-one-note song as time and again they openly stated they had never had problems paying *their* bills. It was a return to the ancient sport of pancratium, with a little biting and gouging added.

And so it was when Arledge and the president of the network, Elton Rule, finally made their way to the Munich tables for their last chance. It was as if they had found "Blake safe at second and Flynn a-hugging third" and all eyes on them as they came to the plate for the last time. The negotiations were delicate. For the first time the rights were but part of the package. There was a footnote. What would the Germans give to ABC in terms of production facilities and housing, and how much would that cost? After an all-day session, the two parties were only separated by a couple of hundred dollars. They had already agreed to $8 million for rights alone.

It now became a question of settling on the amount of moneys for production facilities. Finally, they came close. But the hour drew near when the most influential man on the German negotiating team looked at his watch and announced he had a train to catch. As he put all of his papers in his attaché case, Arledge knew he had been had. If he didn't agree to the German's final figure, and quickly, he calculated the chances were that the Organizing Committee would immediately turn to NBC which had bid $12.5 million. Arledge watched as "Herr Doktor" marched briskly out the door, then knowing those left behind had no power to negotiate—only accept or reject the offer as it had been structured earlier—succumbed and "gave them everything they asked," $7.5 million for the TV rights and $6 million for facilities. For the fourth time in the seven televised Olympics, they belonged to ABC, but the "German closer" had one-upped the "ABC closer."

* * *

The Munich of 1972 was a modern city of more than one million, just nine miles and thirty years away from Dachau. Determined to make the games an example to the world that men and nations can change for the better, the German Organizing Committee set upon a massive building program that cost $650 million and would make the setting much more Hansel and Gretel than Hitler and Goering; a site that would be the place of "The Serene Olympics." There was a deliberate attempt right from the start to mute the pomp and panoply of the games and offer a sharp contrast with the arrogant extravagances of the 1936 Nazi Olympics. Flowers and pastels were to be the dominant theme.

The German state-owned television system had planned to use ninety electronic cameras at thirty-one sporting events, plus twenty more in ten studios, along with fifty videotape recorders (VTR's) and slo-mos. They also had built a technical center for what was to be, after the Olympics, a physical education high school and college. For the time being the gyms would be used for studios.

Unlike NBC, Arledge had negotiated from the very beginning for its own unilateral coverage; coverage that was included in the $6.5 million production figure. This was, in the words of one of those on the negotiating team, "the most important factor to us in our negotiating."

A preliminary survey had been made by Arledge, as the

overall producer of the Olympics, to determine the placement of cameras and production facilities. And now, almost three years before the start of the games, a production team was sent to Munich to implement those decisions. Immediately it became very evident that if ABC had only the amount of equipment allocated by the Germans, their coverage would be no better than NBC's at Sapporo. Production insisted, as was their right, on coverage at five key locations—track and field, boxing, swimming, gymnastics, and basketball—along with ABC's own program assembly studios and additional VTR's, slo-mos, two more film cameras, and two program assembly studios; plus ABC's own television transmission area and two mobile "flash" units for background shots.

Julie Barnathan, head of Broadcast Operations and Engineering, was the man deputized to carry out the production prerequisites. "Part of my assignment was to convince the German engineers that our requirements were not 'ridiculous' and that the designs were based on experience. That the ABC Sports people needed to present to the American people the type of show they would enjoy. It took many meetings," he added, "here and abroad."

The primary problem in conveying ABC's "wants" was that the Americans and the Germans spoke different languages, both literally and figuratively. One of Arledge's assistants, Geoff Mason, called down to the switchboard operator for a wake-up call. "I want one at 7:00 and one at 7:15," he said, very deliberately. "I want two wake-up calls, one at 7:00 and one at 7:15," he emphasized. "Are you sure you understand?" "Of course," came the reply, "we do this all the time. Now which one do you want first?" That episode of international misunderstanding indicated just what ABC was up against in attemping to persuade the Germans that ABC's requirements were not "ridiculous."

In following the production survey, Barnathan soon became cognizant of the fact that the facilities offered him in the studio–high school gym were inadequate. ABC needed fully 15,000 square feet, and there was only provision for 5,000. To position everyone and everything needed in one-third the space would be like cramming twenty-five people into a phone booth.

Barnathan sought out the head architect, "That's OK for the technical facility, but I need 'people space.' What about people?"

The architect smiled and answered, "That's it."

Barnathan returned his ingratiating smile and said very slowly—difficult for the fast-talking Barnathan, "Well, that's not enough." Then, in answer to the architect's hands that were thrown out in the universal symbol that says, "What can I do about it?" Barnathan pointed to a vacant lot he had just espied across the street. "What's across the street, over there?" It was nothing. "Well, why can't we just put a little bungalow over there?" meaning something like they stick up outside the site of political conventions—a trailer-type vehicle. After more discussions with several other efficient-looking architects and builders, they asked Barnathan what he had in mind. He sat down and "on a friggin' little piece of Xerox paper" laid out the space, showing them why ABC needed that much space.

The next thing Barnathan noticed was a building going up on the vacant lot. Walking up to the head engineer, he jibbed him, "See, you ran out of space yourselves and you're going to put a bigger building up." But no, that was to be the bungalow Barnathan had indicated he needed. "What do you mean? My bungalow?" He was told that the architect couldn't put up something that didn't conform to the rest of the buildings.

After this massive "little bungalow" was constructed, Barnathan noticed that it didn't have any windows. "Where are the windows?" he asked. The German demurred in the time-honored German "I-was-only-following-orders" answer uttered so frequently by Helmut Dantine in World War II movies. "They weren't on the blueprints," Barnathan was told. Blueprints Barnathan only remembered having sketched a little diagram on Xerox paper showing them why ABC needed the footage. And so, in the efficient manner of the Germans, they had copied it, line for line, like the Hong Kong shoemaker who mailed two left shoes back to the states because his customer had only sent him one left shoe and wanted a pair made.

Promptly dubbed Barnathan's Bungalow by ABC personnel,

it was immortalized first with a hand-written sign and then with a little gold plaque that hung outside the front door. It not only became "The House that ABC Engineering Built," but home for the 500-man brigade that was in Munich to televise the XX Summer Games.

It was there that Roone Arledge oversaw the action from the many different venues on banks of monitors that looked like Mission Control preparing for a moon shot. It was also there, on the afternoon of Friday, September 1, that sprinters Eddie Hart, Rey Robinson, Robert Taylor and their coach Stan Wright looked up at one of the monitors with unbelieving eyes to see the start of the second round of the quarterfinals of the 100-meter race that they were supposed to be in. Thinking at first it was a replay of the heats they had won earlier that day, they heard Jim McKay from trackside at the 80,000 seat Olympic Stadium tell them that "it looks like the reports about Robinson are true. He did pull up this morning, and now, apparently, can't make it for this round." As an official went out and removed his starting block, there was turmoil inside Barnathan's Bungalow. There was still time to get Robert Taylor to the stadium in time for his heat, but for Robinson and Hart, the Olympics were over. Afterwards, Howard Cosell doggedly pursued the coach, Stan Wright, for an interview. But in spite of a press conference in which blame was passed to some cloudy individuals named only as "those a little higher up," Wright was unavailable for comment. The West German Polizei kept the press away, even taking away the credentials of one reporter who tried to see Wright. Finally, Cosell got to Wright and wouldn't let him off the hook, either for his failure to get his charges to the stadium or his attempt to pass the buck. To Cosell, two wrongs don't make a Wright, and he zeroed in on the poor coach, whose reliance on an eighteen-month-old schedule had proved his undoing.

The remainder of the games will be remembered not for Olga Korbut, Frank Shorter, Dave Wottles, or Kip Keino but for the blunders, bungles, botches, and boors on the part of the United States team. And ABC was there to catch them all. The boor was Mark Spitz, who captured seven gold medals but failed to captivate the press corps with his wise cracks and arrogance, refusing to even pose with his seven medals, already having contracted to sell that pose as a poster on his return to the States. The blunders, bungles, and botches took other forms. Young Rick DeMont, seemingly the winner of the 400-meter swimming event, was disqualified when U.S. officials attempted to conceal his use of a drug prescribed for his asthma. Jim Ryun ended his amateur track career by falling in the semifinal heat of the 1,500-meter race. Vince Matthews and Wayne Collett fidgeted while on the victory stand as Olympic judges fumed and later disqualified them from further competition. The U.S. basketball team lost to Russia in the last three seconds of a game that they had won. The "Serene Games" were fast becoming the star-crossed games as far as the United States was concerned.

* * *

But at 4:09 in the morning of September 5, eight shadowy figures in sweat suits—members of the Palestinian terrorist group called Black September—scaled the six-and-a-half-foot-tall chain link fence around the Olympic Village and turned the Olympics into the "Obscene Games." As they made their way across the sixty-yard expanse to 31 Connellystrasse and the Israeli team's headquarters, they seriously dampened forever the light that burned in the Olympic torch—the flame that had pronounced the Olympics to be one "in the true spirit of sportsmanship." It flickered; never again to regain its former luster.

The ABC team in Barnathan's Bungalow had just finished a long, tedious day. They had been on the air seventeen hours the preceding three days, the Labor Day weekend in the United States, and finally called it a day at 4:00 A.M., 11:00 P.M. the previous evening in New York. Tuesday was a down day, with no track and field or swimming scheduled. Certain personnel, like Jim McKay, were taking the day off. ABC had several soft pieces scheduled, including a twenty-seven-minute film written and narrated by Erich Segal which pitted two former decathlon winners. Bill Toomey and Rafer Johnson, in a re-creation of the ancient pentathlon, filmed on location in the ancient Greek Olympic stadium where it was held. Chris Schenkel and Roone Arledge walked out of the Bungalow on their way back to the hotel, passing the exact spot where just minutes earlier the eight forms had climbed the fence, unaware that at that very moment the trespassers were hovering under a nearby bridge changing their clothing from the track sweat suits they had used to couch their entry into the mufti of the PLO, their own "official" uniforms. Murder was to become the twenty-third sport at the XX Olympics.

Manfred Schreiber, the police chief of Munich, heard that the terrorists had taken the Israeli headquarters and eleven hostages at 5:21 A.M. The ABC personnel, housed at the München-Sheraton, and the rest of Munich found out the chilling news an hour or two later. LeRoy Neiman, the artist sketching the Olympics for ABC, got a call: "Something's going on! It's an emergency." There were other calls at 7:00 A.M. rippling through the seventeenth, eighteenth, and nineteenth floors of the hotel. Cosell was aroused at 7:00 by Harry Curtis, his radio engineer: "Arab commandos got into the Village." Jim McKay, on his first day off in four months, was awakened by the student-driver assigned to him: "The Arabs have invaded the Israeli team headquarters. They've asked me to call you and ask you to stand by." Everywhere there were macabre wake-up calls.

Cosell was one of the first to reach the lobby of the hotel, already buzzing with angry voices. He called Arledge from the lobby, "Roone, have you heard?"

"Yes," replied Arledge, cutting him short. "Find a way to get into the Village right away. Leave immediately. Jennings is already there for news."

As Neiman emerged from the elevator, he could see Cosell pacing the lobby "like a madman," waiting for his car. So, too, were sports correspondents Jim Murray of the *Los Angeles Times* and Shirley Povich of the *Washington Post*. Neiman's car came first and they all piled in, as the driver took off for the Village like an emergency ambulance. "Howard was sitting in the back seat," remembers Neiman, "and saying, 'I'd like to get at them. I want to find out what's going on.' " Cosell was raging mad, a wave of indignation sweeping over him as the young Israelis were trapped inside by men intent on nothing short of murder.

Cosell got out of the car and headed toward the gate to the Village with Tony Triolo, the *Sports Illustrated* photographer. Both got into the Village not because they were newsmen, but on the contrary, because they held themselves out to be Puma shoe salesmen. Newsmen were being barred at the gates; Puma had a shoe store on the grounds and their salesmen were granted free passage to the Village. On the way in, Cosell saw *Chicago Tribune* sports editor Cooper Rollow being summarily thrown out of the Village. Cosell identified him as "one of my assistants" and took Rollow in with him. The German mentality has always understood commercialism better than journalism.

As Cosell and Rollow hit the slope of the hill not thirty feet away from Building 31—soon to join the Texas School Book Depository and Ford's Theatre in the grisly records kept of places where terror has visited innocents—others in the ABC crew were making their advances on the Village as well. Bill Toomey, former decathlon champion and now an ABC expert commentator, put on his American athlete's uniform and trotted past the guards at the gates. Arledge and Julie Barnathan, who had just taken his wife to the airport and put her on a plane (the same plane that carried Mark Spitz out of Munich to London as the committee feared for the young Jewish athlete's life), now sent John Wilcox and Jim Flood into the Village dressed as athletes. There had been a remote truck on the grounds of the Village, but there was no way to get the tape in and out for the Electronic News Gatherer (ENG), a pretentious name for a tape unit. For that purpose they used Puma bags, taking Cosell's and others and giving them to young couriers dressed in Pumas and sweat suits.

As the area reverberated with police sirens that were reminiscent of middle-of-the-night Gestapo roundups of political prisoners, Peter Jennings made his way into the toilet in the Italian Building, which looked directly out onto Building 31. Time and again, he was thrown out. And just as many times as he was thrown out—less one—he made his way back in and finally worked his way to the rooftop, where he was joined by ABC's publicist Irv Brodsky. John Wilcox detached himself from the group he was with and tried to enter the Burmese Building for a better vantage spot of 31 Conellystrasse. He finally made his way into the building by telling the guard he was a United States boxer who had left his credentials inside. He then took his Puma bag stuffed with tape, walkie-talkies, and recorders to the third floor, where he looked out directly into the eyes of the terrorist lookout not fifty feet away.

Jim McKay had been called down to Barnathan's Bungalow early that morning. Although Chris Schenkel had been the anchor man up until that point, the next fifteen hours were to be the anchor of Jim McKay's fame as a sports and news commentator. McKay had been used in place of Schenkel—instead of Jennings and Cosell whom Arledge wanted in the field—because he was a newsman and, in Arledge's estimation, an objective and sensitive reporter. Barnathan adds, "McKay is our key whenever we're doing an ad-lib thing. Schenkel is not the greatest ad-libber in the world." And so Jim McKay, the man who had started as a newsman at the *Baltimore Sun* and been a newscaster for WMAR in Baltimore, reverted to type and took over the news portion of the Olympics.

Barnathan patched Jennings's phone line into the ABC audio console and transmitted his telephone reports as well as those from Wilcox, who was using a walkie-talkie held up to Jennings's telephone, directly out over the airwaves, the mouthpiece held to a speaker in the control room. But McKay couldn't get back to him except over the phone. And he obviously could not hear Arledge's instructions from the control booth. When McKay spoke to Jennings, he would cover the mouthpiece because of the feedback. And so it went all afternoon. From this experience an entire system was devised for the Montreal Games just in case terrorism reared its ugly head again. Not only were the police ready for any recurrence in Montreal, so was ABC.

The continued glimpses of the man in the white hat, German police with their machine guns slung over their shoulders, hooded lookouts, and the plaintive wailing of police sirens all brought a chilling scene to American screens. Never again would we be able to look at a ski mask or hear a helicopter's blades without thinking of Munich.

Schenkel soon joined McKay as the show went on the air live, and they in turn were joined by Peter Jennings and Lou Cioffi, ABC's Bonn correspondent. But no matter how closely they covered the story, there was much we didn't know. Nor were we meant to know. We didn't know that General Zvi Zamir, head of Israeli security, had landed with an entire commando force in Munich to offer his aid to the Germans; aid that they turned down. We didn't know how many terrorists there were. Nobody did. And we didn't know for agonizing moments what the fate of those at the Fuerstenfeldbruck airfield was. In fact, we were treated to the cruelly inaccurate report by the Germans that all of the hostages had escaped. Although he never fully accepted the first report, Jim McKay was later dumbstruck by a communique that read: "We are afraid the information given so far is 'too optimistic'." Then, according to Chris Schenkel, it was "waiting, waiting, and more waiting. Seemed we waited forever." To fill the time there were "long periods of vamping" on air. But, Schenkel vividly remembers, "We knew something was wrong. But no one would tell you what."

ABC, which had already fought off an incursion by CBS to monopolize the satellite by buying up all the time available so that no other network could use it, now preempted the rest of the evening's programming. For McKay, it was to be an exhausting wait until confirmation of the fate of the hostages was given. Nineteen hours ago he had been awakened. And the story was still unfolding. Then, at 2:30 A.M. Munich time, 9:30 P.M. New York time, Arledge called McKay over the headset, "This is important. Tell the stations all along the line that we'll take a thirty-three-second break, then come back and wait for a press announcement of what happened to the hostages."

As the most dreaded of announcements was made over the radio line connecting the press conference with McKay's earpiece, the utterly exhausted features of McKay froze into an "Oh-my-God!" fresco. Then, with as much poise as he could bring to bear, he told the United States that "the worst" had occurred. All were dead. It was a tragic footnote to the games that had started with so much hope. And only Jim McKay could have taken us through that horrible moment, when with solemnity and dignity he transcended the man we knew, the host of "Wide World," and became a respected news journalist, a role for which he was to receive two Emmy awards for sports and news from his peers.

* * *

The Olympics which had started on such a high note, with ABC optimistically playing "What the World Needs Now is Love, Sweet Love," had disintegrated into the grotesque carnage of innocent athletes. Nothing was to be the same. But as with life, things go on. So, too, did the Olympic Games. They had continued up to four o'clock in the afternoon with what now were meaningless events, volleyball and boxing, including the semifinal bout between America's Duane Bobick and Cuba's Teofilo Stevenson. As the exhausted Cosell entered Barnathan's Bungalow, Arledge approached him. "Howard, I'd like you to do the voice layover on the Stevenson-Bobick fight."

Cosell was shocked. "After what I've been through today and what's happened to my people. . . . I'm not doing another thing."

But Arledge consoled Cosell, "Howard, tomorrow several people are not going to read about the terrorist attack, unfortunately, they're going to read about the fight." And so the emotionally drained Cosell went into the control room and called the two-round fight, giving it "everything I had." Then he begged off joining everyone in the control room and went back to the München-Sheraton where "I found my wife in bed crying." He then went down to the bar and drank for six hours as he tried to forget the events of the day. Barnathan and Arledge and company worked almost round the clock, getting no sleep for two days. And Chris Schenkel, in a state of shock, signed off that night mechanically, "We'll be back tomorrow with the memorial services. . . . I know you'll enjoy it."

The 1972 Munich games ended with the electric scoreboard spelling out "Thank you, Avery Brundage." Except the name

"Brundage" was misspelled "Brandage." It was a fitting finale to the Olympics that will always be remembered for all the wrong reasons.

* * *

Chet Forte describes Roone Arledge as "thinking of the Olympics eight years before everyone else. He's there ten steps before them." And even before the closing ceremonies brought the Munich Olympics to a merciful close, Arledge was laying plans for the Montreal Games, four years hence.

But the acquisition of the Montreal Olympics was not so much a factor of Arledge's being there "ten steps before them," as merely "being there." During the 1972 Games, the Montreal Organizing Committee had rented a suite of rooms in one of the Munich hotels and made their presence known loud and clear to the three networks. Surprisingly, only ABC took the trouble to come up and see them. This serious lack of follow-through was to plague both NBC and CBS throughout the supposed race to acquire the 1976 games, as their continued absence prompted members of the Olympic Organizing Committee to ask ABC on more than one occasion, "Where are NBC and CBS?"

By the time the other two networks realized that the bidding for the Montreal Olympics was not to be an open contest, ABC had stolen the march on them and almost finalized the deal for TV rights to the 1976 games. Throughout the fall of 1972, Arledge was officially away from his office several times. His whereabouts was unknown to many at ABC and to all at NBC and CBS. With movements as shrouded in mystery as those of Lamont Cranston, he was simultaneously reported to be in Petaluma, Pendleton, Pittsburgh, and Peking. But in reality, he was in Montreal all the while "romancing" the Olympic Organizing Committee. The romancing took the form of show and tell: not only telling the committee but showing them how ABC would do a better job for them. To support his point Arledge came equipped with reel after reel of tapes from the Mexico City and Munich games attesting the artistic achievement of his sports department, an achievement that not only won rave reviews from critics but thirty-eight Emmys as well.

Then, in a meeting on November 18, 1972, attended by

Arledge, Jim Spence, his vice-president in charge of Sports Planning, and three members of the Montreal Organizing Committee, an agreement in principle was worked out. As the all-day meeting stretched into night, Arledge asked the head of the committee, Paul Durocher, "what it would take to 'do' the deal." Durocher threw out a figure—$25 million. Arledge and Spence looked at each other, remembering that the Munich figure was $13.5 million, about half that, and suggested an addition: that the Montreal Organizing Committee throw in roughly $2 million of custom-made production facilities for ABC. Agreed.

They parted company sometime after one o'clock in the morning, with the stipulation that they would reconvene at 10 o'clock the next morning to present the accord to a meeting of the whole Olympic Committee. Arledge and Spence then went back to their hotel, the Queen Elizabeth, and called ABC President Elton Rule to fill him in on the details. He approved them on the phone. Next they tried to reach one of ABC's attorneys to work out the language of the agreement. Finally, after discovering that the one they had been working with was out on the West Coast, they roused Allen Morris, who fed back the necessary legal language to Spence, who took it down in longhand. Now it was after three in the morning, with the meeting less than seven hours away.

In a scene right out of *Grand Hotel,* Spence called down to the front desk to see if they could find a public stenographer at that hour of the morning. But all the hotel could provide them with was a typewriter and some carbon paper. And so, at four in the morning, Spence sat down at the typewriter and started to type a short legal memorandum on the back of Queen Elizabeth stationary. As he laboriously worked his way through the short memo spelling out all the main points of the accord, each mistake was punctuated by a "Damn it!," and Arledge would invariably ask, "Are you *sure* we can't get anybody to type this thing?" And so it went for two more hours, as Spence mustered almost enough typing speed to rival Elizabeth Ray's top speed of eighteen words a minute, with almost an equal number of errors. As part reward and in part because he couldn't stand to see a grown man cry, Arledge volunteered to go out and get Spence some food. As the vice-president–typist continued to hunt and peck away, the president–messenger boy went out for scrambled eggs and coffee. Finally, with dawn breaking through the hotel window, two copies of the two-page memo agreement were completed. After freshening up, Arledge and Spence took the magnum opus to present it to the committee for their approval and signature.

But the two-page-memo agreement did not finalize the negotiations, for a memo agreement lies somewhere in that legal never-never land between an agreement to agree and a contract, which is fully enforceable in a court of law. ABC dispatched a full regiment, including attorneys, to a top-secret meeting in Montreal the day after New Year's Day, 1973, a national holiday in Canada. One executive wouldn't even tell his secretary where he was; he was "merely out of New York."

As everyone gathered in the offices of the prime minister of Quebec, in Montreal's Hydo Building at 9:00 A.M. on January 2, in walked Marvin Josephson, president of one of the largest talent agencies in the world. Josephson, following a long and honorable trade, had approached the Montreal Organizing Committee sometime between November 18 and January 2 to offer his services. He wanted to agent the Olympics on a worldwide basis. In response to his offer to make them, as Dr. Samuel Johnson had told the brewer's widow, "rich beyond the dreams of avarice," the committee informed Josephson that they had already made a deal with ABC.

Josephson, who had the technical knowledge that many of those on the Organizing Committee, albeit sophisticated businessmen, didn't possess, had told them, according to one committee member, "You've only just begun. You've agreed to some very general terms and a number. But now the real crunch comes. And for that, you'll need a man of my skill and stature." And so, the Organizing Committee took on Josephson, who didn't get a commission on the ABC contract, but threw in his services to finalize the ABC agreement. His oyster was to be the merchandising and television rights for the rest of the world.

Josephson took the position that the two-page memorandum agreement was not binding on his client. And he told NBC and CBS, who had learned of the deal with ABC and started crying something that sounded like a cross between just plain "foul" and a more aggrieved "murder most foul," that although ABC definitely had the inside track and was in an advanced stage of negotiations, the deal wasn't totally closed. His deal with the Olympic Committee was that if the ABC negotiations fell apart, he could represent them in making a deal with either of the other two networks.

In this atmosphere, the three members of the ABC team, Arledge, Spence, and attorney Richard Burns, and the committee met to consummate the short strokes of the agreement. Some points were easy to deal with, such as what production facilities would the Organizing Committee provide ABC. Some were lighthearted. Gerry Snyder, the chief revenue officer for the committee, probably only 40 percent in jest, said "One of the conditions of the deal is you've got to keep Cosell out of Canada."

The most difficult area to be worked out was that of merchandising rights. While ABC accepted in principle the fact that there were to be no merchandising rights included in their purchase of the TV rights, they needed the latitude to allow their advertisers to use the Olympic seal for self-liquidating premiums and in their advertising. This minor ancillary right, distinguishable from the overall merchandising rights, took several hours to work out in concept. As the cold early morning hours continued to tick by, the Organizing Committee subtly let it be known that they had scheduled a press conference for 10 o'clock the next morning, which was fast approaching. In preparation for that meeting, they had two press releases printed up. One said, "The Organizing Committee announces with pride. . . ." The other, "The Organizing Committee announces with regret. . . ." The Organizing Committee was either going to have a completely agreed-upon contract, in detail, or they were going to call it off. And so, with no breaks, the meeting continued until just before the 10 o'clock cut-off time—twenty-five hours in all. Then, less than an hour before the scheduled press conference, the detailed agreement for $25 million was signed by all.

* * *

In contrast to the 1976 Summer Games, which had been awarded to Montreal as far back as 1971, the site of the 1976 Winter Games was not settled upon until late January to early February of 1973. Originally, the games had been awarded to Denver, Colorado, but environmentalists had forced the hand of the local Organizing Committee and the local government, mounting a successful campaign to vote down the bonds necessary for the building of facilities. In January 1973, the Denver Organizing Committee had relinquished their rights to the games, and the IOC was forced to find a site, posthaste.

With no time to spare, the IOC reversed the traditional roles and petitioned the obvious selection, Innsbruck. The Tyrolean city at the foot of the famed Brenner Pass which connected Northern Europe with the Mediterrean, the crossroads of Europe, had hosted the IX Winter Games in 1964 and retained most of the physical plant to host another. And so, without an Olympic Organizing Committee, Innsbruck was awarded the XII Olympic Games in 1976. In a rush-rush atmosphere, a committee had to be formed, a job as difficult as the scaling of the peaks surrounding the resort city. It took time to put together such an organization, and four months went by while one was being organized. During those four months, the three networks were also preparing to mount their attacks. NBC and CBS were determined not to be left standing at the starting gate on this one. But ABC, which had televised the 1964 Olympics from Innsbruck, found friends in the Olympic Organizing Committee. One of these. Dr. Klee, the secretary-general of the committee of the 1976 games, was their attorney during the 1964 games.

ABC's biggest problem came not in winning the television rights to the Innsbruck games, which they did with a bid of $10 million, using the exact contract they had used in Montreal, word for word, except for the dollar amount (outbidding both NBC and a surprisingly quiescent CBS) but in working out the intricate details for the coverage of the games. Having won their third Winter Olympics and their fifth in the last six of all Olympics televised, ABC immediately dedicated itself to the meticulous planning necessary for producing the finest technical and artistical games yet. Combining the knowledge they acquired in televising the 1964 Olympics at Innsbruck with their several "Wide World" dry runs, they were able to begin plotting their coverage of all thirty-seven events a full three years ahead of the actual games. Each Olympics had now become, in fact, a rehearsal for the next.

Their precise planning took the form of sending those in the trenches, the engineers, over to survey and resurvey each and every avenue. They left nothing to chance, investigating every possible camera position, camera angle, and lens. Local experts were even brought in to find out how a given course should be run in every climatic condition. But perhaps ABC's most ambitious act of preplanning was to persuade the Organizing Committee and the International Federations to stage what were billed as championships in ski jumping and downhill races at the very sites they would be run one year thereafter. While these championships were in reality dry runs for the Olympics, they gave ABC three full "Wide World of Sports" shows in the bargain.

Because of the complicated logistical problems involved, many meetings were held with the Austrian Organizing Committee to work out the details. At one such meeting, Roone Arledge was going over the camera positions, what ORT, the Austrian state-owned television network, would be responsible for and other items that had to be not only agreed upon, but acted upon for the production to work. As he went through page after page of extremely technical notes, he noticed that the head of the committee did not have an interpreter. He diplomatically suggested that such an addition would facilitate the meeting. "Oh, no," answered the proud Austrian, "I understand perfectly." Arledge, satisfied that the complicated instructions he was reading were being understood, returned to his note pad. Finally, after a session lasting over four hours, the Austrian stood up, stretched, and looked at his watch. "I see, by looking at my watch," he said as he moved to the door, "that it is time to say 'Hello'."

The planning wasn't restricted to the site of the Olympics alone: it was taking place back in New York as well. And once again the man in charge of much of the nuts and bolts preparation pursuant to Arledge's instructions was Julie Barnathan, a veteran of twenty-three years of service with ABC. Barnathan is one of those anomalies in the clubby world of broadcasting who obviously didn't get where he is because of his Ivy League ties or the cut of his clothes. This product of Brooklyn College, who wrote his doctoral thesis on the probabilities of dice and looks like his clothes wear him as much as he them, climbed the ladder on ability alone. Joining ABC as a researcher in 1954, "one month after Walt Disney went on the air," he became director of research in 1957. Thereafter, he touched every facet of ABC's operations, becoming, in turn, vice-president in charge of Affiliated Stations, president of Owned & Operated Stations, vice-president–general manager of the Network, and in 1965, vice-president in charge of Broadcast Operations and Engineering.

Barnathan is an energetic and feisty man of swarthy complexion whose strong and compact no-neck frame gave him the appearance of the bottom man on a human pyramid. During one of the strikes by ABC's engineers, Barnathan went out on the street to talk to his men to explain what the issues were and should be. The union refused to negotiate until Barnathan stopped talking to the men and even dressed up one of the pickets in a gorilla suit with the sign "Barnathan" hanging around his neck. A no-nonsense guy, he is as quick to tell a story on himself as on anyone else and accentuates his story-telling with cackling laughter, continual hand movement, and an affable smile. One of his associates remembers Barnathan animatedly poking Jack Kennedy in the chest to emphasize one of his points about the Kennedy-Nixon debates at the 1961 National Association of Broadcasters Convention in Washington, while secret service men stood there aghast. Throughout his career he has approached every job and every man with the same lack of inhibition.

Barnathan had surveyed Innsbruck, both in 1964 and throughout the intervening years. He knew that "each event, each mountain, each length, and each environmental condition is different" and sculpted his plans to accommodate them all—and later Montreal. He designed the facilities for both cities, Innsbruck and Montreal, constructing a prefabricated production center in component parts, which he referred to as "a very large erector set." The production center was built in New York and crated and sent to Innsbruck to be set up. After Innsbruck, it would be dismantled and sent on to Montreal. The cable lines were calibrated and cut to the distance needed for the longest possible place from the center. Everything was precut and preset. Barnathan also organized the shipment of mobile units, the studios on wheels, so that they could be in Innsbruck in ample time for setting up. It was a masterful feat of organizing his landing troops and battle stations far in advance of actual D Day.

* * *

As D Day approached, 350 technical people landed at Innsbruck. They had to construct platforms, make sure the cabling—which had been laid the previous year before the ground froze and was covered with snow—was operative and could be linked into their cameras, and move cameras to positions by helicopter, snowcat, or carrier. In short, every run had to be precabled, prechecked, and preset for the events. And the technicians, "all pros," according to Barnathan, "have to know where the buttons are, they've got to know how the phones work, and where things go. It's a tremendous educational process that goes on up to three weeks before the games."

But as the countdown to the games continued, something else was happening on the home front: For the first time in their corporate history, ABC was winning the weekly Nielsen ratings race. For two straight weeks the network that had never even been number two had catapulted to the heady position of number one on the Neilsen charts on the basis of several sitcoms like "Happy Days" and "Welcome Back Kotter." And the momentum was growing, as they kept and then increased their weekly lead. They were on their own Mount Olympus.

But the Olympics, scheduled for twenty and a half hours in

prime time as far back as 1973, when the games were first acquired, now threatened not only that momentum, but their number one ranking as well. *Variety's* Frank Beermann, who covers ABC specifically and television generally, remembers "anybody who was out of sports being afraid they were going to lose momentum." The ABC executives were dying, not having expected to do that well in prime time in January. And now they were stuck with "these goddamn Olympics," which they were committed to, but had no faith in. Beermann remembers one of them, head in hands, telling him privately, "Jesus Christ, I hope it doesn't bomb!"

The shoe was on the other foot. Entertainment, which so badly needed sports to provide credibility to its faltering operation for so many years, was now afraid of it. Executives on the upper floors were telling those on the twenty-eighth floor that "nobody cares about winter sports in the United States." ABC was committed to almost thirty hours of prime time coverage over fourteen days to esoteric sports that, in their mind's eye, didn't appeal to almost three quarters of the country, particularly the populous Sun Belt, with no identifiable athletes with whom viewers could relate. They were, in the words of one of those in Entertainment, "scared shitless." Everything they had ever worked for—becoming number one in programming—was "in danger of going down the crappers." The pressure on the twenty-eighth floor was tremendous, magnified by an article by John O'Connor in *The New York Times* the day before the opening of the Innsbruck games chiding ABC for sacrificing their recently won top ratings.

Accepting the tremendous pressure, the sports department was up for what they called "The Winters," as opposed to "The Olympics," which refers to summer Olympics. Coming off the Grenoble games, their last Winter Olympics, which were, in the words of Producer Doug Wilson, "flat and lackluster, without the sparkle, the excitement, and the vitality" ABC Sports was capable of, they had returned to the spot of one of their greatest triumphs, where they had pioneered in Olympic coverage back in 1964. This time they were determined.

For some, Innsbruck was a chance to show everyone, particularly ABC Entertainment, just how good ABC Sports really was. To others, it was a challenge to technically surpass their first Olympics and to make winter sports as fascinating, interesting, and exciting as any other sports. And for some, like Doug Wilson, it was an opportunity to show just how far both they and ABC Sports had come in a dozen years. "The first thing I did in 1976 when I went back," Wilson remembers, "was to go into the basement of the Ice Stadium, where I had spent fifteen days without sleep and food in a Stalag 17 atmosphere, complete with one bare light bulb and three antiquated billiard tables, open the door, and spit on the floor." Now Wilson was ready to surpass his previous efforts. All were. And all succeeded.

From the very moment the cameras swooped down over the Tyrolean Alps in a *Sound of Music* opening shot of mountain upon mountain, accompanied by the "Olympic Fanfare," the official ABC Sports Olympic theme excerpted from "Bugler's Dream" and used since Innsbruck, the 1976 Winter Games were a smashing artistic success. The camera work was raised almost to the level of an artform. Roone Arledge had determined that the downhill, a straight race down the mountainside, could be covered from the side, with the perspective and feel for the event preserved. However, the same angle would not provide proper perspective for the slalom. *Slalom*, a Norwegian word for "turn," pits a skier against the elements, himself, and seventy gates. In order to capture this challenging sport from start to finish, Arledge positioned fourteen cameras from the top of the hill to the bottom, including a camera with an 18–1 zoom lens, one of the longest lenses imaginable on a zoom basis, from across the twin mountains of Axamer-Lizum to catch all of the action. For events on the other mountain face or at Patcherkopel, the camera with the telephoto lens would be airlifted by helicopter. For the first time you saw all the events from start to finish, including Franz Klammer winning the Downhill in dramatic fashion, beating the Swiss gold medalist of 1972, Bernhard Russi, by only .33 of a second. It was sensational enough to inspire Jim McKay, sitting up in his announce position, to add, "It's something that should not go unnoticed a second time," when telling everyone that Klammer's gold medal run would be repeated on tape the next night.

Klammer's heroics were followed by more of the same by Rosi Mittemaier, who won two gold medals and barely lost the third instead winning a silver. When the home town crowd, cheered her wildly at the finish of the third race, ignoring the skier who had won the race, someone in the crowd handed her a bouquet of tulips. Mittemaier took a single tulip from the bunch and presented it to the gold medal winner, Kathy Kreiner of Canada, in a gesture of graciousness and sportsmanship that is the raison d'être of the Olympics. In one poignant moment, captured by ABC, she said it all.

Mittemaier, Sheila Young, and Dorothy Hamill embodied the coming out of the woman athlete in the Olympic Games. It showed in the ratings, as ABC averaged a 35 share (34 on prime time), better than the entertainment fare they had replaced. And for the first time in sports history, the majority of the audience watching a sporting event were women.

ABC also didn't suffer from the fact that the United States, which went in with no identifiable performers—with the possible exception of Dorothy Hamill, who was expected to finish behind the favored skater Deanne de Leeuw of the Netherlands—won eight medals in the first nine days of coverage, including the first one ever in Nordic cross-country skiing by twenty-year-old Bill Koch of Guilford, Vermont.

It was a magnificent event for ABC, the most significant one in their history of Olympic coverage as they once again reestablished their place in the hearts of the viewers and in the minds of the executives of ABC. Particularly those who doubted that a Winter Olympics without identifiable American athletes, without sports that appealed to the majority of the country, and against the other two networks' regular prime time programming could carry the day. ABC Sports handed Entertainment back its programming with the number one position well entrenched.

McCann-Erickson reviewed ABC's performance in the following terms: "The 1976 Winter Olympics from Innsbruck, Austria . . . were probably the best sustained telecasts of a sports event in the history of television. . . . ABC's coverage ran to virtual perfection." They had their gold.

* * *

It's impossible to remember the 1976 Montreal Olympics without remembering the TV coverage of the games in what has now become a TV Olympiad. Shots of the little nymphet Nadia Comaneci; America's Clark Kent, Bruce Jenner; the mustachioed and wet John Naber; Princess Anne and her horse, Goodwill, going down over a hurdle; Alberto Juantoreno becoming the "World's Fastest Human"; Edwin Moses and Mike Shine, finishing one-two in the 400-meter hurdles, or sticks as they're called in the track and field world, with their arms wrapped around each other; and five American gold medalist boxers, all interwoven into a mosaic that served as a magnificent showcase for them—and ABC television. They converted a whole new "Jenneration" to the leap year spectacle known as the Olympics.

Just as John Naber had "no regrets about spending seven years of my life training" for his four gold medals, claiming, "It's worth it," so, too, was ABC's three-year preparation for the coverage of the Montreal Olympics.

Those preparations had included the expertise of Julie Barnathan, the skill of Roone Arledge, and the efforts of over five hundred ABC people who had worked up to eighteen hours a day for the seventeen days of the games and months beforehand—over 100,000 man-hours for the seventy-five hours of air time, almost 1,500 man-hours for every one hour on air.

Fully a year before the start of the Olympics, July 17, 1976, two film crews had gone around the world shooting the vignettes that would appear as "Up Close and Personals" on the athletes in the games. They were, as one of the producers, Brice Weisman, called them, "the face on the other side of the gold medal, the human being." When they were brought back to New York and edited to an approximate two-and-a-half minutes, with music put behind them, they would be brought into a studio in New York and Jim McKay would take a look at them and then write up his narration for later recording. There were seventy of them for the Montreal games and McKay recorded ten or eleven a day for a full week, serving as his own editor and copy editor, something akin to devouring one's own young. But McKay's newspaper background served him well, as he rapidly wrote each one in longhand on foolscap paper, working quickly, yet precisely, to fit his words into the picture and time frame allowed.

Over a year before the Olympics, Arledge had commissioned Peter Diamond to put together what amounted to an Olympics *Playbook,* something that included a personal and achievement profile on every one of the over 8,000 competitors. The *Playbook* not only became the bible of the Olympics for the ABC staff, but its possession was as zealously guarded as were a maiden's worldly goods.

As the time for the Olympics neared, each of the ABC announcers was fitted for his banana-yellow ABC blazer, with the Olympic patch sewn on its pocket, trading in the turtlenecks of Innsbruck. The personnel would almost be the same as appeared in Innsbruck and in Munich. Jim McKay would serve in the capacity of ringmaster, trying to make one story out of twenty-one different sports: Keith Jackson with O. J. Simpson would cover track and field; Mark Spitz, the swimming; Frank Gifford would do the wrestling, the rowing, and the marathon bicycle race; Bob Beattie, the weight lifting; Chris Schenkel with Bill Steinkraus, the equestrian events; Gordon Maddux and Kathy Rigby Mason, the gymnastics; Howard Cosell, the boxing; Bill Flemming, assisted by expert commentator Mickey King Hough, the diving competition; Bill Russell and Curt Gowdy, the basketball competition. And Pierre Salinger would gadfly around Montreal for local color.

One on-camera performer who wouldn't be clothed in a jacket was LeRoy Neiman, who had sketched the Munich Olympics for ABC and become incensed when Peter Jennings introduced him as "the famous sports artist who's going to be working with us throughout these games, LeRoy Seamon." Neiman had come off-camera sputtering, "Did you hear what that fuckin' phony called me? What are my friends in America going to say? What am I going to do? How can I go back to my country?" Now, he wanted to do a large eight-by-twelve-foot mural of the games and approached the man he calls "the Redhead," Roone Arledge, to propose it. "Great idea! let's do it," was all Arledge said, coming to an immediate decision and Neiman became a salaried celebrity announcer, receiving a contract which called for exactly what Bill Russell, Mark Spitz, and other celebrity commentators received.

The members of the production staff also had their battle stations. Dennis Lewin was to be the producer of the gymnastics; Chet Forte, the swimming; Chuck Howard, the track and field and the opening and closing ceremonies. Howard also served as second in command to Arledge. It was hard to tell where everybody went without a scorecard.

But one thing you could be sure of—Roone Arledge would sit in the "chair" overseeing all of the activities, the thirty-two monitors, and a myriad of problems. He was there at 2:30 P.M. on Saturday, July 17, as the XXI Olympic Games began with the lighting of the torch, for the first of 73¼ hours of coverage, the most ever devoted to what seemed to be part of ABC's permanent programming.

The CBC studios given over to the ABC team were originally the International Broadcasting Center for Expo, then the facilities for the French Broadcasting Division, located near the old soccer stadium and equidistant from the Holiday Inn Hotel, where they were staying, and the Olympic Village. Seated in the glass booth overlooking the floor area were Jim McKay, Arledge, an AD on the headset with New York, timing everything, Don Ohlmeyer, who was the studio director, a technical director, an audio man, and occasionally Lewin, Howard, and others. There was also another glass booth for clients and celebrities, which the Kennedy family made frequent use of. Off to McKay's right, approximately six feet away from him, was Neiman, who was continually cued by McKay, "LeRoy, we may come to you." But invariably something would happen somewhere else and Neiman, always ready with his cigar in his mouth, would disappointedly go back to painting the Olympic mural. Working diligently at his oversized mural, Neiman finally finished in tandem with the ending of the games. As it hung proudly on the wall, Frank Gifford marched into the central broadcasting area and espied the multicolored painting. "What happened?" he asked Jim McKay. "Did the pizza factory blow up?"

McKay was constantly being fed stats and stories by Diamond and another young PA in the studio and was receiving input from Arledge and others as to what was coming up. Several times during the next seventeen days he would punctuate an event with a comment like "The Marathon Bicycle Race is 180 kilometers, approximately the distance of the train I often take between New York and Philadelphia" to put distances and records in perspective. But most of the time it was his task to throw the coverage to another venue or to bridge the events with an introduction to a station break or commercial, which ran like strings of pearls for such sponsors as Burger King, Coke, and Chevrolet, all specially made for the Olympics and costing $72,000 a minute.

But the hub of activity and the overall coordinator was Arledge. Everything went through him, and as one of his producers said, "Roone's the man. His word's final." Arledge would be confronted by a multitude of decisions and would turn to his producers to give him some input on what was important at that moment. Should he go to swimming, track, the fight, gymnastics or hold it? Added to this was the timing element; Did he have too much or not enough material? One of them, Chuck Howard, would call him and say, "Roone, here's what I've got. . . ." And then in response to the inevitable query, "How good is it?" Howard would respond, "I think that on a scale of 10 that the first one is 8.5 and the second one, 9.5. I think that if we have a time problem, this is what we ought to cut out. . . . And if you're short the other way, I have an eight minute segment. . . ." It was madness, but Arledge, as usual, had a method to it. His judgments were instantaneous and instinctively correct.

On one occasion the power on the Toronto-to-Buffalo leg of the line to New York was lost for nine minutes. Six minutes were filled with those ever-present fillers called commercials. The other three minutes were covered in part by feature material prepared for just such an exigency. During the power failure, Barnathan came up to Arledge and said, "Roone, there's a problem," meaning there was a problem with the whole system. It wasn't just ABC who was out—it was everybody. Arledge, cool in the eye of a storm, then threw on his IFB mike to

McKay and said, "Jim, I just want you to know that the vice-president in charge of Broadcast Operations and Engineering has just advised me that there is a problem!"

There were people constantly submitting creative ideas and tapes to the afternoon's activities for him to look at. He'd look at everything, weigh it, and allot time. But there was always something that came up unannounced, and Arledge would strike the previous schedule and go directly to the happening, leaving in his wake several unused segments and several disappointed people who had perhaps stayed up all night working on the little "three or five minutes bit" that had just been jettisoned.

The man sitting to Roone's right was director Don Ohlmeyer, a thirty-year-old producer-director who had come to ABC directly from Notre Dame in 1967 and worked his way up in the traditional go-fer-to-PA-to-AD-to-director-to-producer fashion. Ohlmeyer had been found in one of those classic right-place-at-the-right-time scenarios that would make a Hollywood picture; he was playing pool at the Notre Dame Student Union when he was joined by another graduate from Notre Dame who just happened to be an ABC unit manager. As pool talk changed into shop talk, the unit manager–friend asked him why he didn't "come over and serve as a go-fer for the weekend" for the upcoming Notre Dame–Purdue football game. Ohlmeyer threw in his cue stick immediately. After two more stints as a go-fer, ABC called him up and offered him a job in New York as a PA. Eleven months later he traded in his PA stripe for an associate director's epaulet. Eight months later he became a director. By 1972 he was the producer of "Monday Night Football," and in 1980 he will be NBC's "chair," joining the red and blue N network to oversee the Moscow Olympics.

In a takeoff on the old army bromide, anything that moved was taped. And as the crunch of tapes came into the control center from every venue, somebody had to allocate the proper editing facilities and arrange the necessary priorities. That somebody was Ohlmeyer, who constantly juggled the twelve tape machines and two people working them to come up with the tapes in time for their inclusion in the broadcast every night. But it was not merely Ohlmeyer's orchestration of the machines alone that brought order out of chaos—it was the two people who handled them, associate directors Joe Aceti and Carol Lehti. The twosome, who sound like a vaudeville dance act, "really got us through the Olympics," in the words of Chuck Howard. But editing was not without its problems. The problem that occurred most frequently was one that the colorful Aceti termed for all time, "the bat," as in "hit with the bat." It signified a sudden change in the order of the tapes commanded by God-knows-who in the tape room. The rearranging would invariably precipitate a mad scrambling of tapes and a different piece of tape would mysteriously appear on the machine as Aceti and Lehti scrambled *ABCDEF* to become *ABDECG* in under a minute. They were hit with so many "bats" during the games that they became known as Hillerich & Bradsby, in honor of the famous bat manufacturer.

Nicknames weren't confined to the control room. They also pervaded the events themselves. Howard Cosell, whose hobby seems to be giving nicknames to everyone around him—Giff for Gifford, Danderoo for Meredith, and Dendoo for Dennis Lewin—had applied his own verbal shorthand to the events. The oars were rowing, the blades stood for fencing, the sticks for field hockey, the wheels was bicycling, the gloves was boxing, and so on down the line, putting into succinct words every symbol used by the Olympics for each and every event. As Gifford came up to complain to Cosell, "I don't know what I'm doing here," Cosell would reply, "For Christ sake, you're on the paddles." Gifford would shrug and tell Cosell and his wife, Emmy, "I don't know anything about the paddles."

Cosell was back in form. During the Innsbruck games he had stayed behind, serving as a visiting lecturer on the Yale faculty for the spring semester, one of the few such offers he had accepted. He had turned down several other endowed chairs "open to distinguished men and women in a variety of fields with an inter-disciplinary outlook and interest in their professional endeavors." But Cosell was forever a teacher, and at Montreal his willing pupil was O. J. Simpson. Everywhere

Howard went, OJ was sure to follow. It seemed that whenever Cosell would stop to sign autographs, OJ would also stop to sign. Howard would look at his watch, put his everpresent cigar in his mouth, and say, "OK, OJ, let's go." Cosell, the instructor, has said, "No reporter is better than his connections." Now he had formed one with an almost invisible umbilical cord.

Cosell's office wall bears a signed Olympic poster from the 1972 Olympic boxing team, signed "in appreciation" to the man they viewed as having been as much a part of their team as the eleven men themselves. But the 1972 team produced merely one gold medalist, Light Welterweight Ray Seales. Now, in 1976, as the final evening's program neared completion, it became apparent that the fighters representing the red, white, and blue would take away the lion's share of gold, silver, and bronze. Six finalists, as many as any team in Olympic history ever had in the final round, went in and five came out with gold—Randolph, Davis, Leonard, and the Spinks Brothers.

The five American gold medalists had given the bouts and the Olympics a meaning of their own. And Cosell had shared in their glory with his own enthusiasm. For once, the man who had been attacked by many after he championed and was identified with Muhammad Ali was now adored by the very same people who had once accused him of something less than Americanism. The mail came flooding into his New York office. Even one from the commandant of the Marine Corps, General Wilson, thanked him "on behalf of all Marines" for "taking time to include mention of the fact that Corporal Spinks is a United States Marine." Then General Wilson's letter went on "to add, moreover, that your own characteristically professional performance added greatly to the enjoyment of the evening."

But even with all the bouquets, Cosell still got brickbats, including one from *Chicago Tribune* columnist Gary Deeb. It seems that Cosell is sensitive years afterward, to everything written about him, particularly those reviews that are less than favorable. He recalls, word for word, Deeb's column. "Two days after I got back there was this column, 'Howard

Cosell should be muzzled and fired,' and carried in almost every newspaper in the country. How I was a superpatriot. . . . Didn't even talk about the fighters. Can you imagine doing a fight between amateur kids where you're saying the Polish fighter against the Soviet fighter?'' and here he injected three-syllabic names of two never-again heard-from fighters, "like it would have meaning for the American people?'' But Deeb did praise Arledge's presentation of the Olympics, even though each and every show closed with a shot of the American flag and Lou Rawls's infectious rendition of "America the Beautiful.'' It was pure jingoism and it worked.

Unlike Munich, where ABC had lost $1 million on their Olympic's coverage, they made over $1 million, partially on the allowance of $2 million by the organizing committee when ABC built its own facilities. But beyond the debits and credits, they capitalized on the prestige that comes with being associated with the Olympics. In the climate of summer reruns, they had dominated the ratings. The second week their seven nightly telecasts of the Summer Games captured the seven top spots on the Nielsen top ten show chart, delivering an average of seventeen million homes and over forty-two million viewers each night. Added to that, it carried ABC to a permanent first place victory in the year-long ratings race and supplied enough of a carryover to insure that the fall's new programs, hyped throughout the games, would receive sufficient sampling by the viewers. ABC Sports had once again pulled the network through as they had for sixteen years. They reigned once more as king of Mount Olympus.

As the XXI Olympics closed on a high note for American athletes and ABC, the electronic scoreboard at the far end of the stadium flashed "Moscow, 1980.'' Now the real "games'' would commence—the scramble to acquire the 1980 games.

* * *

In Paddy Chayefsky's *Network*, the Chairman of the Board Arthur Jensen delivers a pontification to his quasi-lucid newsman Howard Beale that goes: "What do you think the Russians talk about in their councils of state—Karl Marx? They pull out their linear programming charts, statistical decision theories, and minimax solutions like the good little systems analysts they are and compute the price-cost probabilities of their transactions and investments just like we do."

When the IOC awarded the 1980 Summer Games to Moscow in October 1974, it began a romantic tale of international suspense and backroom maneuvering that would have made the plotline of a great television soap opera, as three swains fluttered around the flame that was to ignite the torch in Moscow in August 1980. It was an old-fashioned potboiler with covert schemes made up of equal parts international intrigue and international monopoly in megabucks and megarubles that pitted the prototypical capitalist businessman against the archtypical Russian bureaucrat.

But the distinction between those two bastions of competitive economic systems sometimes blurred. For the communist bureaucrat was not substantially different from his capitalist counterpart in one respect, they both understood hard currency. Money has an importance to the Russians it doesn't have to the Western world; it is convertible currency necessary to their trade balance and to their economy. In a faint echo of *Ninotchka*, for a price they were willing to discard their Russian serge for Paris silks.

Representatives of ABC as well as those of the other two networks met with those who would have the most to do with awarding the U.S. television rights to exchange hellos and *preavets* in Vienna that October. It was to be the beginning of one of the longest and most determined romances in the history of television. One that would last over fifteen months and see the trio fly in and out of Moscow's Sheremetyvo Airport with the regularity of one of Henry Kissinger's shuttle diplomacy missions, bringing gifts to the doorstep of those they were pursuing, seeking their favors.

Some of those favors included ABC's dispatching its entire "A.M. America" show to Russia for a week of morning programming, CBS's packaging of the Bolshoi Ballet with Mary Tyler Moore serving as the insert embroidery to stitch together the special, and NBC's initiating a contract to broadcast the USSR Festival of Music and Dance.

Each of the three networks believed themselves to be worthy of the hand of the Organizing Committee. ABC considered itself to have the inside track on the basis of their excellent track record over six of the last eight Olympics and their continuing relationship with the Soviet Sports and Television committees through their "Wide World" coverage. CBS, which had not carried an Olympics since 1960, had the benediction of patriarchal William Paley, the aging founder-president of the fifty-year-old network, who saw the Olympics as something of a monument to himself. And NBC, the continual bridesmaid, suffered from the stuff dreams are made of, infatuation with and for an Olympics of their very own. It was to become an absorbing drama as all three pursued their desire—the 1980 Olympics.

But that pursuit was not without its problems. In the highly charged atmosphere of international relations, many voices were heard, including that of *TV Guide* which offered the three suitors advice: Don't allow the Olympics to become a propaganda forum. The dilemma was quite evident to those at ABC. If they merely presented the Olympics as they had previously, with up-close-and-personal profiles and scene sets, they would be accused of propagandizing. And if they ignored the ambience and the surroundings, they would leave themselves open to charges of poor production. Their plight of wooing and winning the rights was compounded by the problem of what those back home would say.

The reason for the romancing of the State Committee for Television and Radio and Moscow's Olympic Organizing Committee were two new rules promulgated by the IOC. These new regulations had come as a result of the furor NBC and CBS had raised after the Montreal rights were awarded to ABC and said, in effect, that no organizing committee could award television rights until the preceding Olympics had concluded and that all bids were to be made by a bidding procedure rather than by closed, unilateral offers. The favors of the Moscow Olympic Organizing Committee were for sale—at the right price.

A few of the American TV executives could speak Russian.

Hardly any could read it. But they all could drink it fluently. And they got their chance to do so on one of the last nights of the Montreal Olympics, when the Russians hosted a lavish, almost czarist, feast aboard their ship, the *Alexander Pushkin*, moored in St. Lawrence Harbor. The Pushkin party was by invitation only, but it clearly was a command performance, as bigwigs, including Arthur Taylor, president of CBS, flew up to Montreal. The eyes of the networks' executives reached the same distended proportions of their stomachs, crammed with Russian sturgeon, caviar, vodka, and cognac, when they heard the opening demand made by the Russians—$210 million, payable up front in cash. It was almost as indigestible as the rest of the lavish spread. Most knew it to be the opening gambit of a very long struggle, figuring it would settle somewhere in the neighborhood of $75 to $100 million. Still some neighborhood, but nearer lox than sturgeon.

After that first taste, the Russians threw in one more demand as food for thought. Not discerning the difference between news and propaganda, they suggested, as subtly as a Russian tank attack on a small village, that the Olympic carrier show Russia in a favorable light. The Americans choked over the request and returned home to consider their next moves.

* * *

But in spite of the overt romancing by the three networks, one of them had a matchmaker as effective as any since Dolly Levi Gallagher. His name was Lothar Bock, and he was one of those many men who surface every four years on the scent of big money and run with the hounds and the hares in pursuit of it. Others like Samuel Pisar, Sargent Shriver, and Marvin Josephson, had attempted to sell their services and their influence, but none was as successful in what was fast becoming not only an Olympic "Who's Who," but an Olympic "Who Knows Who" as Bock.

Bock is a thirty-eight-year-old self-described impresario, who makes his headquarters in the show business community of Munich and his hindquarters in Moscow almost as much. A smallish man who sports long hair, speaks in clipped English, and wears an ingratiating smile, Bock is a charmer, described by some who've dealt with him as a "straightforward-seeming guy who is very intelligent." Others have described him as a sort of "German Sammy Glick." His foundation with the Russians seems to have been built on the fact that they can trust him because he stayed with a bad deal for a long time, the importation of several cultural shows into Western Europe on which he lost $50,000. They "trusted his endurance and persistence," said one network official who dealt with him.

But this story of trust and credibility of those stateside is not universal. Several of those in the emigre community of Munich attribute his comings and goings into Moscow to the fact that, alternately stated, either he and/or his wife, Ingrid, are single, double, or triple agents; choose one of the above.

Bock's ready access to the Soviet Government is rumored to have grown out of a contact of his wife's, Vladimir Golovin, a Deputy Minister of Culture. Whether the contact with Golovin social, romantic, or ideological is not known: But what is known is that it provided Bock with an entree that he exploited to the fullest. Moreover, among the producers and money people in the movie community that thrives in Munich, Bock's reputation is somewhat tarnished. Depending upon whom you speak to, you get everything from his having suffered financial problems to bankruptcy. But Bock smilingly denies all of this. And well he might. For from May 15, 1975 on, he no longer had to worry about his background; it was his future that mattered. And the future of the network that tied their wagon to his Soviet-directed star.

On that May day in 1975, Bock came to see film producer Bud Greenspan at his Madison Avenue offices. Greenspan had gotten to know Bock the previous year when he was over in Munich filming his ten-part series, "The Olympiad." A 20th Century Fox representative had mentioned Bock's name as someone who could be "very important in opening up East European countries." Greenspan found that Bock could "do everything they said he could" and became immediately Bock's American connection. Now as Bock resignedly fell into one of Greenspan's soft office chairs, he was disappointed he hadn't been "able to see people." The people he was referring to were the network programming heads he wanted to sell properties he represented to, including the Bolshoi Ballet and the Moscow Circus. Between his lamentations Bock idly asked Greenspan, "What are all the Americans doing in Moscow?" Greenspan told him he thought they were trying to get the rights to the Olympics. "Oh," said the suddenly alert Bock, "I could help them," and he proceeded to rattle off the names of Russians who were the "same people who gave me the Bolshoi Ballet." Everyone of them was recognizable to Greenspan as those in charge of also bestowing the rights to the 1980 Olympics.

Greenspan grabbed the telephone, "That's the way to get the Bolshoi Ballet on the air." He called the sports head of all three networks—Arledge at ABC, Chet Simmons at NBC, and Bob Wussler at CBS. Simmons was out of town. Arledge characteristically never returned his call. Only Wussler did. Greenspan told him, "If you're really serious about the Olympic Games, here's the man." Wussler, as head of CBS Sports, was quick to see the wisdom in allying his network with Bock, and just as quick to sign him personally to a six-figure contract, ostensibly for a Bolshoi Ballet show.

Nothing any of the three networks had done up to that point, or would do from then on, would further their cause any more than that one phone call. He was to serve as chaperon, matchmaker, and duenna to the Russians and ultimately guide their choice. He was the man of whom the Russians were to say to CBS, "All American TV networks are bad; you are less bad because you have Lothar Bock."

* * *

As the first flakes of snow started to descend on Red Square, planeload after planeload of network executives started to descend on Moscow. They had already made their preliminary bids in early September—CBS came in with the high bid of $71 million, ABC matched them and NBC followed closely with $70. But now they were attempting to add leverage to those inanimate pieces of paper by personally pleading their causes.

One of those who came to Moscow was William Paley himself, who flew in to meet with the chairman of the Organizing

Committee, Ignati Novikov, in early November. Once before CBS had been close to closing the deal, but just prior to President Arthur Taylor's going over to endorse the terms Novikov and Bock had worked out, he had been fired. Firings, like purges, don't sit too well with the Russians, who understand their meaning all too well. And so it was now up to Paley himself to turn the red tide in his network's favor. After two days of head-to-head meetings between Paley and Novikov—the two venerable heads of the two divergent systems they represented—an agreement was reached. There was a firm handshake and a memorandum initialed by both. Contained within the memorandum was a "topper" contract, giving CBS the right to top the highest bid of either of the other networks by $1 million.

All that was needed was to prepare and sign the formal agreement. Although all business in American television is done with a handshake, the Russians place absolute faith only in the printed word. Not merely memoranda, but long, involved printed documents the size of the Magna Charta. But memorandum or long contract, Paley felt that his agreement with Novikov was an absolute bond.

* * *

And so, on December 8, when CBS, as well as ABC and NBC, received detailed bidding instructions from Moscow pursuant to the IOC rule, they were positive it was going to be merely a charade. They would go over and take their place, believing that the deal was firm. The Russians entertained no such idea, planning instead a surprise party consisting of Russian roulette to commence on December 17 in Moscow between the three networks.

ABC's contingent was Roone Arledge, Jim Spence (vice-president in charge of Sports Planning), John Martin (vice-president of Program Development and Assistant to the President), Chuck Smiley (vice-president of Legal and Business Affairs). They were joined there by Georges Croses, vice-president of European Affairs. All were housed, together with CBS, at the Sovietskaya Hotel, an old Guard's Palace with thick and formidable walls. Many thought that their sitting room accommodations were bugged, and consequently informal meetings were continually held in the corridors. Every now and then one of the executives from one of the networks would stand up on a chair near a vent or a light and scream, "Let me repeat that in case you missed it the first time."

The Russians held daylong meetings with each of the three networks. In each meeting the executives were told the new ground rules. Arledge, Spence, Martin, Smiley, and Croses were told that they would have to pay $50 million up front for the acquisition of new equipment, the mere ticket to the ball to get into the bidding. Then, the Russians, as is their wont, again changed the ground rules and informed them that it would be $50 million over two years—$20 million in 1977 and $30 million the year after. Then again they changed, saying that the networks could supply equipment instead of cash. Then it was no, cash only. And so it went. The capricious and fickle Russians were making the chase all the harder. And everybody was getting the idea that they were being jerked around.

Then the Russians dropped the other shoe. There would be a continuing auction of the rights, with a series of sealed bids submitted every twenty-four hours until only one was left standing. There was also a "kicker." Any loser could get back in by coming up with at least 5 percent more than the previous so-called winning bid, ad nauseam. Arledge analogized it to three scorpions fighting in a bottle, with the two losers "dead and the winner exhausted."

But none was more nauseous than CBS's Wussler. He had come to Moscow certain that he had the rights and now was told he had to participate in a suicidal auction. He requested a private meeting with Novikov during which he produced a letter from Paley reminding him that he had a commitment. Novikov only answered: "It's a pity."

That night the Russians threw a lavish bash in the lobby of the Sovietskaya, calling all three heads of the delegations together like Roman gladiators in a salute to those who seemed about to die. Novikov advanced to the middle of the floor with a vodka bottle in one hand and a glass in the other. Bob Howard, president of NBC, Wussler, and Arledge all tentatively advanced to the center of the floor. Novikov then poured each a glassful of vodka and raised it for a toast.

Wussler whispered, "I wish I had a photographer," but the rest thought it was too degrading to even remember, let alone photograph. Whatever else it did, it gave the three combatants a rebellious spark of life; something the Russians hadn't expected.

Minutes after the Russians had tried to apply Darwin's theory to Olympic bidding, Wussler approached Jim Spence and tugged at his sleeve to get his attention. Spence, in conversation with someone else, excused himself. Wussler asked him to join him in the corner to discuss something. Unbeknownst to ABC, that afternoon after hearing the bad news from Novikov, Wussler had called Jack Schneider, the corporate president of CBS at his home in Greenwich, Connecticut, to fill him in on the details and to broach the subject of setting up a multinetwork pool; something that hadn't been done in sports since the first Super Bowl game. Spence told Arledge something was up and both Arledge and Spence adjourned to the corner along with Wussler and Al Rush, NBC's chief Olympic negotiator.

The subject matter of the confab was pooling. Wussler told them that he had already discussed the idea with Schneider and that CBS was in favor of it. But that was "now." ABC had once been opposed to such a pool while CBS and NBC had been for it. Then CBS, thinking they had the Olympics, was against it. It all depended on who for that moment thought they had the best shot. The haves were rarely in favor of a pool, the have-nots ardently embraced it.

Arledge looked over at Wussler and giving him one of those "Is-you-is-or-is-you-ain't" looks, said, "Bob, don't give me any bullshit now. Are you in this thing or are you not? You were in favor, then you were opposed, and now you are saying you're in favor of it." Arledge's spinal tap seemed to work. Wussler said, "I've got to make some calls, but I'll call you by one o'clock and let you know for sure." Wussler thereupon left the so-called party and went back up to his room in the Sovietskaya to call Schneider and tell him about the three-way conversation and to get the go-ahead. At 1:30 A.M. Moscow time, 6:30 P.M. New York time, he came back down. "Yep, it's all done!" Confronted with a fait accompli, although he still thought he could win it all, Arledge agreed to pull out and form a united front with the other networks.

What was "all done" had been a conference call linking the spokesmen of the three networks: NBC General Counsel Corey Dunham, Elton Rule, president of ABC and Jack Schneider of CBS. For forty-five minutes the three network representatives dickered over how to proceed, or in the words of that old limerick, "Who was to do what and to whom." Finally, after many "whereases" and other contingencies, Rule cut through the bullshit and said, "Well, if we're going to pull out, we're going to pull out. Why don't we just have a verbal handshake over the phone and forget all the covenants." Schneider replied "All right," and Dunham concurred. It was agreed that the three networks would pool their facilities and petition the Justice Department for a dispensation from the antitrust laws to form a pool for the 1980 Olympics.

And so the cocktail party that had started with the three gladiators saluting each other on their supposed death struggle, became instead the rallying point for the three networks to tell the Soviets what they could do with their Olympics. Now it was the Soviet's turn in the barrel.

As a postscript to the Americans stealing a page from the Russian's diplomatic book of tricks and walking out during the negotiations, Novikov panicked. First he told all of them that if they walked out they wouldn't be allowed back in. Then, he met with Arledge, at a meeting arranged the day before, and told him that if he wanted the Olympics all he had to do was "sign the dotted line." But Arledge was bound, both by his agreement and by his network's. Finally, as a face-saver, Novikov turned to a fourth group that had been represented in Moscow, the Soviet-American Trade Association, known as Satra. And eight days later they announced that they had signed a protocol agreement giving them the rights, an agreement that only awaited the IOC's ratification—that would never come.

ABC had earlier bid $33.3 million, based on a pooled effort. If a pool was arranged, with like rights for each of the three networks, ABC believed it would benefit from its past record, with many viewers turning to ABC as the "Network of the

Olympics." But now it refrained from going back with any bid, in light of its agreement. Then two days after the pullout, ABC picked up disturbing information from its spy network, a network peopled by Slovaks, Russians, and many other nationalities. According to their information, during the joint evacuation, Lothar Bock had been in Moscow and continued the courtship, negotiating with the Russians. Moreover, ABC was informed that he was negotiating in CBS's name. ABC had caught CBS with their hand in the proverbial cookie jar.

While Lothar Bock was calling Wussler and telling him that "the Games are yours if you want," having obtained a letter from Novikov giving them to Bock's principal for $82 million, ABC was also calling Wussler, telling him to call Bock off. Either repudiate him or acknowledge his activities in your behalf. When Wussler denied that Bock was acting on behalf of CBS, Arledge demanded a letter be sent to that effect either directly to Bock or to the Russian Organizing Committee or at the very least to ABC. The implication was very clear: Make a clean breast of it and admit your wrongdoing.

Faced with disappointment after disappointment, including contract repudiations, ground rule changes, insulting and demeaning behavior by the Russians, and now this, CBS decided in an all-day meeting to throw in the towel. In a statement dated January 25, CBS announced their withdrawal from the pool, attributing it to "many imponderables." Now it was every man for himself.

Lothar Bock, the man who had kept his hand in the pot throughout the negotiations, now stirred again. After a full twenty months of courting the Russians, he finally had the Olympics and his sponsor was pulling out. He sought a new one. After gaining his release from his contract with CBS—as well as $140,000 as part of a settlement by CBS, even though they were under no obligation to do so, and were sarcastically charged by one congressman with being "the biggest tipper of all time"—he approached NBC the very next day and offered them the Olympics, lock, stock, and television rights. The network that was never really in the picture until Bock focused them in on the Olympics bit and immediately signed him to a $1 million finder's fee contract plus a guarantee to buy three shows a year from him over the next five years. Within a day after the signing and two days after CBS pulled out, Bock was on his way back to Moscow. This time he carried the NBC banner.

Knowing full well that Bock had aligned himself with NBC and was enroute back to Moscow with more than just love, Arledge hurriedly made preparations to return to Moscow that very weekend to hopefully pick up the pieces. It had become a game just as deadly as any concocted by Agatha Christie as now only two remained.

But even as the airplane filled with ABC executives was airborne, Bock had delivered. First announced on Sunday, January 30, 1977, by NBC, it evoked immediate denials from the Russians, who claimed "the rights are still open." However, they had also sent a wire to Paris cordially disinviting the ABC contingent. But ABC was already on its way, hoping to snatch victory from the jaws of defeat.

In fact, Georges Croses had already arrived and met the IOC Executive Secretary Monique Berlioux at the airport upon her arrival from Lausanne, as she sped to Moscow to provide a benediction over the shotgun marriage of NBC and the Moscow Organizing Committee. Croses intimated strongly that ABC would even go higher than the $82 million Bock and the Russians had settled on. Madame Berlioux immediately sent a telegram to Lord Killian stating that they should make sure the Russians were getting "as much as they can," especially in light of the fact that ABC would go even higher. The Russians did get as much as they could, eking out another $3 million from NBC rather than going back to ABC. The home court advantage belonged to Bock's team even though ABC was there ready, willing, and able to pay at least that.

And so, on Tuesday, February 1, 1977, a formal contract was signed with the two stern septagenarian bureaucrats straight out of central casting, Sergei Lapin of the State Committee for Television and Radio and Ignati Novikov of the Olympics Organizing Committee, signing for Russia and Bob Howard of NBC signing for the network. It was approved on the spot by Madame Berlioux. The provisions included clauses for the payment of $85 million by NBC, with $50 million for the "technical aspects of broadcasting," the remaining $35 million for rights—to be split between the Moscow Organizing Committee and the IOC, $22.4 million and $12.6 million respectively. The $85 million is to be paid in progressive payments over the next three years, all in advance of the start of the Olympics. NBC, which was paying more than three times its entire sports budget just ten years before, had an option of supplying television cameras in lieu of a portion of the $50 million, which were adaptable to the Russian "secam" system. It was an arragement similar to what they had worked out with the Nebraska Educational Television Network for their infringement of their N just a year earlier. And finally, the contract provided that no matter how many countries pulled out, so long as the U.S.A. and the USSR still participate, it is a valid and enforceable contract.

But the most intriguing portions of the contract are not what it said but what it didn't say. For nowhere in it are there any provisions demanding or suggesting that NBC show the Olympics in a "favorable light." Conversely, there is no clause giving NBC the right of approval over what goes out over the airwaves before the Russians "pull the plug." This omission some NBC executives feel is based on an intangible known as trust, an unenforceable bond anywhere in the world, but particularly in the context of a contractual agreement between an American corporation and the Soviet bureaucracy.

The biggest event in United States television history was over and the media had indeed become the message. The acquisition of the rights to the Olympics was a media event unto themselves. NBC had committed to paying more than 154 times the amount paid for the rights to the 1960 Rome Olympics, even measured by the fact that $85 million in January 1977 would be worth "only $64.1 million in 1980 dollars."

For ABC it was a tremendous disappointment. One of their executives said, "The best thing we could have done was to get the Olympics; the next best thing was not to get them." Editorials in several papers throughout the country echoed the sentiments of ABC President Fred Pierce, who said, "We deeply regret that the American viewing public will be deprived of the experience and expertise gained by ABC Sports in televising six of the last seven games." One paper, the Morris County, New Jersey, *Daily Record* bemoaned their loss by writing, "The worst part of NBC's questionable coup is that we will no longer be treated to ABC's superb coverage of the quadrennial event. An Olympics without ABC Sports President Roone Arledge at the helm and Jim McKay in the broadcast booth is as bleak a prospect as the Miss America Pageant without Bert Parks." And the Chicago *Daily News* wrote, "Such popularity as the games do enjoy is based solidly on the superb job American Broadcasting Company has done. Based on ABC's past coverage, Moscow and the Russians need ABC more than ABC needs the Olympic Games." But perhaps Jim McKay, as usual, put it all into its proper perspective: "If there is an Olympics to miss, it's Moscow."

* * *

But if the event-getting of the networks is part of the story, the escalation of the price is the other. The Summer Olympics' costs had soared an incredible 154 times since 1960. But the Winter Olympics had escalated an even more astounding 310 times.

Despite the loss of the Summer Games to NBC, ABC has the Winter Games in Lake Placid, New York, to look forward to and to supersede their award-winning coverage of the Innsbruck games of 1976.

ABC had originally approached the Lake Placid Organizing Committee early in 1976 through their comrade-in-mikes Art Devlin. Devlin not only worked for ABC but had also worked for NBC. There was no outright collusion involved, but perhaps a small amount of favoritism.

NBC had also shown interest in acquiring the games, but it was minimal. They had sent executives up to Lake Placid dressed in business suits to make a survey in the snow. It was like Calvin Coolidge showing up to pitch hay in his patent leather shoes and as patently ridiculous to those members of the Organizing Committee who couldn't believe what they were watching. On the other hand, ABC went after the games "balls-out" and acquired the U.S. and Canadian rights on

February 13, 1976, for $10 million before any of the other networks had even bid.

The contract came to light when one of the members of the Organizing Committee walked into the offices of the editor of the local weekly and told him "the TV contract's out in my car. It's not locked and if you happen to take it out of my car, I'd never tell." The editor not only found the contract, he found that the bid had been made without any competitive bids from CBS or NBC—shades of Montreal. The Organizing Committee also sold Canadian rights. Just as important to the editor, ABC was under no contractual obligation to provide coverage of events that other portions of the world might wish—such as the biathlon and Nordic events.

The publication of the contract in the paper cured those problems. ABC had to ante up $5.5 million more dollars, which was *not*, as ABC vice-president for sports and attorney Chuck Smiley later confirmed, "a $5.5 million bonus," to meet the competitive bids from the other two networks. Additionally, ABC agreed to provide worldwide coverage of each and every one of the thirty-four events.

As Julie Barnathan says, "It's a thankless task and one that will present problems."

But then, the history of the modern televised Olympics Games has not been without its problems. It is the mastery of these very problems that has led to the majesty and madness of the five-ringed circus known as the Olympics—spelled with an M for money and media.

8
Monday Night Madness

The line feed comes into the New York offices of the American Broadcasting Company a full twenty seconds before 9:00 P.M. The transmission is immediately analyzed by a team of ABC technicians to make sure that it is free and clear of interference. Five hundred miles away, at Cincinnati's Riverfront Stadium, other technicians are giving their cameras, monitors, microphones, and other equipment a final once-over.

Then suddenly it's 9:00. A button is punched in the New York control center and a tape begins to roll. The tease for the top of the show fills the screen, accompanied by the kind of rousing music that might have guided Ben Hur on his victory lap around Rome's Circus Maximus.

The time is now 9:00:30. The music fades and a new sound fills the air. It's a voice—a voice that stands out like an oak tree in a wheat field. It's Howard Cosell announcing the upcoming gridiron battle between the AFC Central Division's Cincinnati Bengals and the NFC Western Division's Los Angeles Rams.

Another tape is punched up and the show begins its stylized cadence: "Stand by . . . ten seconds to air. . . ." Seven images flash over the screen: pictures of Director Chet Forte, Producer Dennis Lewin, Howard Cosell, the slow motion machine, Frank Gifford, an operating tape machine, and Alex Karras.

All the images move quickly toward their designated places on the screen.

Then the words "You're on the air," music, and twenty-two X's and O's magically form a chorus line of characters that eventually spell out the words some forty million fans have been waiting to see: "MONDAY NIGHT FOOTBALL."

In the control truck parked just outside the stadium they're counting down over their headsets: "10 . . . 9 . . . 8 . . . 7. . . ." Silhouetted players race across the screen. Then the words "Executive Producer—Roone Arledge, Producer—Dennis Lewin, Director—Chet Forte" flash by, and suddenly "5 . . . 4 . . . 3 . . . 2 . . . 1," it's live!

* * *

The clash between the Bengals and the Rams took place on the night of November 8, 1976. Both teams were potential Super Bowl contenders. And neither the players, the managers, nor the 56,000 fans who jammed Riverfront Stadium could disagree with Howard Cosell when he said at the top of the show, "Big game tonight!"

But if there was a big game on the field that night, there was an even bigger game going on off the field. It was a battle of the giants—the three big television networks, and it was waged during the prime viewing time of every American with a working television set. At stake were millions of dollars in revenues from TV commercials, as well as less easily understood but equally important factors such as rating points, share of audience, network prestige, and power.

ABC had built its entire evening programming around "Monday Night Football." Meanwhile, CBS was fielding its standard Monday night comedy lineup, "Rhoda," "Phyllis," and "Maude" in front, "All's Fair," split wide, and "Executive Suite," in the backfield. But CBS wasn't a major problem. "Monday Night Football" had played opposite the CBS team many times before and always emerged with a good share of the ratings. Putting a professional football game into prime Monday night viewing time was considered unorthodox as early as September of 1970. It was an audacious move at best and a dangerous gamble at worst. ABC took the chance, however, and the gamble paid off handsomely.

The real threat that November night in 1976 was NBC and its Monday night movie. The National Broadcasting Company had brought in some real first-team muscle—*Gone with the Wind*. For years *GWTW* had held the number one spot in dollars and cents rating of all-time box office successes. And now, for the hefty sum of $5 million, NBC had bought the right to show it on national television for the first time.

With the story of Scarlett O'Hara, Ashley Wilkes, and Rhett Butler unfolding against a background of the antebellum South and the entire Civil War on NBC, ABC's "Monday Night Football" faced the stiffest opposition in its seven-year history. Only once before had ABC met such a formidable opponent. Two years earlier it had squared off in a head-to-head confrontation with *The Godfather*. It was a confrontation in which, as Howard Cosell would have put it, "ABC bent, but didn't break."

* * *

It's difficult to imagine network television without a regularly scheduled weekday sports night. Today baseball, basketball, football, boxing, and bowl games can be seen during the 9:00 P.M. to 11:00 P.M. Monday through Friday period called prime time. But, hard as it is to believe, regularly scheduled network sports programming in prime time was once as unthinkable as a President of the United States resigning. It wasn't to be. Or, at least, we thought it wasn't.

Years ago, prime time was the exclusive preserve of the network entertainment divisions. Sports was thought of only in terms of weekend fare. But then a shotgun marriage between the National Football League and the American Broadcasting Company gave birth to "Monday Night Football," and the revolution was under way.

The prime time series was an idea that NFL Commissioner Pete Rozelle had long nurtured, one that went as far back as 1964. That was also the year of the big bidding war between the three television networks for the rights to televise the NFL games.

Long before the sports-TV connection became a "thing" with television paying professional football some $54 million annually for the rights to televise their games, pro football was just a glint in television's eye. In fact, before Pete Rozelle was elected Commissioner of the NFL on January 8, 1960, the National Football League did not even have a league-wide contract with the television industry. All television contracts were on a market-by-market basis, with each team hustling to make the biggest and best pact for itself with the strongest television carrier in that local area. But whereas the New York market was a huge plum for the Giants, the smaller Green Bay market was less than sweet for the Packers. And of the three— or more properly, the two-and-one-half networks—CBS first cast its stylized black-and-white eye on professional football in the late 1950's, tying up the then twelve teams in the belief that the day would come when its faith in pigskin futures would pay off.

Madison Avenue discovered pro football sometime during the 1958 season, when the New York Giants, in the final seconds of a must game, blocked a sure field goal by Detroit's Jim Martin. The goal preserved a 19–17 win and the Giants were one game behind the Cleveland Browns with one game left to be played—against those same Browns—in the friendly confines of Yankee Stadium. In that confrontation, the Giants rallied to beat the Browns, 13–10, and force a play-off for the division championship, again to be played at Yankee Stadium. Again they beat the Browns, 10–0, and won not only the championship but the right to play the Western Division champion Baltimore Colts for the pro championship as well.

In what has come to be known as the "Greatest Football Game Ever Played," the Giants lost their first game in four weeks (and the championship) in overtime, 23–17. It was truly one of the most heroic and electrifying spectacles in the history of pro football, converting millions of TV viewers and, not incidentally, the TV and advertising communities of New York into pro football fans.

There was no longer any doubt. Pro football, after thirty-nine years and over sixty franchise changes, had finally arrived. It would never again take a backseat to college football—or, for that matter, to baseball.

Alvin "Pete" Rozelle, the handsome, promotionally minded executive who took over the NFL after Bert Bell's death, understood television and its power as well as, if not better than, the television and marketing executives along Madison and Sixth avenues. He quickly attempted to both equalize and maximize the clubs' earnings by pushing through a league-wide TV contract with CBS for the 1962 and 1963 seasons at the then munificent amount of $4,650,000 a year. In one quick move, he sold both the owners of the clubs and Congress on the advisability of allowing the NFL to sign a single-network television contract, gaining a dispensation from the owners that put the minor-market have-nots on an equal footing with the major-market haves as well as another dispensation from Congress that put the National Football League's dealings safely outside the bounds of the Sherman anti-trust laws.

But Pete Rozelle's most magnificent manipulation of the media came when he announced that he would accept sealed bids to televise the 1964–65 regular season NFL games on the morning of Friday, January 24, 1964, at a televised press conference. Naturally.

CBS, which had telecast the previous two years' games, and NBC, which had purchased the 1963 NFL Championship for just under $1 million, were considered by all observers to have the inside track. The third network, ABC, had made a five-year commitment to something called the American Football League just four years prior and was not considered to be a contender. Or so the form sheet said.

The talk along Broadcast Row and in the watering holes that the executives of the three networks frequented was that the winning bid would be somewhere in the neighborhood of $18 to $20 million. But when the envelopes were opened at Rozelle's 11:00 A.M. press conference, almost everyone was in for a surprise.

The only cameras there to record the event for posterity were those of CBS, which was to be expected since the network assumed it would win the bidding. The surprising facts were that CBS had bid an astounding $28.2 million for the two-year pact and that ABC came in second with an offer of $26.1 million. What was going on? Why were the two offers so far above the experts' estimates?

One person who would have liked to have known was NBC's head of sports, Carl Lindemann. His network's bid of $20.6 million came in an embarrassing third. Did the other two networks know something he didn't know?

Yes, as it turned out. Buried amid the "whereases" and "therefores" and ponderous legalese of the bidding specifications booklet the NFL sent to all three networks was a little nugget.

ABC Programming Chief Edgar Scherick found it first. He promptly took it to Network President Tom Moore. "Here, read this damn thing and see if we can't do doubleheaders."

Moore read it. He read it again. And sure enough there was a loophole, whether intentional or not. There was nothing prohibiting the telecasting of doubleheaders: one from the East and one from the West Coast on Sunday afternoons. ABC had struck a vein. Moore and Scherick sat down, figured out the economics, and came up with an affordable figure of $26 million. But $26 million was a lot of money, particularly to ABC, which up until then had only turned a profit one year in its entire history.

Moore convened a board meeting to discuss not only his discovery, but more importantly, the economics of the situation. They met all day and finally at 3:00 P.M. instructed Moore to confirm his finding personally with Rozelle. It was not to be done on the phone. They would wait for his return. Moore hurried over to the NFL office, then at Rockefeller Plaza, and laid his case on the table. "Pete, we're ready to bid on this thing, and it's a very big item. If we read this right, we can have doubleheaders."

Rozelle stared at Moore and replied, "There's nothing in there to prevent it."

Moore then asked Rozelle for a favor. "Pete, if no other network has asked you up to this time about this thing, you won't call them and reveal what I've asked you."

Playing his hand carefully, Rozelle replied, "I've no reason to."

Moore returned to the board members and reported Rozelle's reactions. Doubleheaders were to be tolerated, if not encouraged. Unfortunately, CBS was also aware of the loophole—and, mysteriously, the magnitude of ABC's offer—and bid accordingly. As a result, it would own the rights to the NFL games for another two years.

After the bidding, NBC's Carl Lindemann returned to his office. By now he knew of the loophole and was feeling very embarrassed and depressed. But then he was handed a note, and he visibly brightened. The note read simply; "Call Joe Foss." And since Joe Foss was commissioner of the AFL, those three words translated into three others—the American Football League. The American Football League, which had been with ABC since its inception in 1960, now wanted some of the megabucks being ladled out by the networks. Their existing deal at under $2 million a year faded by comparison to the NFL's deal. But more importantly, big league money would mean the big league status they so desperately craved. Sonny Werblin, the former head of MCA who had packaged such shows as "The Ed Sullivan Show" and recently purchased the New York Jets and Joe Willie Namath, met with Lindemann and Foss and quickly struck his own deal: $42 million for five years. The deal was hurried through so that there would be no leak back to ABC through the notorious TV and spy-network grapevine.

Although Joe Foss was neither part of a grapevine nor a spy network, he did have his loyalties. As ABC had been the network to give the AFL its start, Foss decided to give it a chance to match NBC. During the final negotiating session, while all the lawyers busied themselves dotting i's and crossing t's and generally trying to earn their "Uriah" keep, Foss took a copy of the contract, slipped out of the room, and hurried to the nearest on-the-street phone booth. He asked ABC President Tom Moore to come down and meet him right away. Moore caught a cab and met Foss in a drugstore on Sixth Avenue across from the Time-Life Building. There, over a cup of coffee, Moore pored over the contract as Foss kept a furtive watchout for a familiar face.

Moore could hardly believe the contract. It was over five times what ABC was paying them. It was also very obviously over the head of ABC. They simply would not be able to afford to compete. Ruefully, Moore wished Foss and the AFL "godspeed."

Now representing the only network without professional football on its roster, Moore returned to the drawing board and Pete Rozelle. All bidding had been on Sunday football. What about Friday? Rozelle seemed interested, but even more importantly, Danny Seymour, president of J. Walter Thompson, the world's largest advertising agency, was able to commit his largest advertiser, the Ford Motor Company, to sponsorship. The plot was thickening, and news of it was slowly making its way through the broadcasting grapevine.

Before Moore knew it, he received a phone call from the venerable head of NCAA, Asa Bushnell. "I hear a rumor," he said. "Are you going for Friday night football on the professional side?" Naturally, ABC, which had once carried college football on Saturdays, and hoped to acquire it again, would be wary of making a move that would affront the collegiate powers-that-be.

"I can't confirm or deny it," the noncommittal Moore responded. But it was no use. Word had leaked. Letters began pouring in. Suddenly it seemed as if every college and then every high school in America were writing to ABC and the NFL protesting the possible telecasting of pro football on Fridays, the evening they held their own games. ABC was under a barrage on two fronts.

Within a week, Moore, Rozelle, and Seymour met over lunch to discuss the situation.

Rozelle said that Fridays wouldn't work, but, realizing a good idea in whatever form, he added, "How about Monday?"

It seemed impossible. Monday night was just beginning to show some signs of life with "Ben Casey," "Cheyenne," and "The Rifleman." "What about Thursday?" Moore responded. "The Untouchables" could be moved.

And so they went round and round, but it wasn't Thursday nor Friday nor in 1964 that weekday football was to make its debut.

* * *

In 1966 the National Football League, using that old professional ploy called "up your income," bluffed CBS into coming up with more bucks for the next two seasons, a skillful achievement, since at that time only CBS remained in the bidding game. NBC had committed itself to the American Football League, and ABC was "not terribly interested," having just signed a two-year contract to telecast NCAA, with a gentlemen's agreement not to bid for pro games during the life of the contract. But the NFL, with Pete Rozelle negotiating as skillfully as a poker player, did not throw in its hand in a buyer's market. Instead, it commissioned a study on the feasibility of putting together an ad hoc sports network on a station-by-station basis. Armed with the results of that study and faced by CBS's obvious reluctance to throw more in the pot, they entered into negotiations with Dick Bailey of Sports Network to establish an independent football network. All the establishment of such a network would take, or so the reasoning went, was a product—in this case football. Telco loops from the phone company would carry the broadcast to a group of stations who would agree to put it on the air.

Not quite by accident, the news leaked to CBS. That maneuver worked as well as any well-executed bluff. CBS gave Rozelle everything he wanted, and more, anteing up $37.6 million ($18.8 per season) for the next two years for the privilege of televising NFL games. This 30 percent rise did not come, however, without CBS extracting some quid professional quos for itself. The number of doubleheaders was increased from five to eight per year. And the NFL lifted its time-honored home game broadcast blackout, allowing CBS to pipe a game back into the territory of a home team.

But beyond the more than $1.2 million a year for each of the fifteen NFL teams, Rozelle came away with an even bigger prize. The 1966 season would have four preseason games televised on Friday nights, one regular season game telecast on Thanksgiving evening, and one regular season game—the Chicago Bears–St. Louis Cardinals game—televised on the evening of Monday, October 31, 1966.

CBS, which had been unwilling to tinker with its highly rated Monday night schedule of "Gunsmoke" and "Lucy," finally capitulated and gave Rozelle what he had wanted since he first heard the idea two years before: prime time football. It

A crane hoists an ABC camera and cameraman high over Philadelphia's JFK stadium for a few panoramic shots of the crowded stands at an Army–Navy game.

The NCAA college football team: Bud Wilkinson; Chuck Howard, producer; Andy Sidaris, director; and Keith Jackson, the "Voice of the NCAA."

Keith Jackson and Ara Parseghian.

The widely regarded twosome of Curt Gowdy and Paul Christman, who broadcast both the NCAA college football games and the early AFL games.

The two men responsible for "Monday Night Football",— Roone Arledge and Pete Rozelle.

"Monday Night Football's" first team of announcers in its inaugural season, 1970, go over the game plan with Roone Arledge, executive producer; Don Meredith, Howard Cosell, and Keith Jackson.

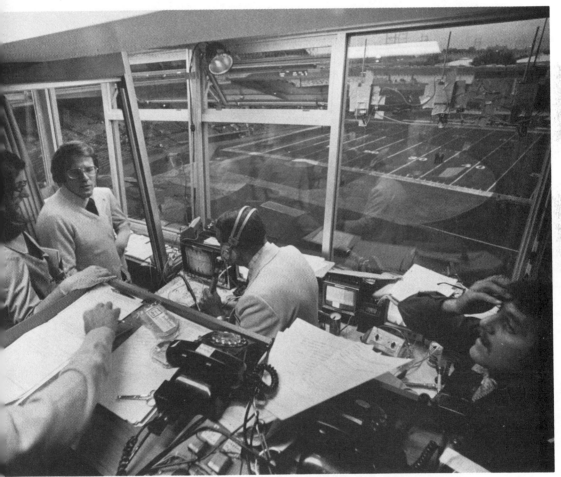

The "Monday Night Football" booth a few hours before a game as Frank Gifford (left), Howard Cosell (with headset), and Don Meredith are occupied with their own versions of pregame exercises.

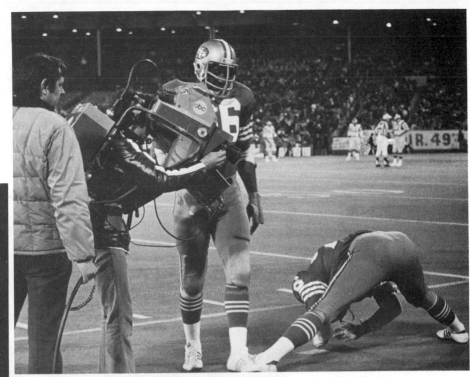

A hand-held mini-cam captures one of those "up close and personal" shots for which "Monday Night Football" is famous.

Two Luv trucks transport their human cargo and cameras up and down the sideline of a "Monday Night Football" game.

Rick LaCivita (on headset), the production assistant, gets some last-minute instructions straight from the truck while "Monday Night Football" announcer Howard Cosell attends to his own last-minute preparations.

Typical of the many signs hung by "Monday Night Football" fans to lampoon the visiting announcers and gain national attention is this decorated bed sheet in Denver's Mile High stadium.

Frank Gifford.

The "Monday Night Football" team of Alex Karras, Howard Cosell, and Frank "the Giffer" Gifford.

Cosell, Meredith, and Gifford.

Meredith and Chet Forte, director of "Monday Night Football."

Fred "the Hammer" Williamson with Roone Arledge at the press conference held at "21" to announce his appointment to the "Monday Night Football" team in 1974, an appointment that lasted for just three exhibition games.

gave the NFL, as Rozelle said at the time, "Broader audiences and prestige." It also gave network television the first prime time football game in its history. "Eventually," predicted CBS's Vice-President for Sports Bill MacPhail, "there may be a sports night on a network."

The 1966 Chicago–St. Louis Monday night game was the first of four that the NFL tested. It was followed by one more in 1967 that pitted the Rams against the Cardinals in St. Louis and two more in 1968 and 1969 during which Green Bay met the Dallas Cowboys in classic rematches of the previous year's two championship teams. The shares of all TV sets turned on for the four games—where 30 is the make-or-break magic criterion for success or failure in broadcasting circles—were 31, 26, 36, and 42 respectively—an average of almost 34. The test was a success! Prime time football was workable, and a sports night was not far behind.

* * *

Convinced that further warfare was economically suicidal, the two warring football leagues buried the hatchet on June 7, 1966. The NFL and the AFL would become one happy family. Their peace treaty contained provisions for separate schedules through 1969, with a combined league of twenty-six in 1970 and a championship game to begin in 1967. CBS would continue to be the standard bearer of the National League—re-upping in 1968 for two more years—and NBC would continue to telecast the games of the American League, as they had the previous year, for the remaining four years of their five-year contract. Then with the merger scheduled for 1970, all contracts, according to one league source, would be "torn up."

Rozelle believed that the doubleheaders on both networks then carrying the pro games were working at cross-purposes by reducing the ratings on both networks. After his testing of prime time television proved successful, he approached the two networks in the spring of 1969 to sell them on the idea of a prime time football schedule. He sought both more and less exposure—less on Sundays; when the doubleheaders were depressing the ratings (ergo the advertising revenues) and more on weekday nights, when they could possibly attract a new audience: women. It had long been undisputed that

women did not watch football in the Sunday afternoon group-
ings. Rozelle was determined that the new audience, attracted
on a family viewing night, could be used as leverage for the
advertisers who sought the female head of the household.

He first presented his plan to CBS, the biggest rights spender
for pro football. But top management firmly believed that their
Monday night schedule, from their "Gunsmoke" lead-in at
7:30 through "Lucy," "Mayberry RFD," "Family Affair," and
the "Carol Burnett Show" right up until 11:00, comprising
their most successful night of the week, should not be tampered with. They rejected the proposal. Next, Rozelle went to
NBC, second in the pecking order of the rights spenders. But
they too had a programming problem. NBC recently had purchased a sizable package of films for "Saturday Night at the
Movies." Their inventory was so huge, however, having had to
purchase many B, C, and D pictures just to get a few block-
buster A's, at a cost of many millions, that they had had to
schedule another night at the movies—Monday. Combined
with the popular "Laugh-In" show, the night was successful. They, too, were reluctant to move their traditional
programming.

Undaunted and still feeling very strongly about the wisdom
of placing a football series on prime time television, Rozelle
simultaneously called on ABC—then running, at best, fourth
in a three-network race on Monday night—and Dick Bailey's
Sports Network. Bailey recently had been purchased by
Howard Hughes for over $18 million, a fact that hadn't gone
unnoticed by the NFL, and Sports Network, Inc. was now officially called The Hughes Sports Network.

ABC was having about as much success with its Monday
night schedule as the Buffalo Bills were having on the gridiron.
Their vapid shows had cost them many millions of dollars and
included such soon-forgotten fluff as "The Outcasts" and the
B-grade "continuing drama" called "Peyton Place," which
had continued so long that it was now scoring C's on the
Nielsens. In fact, one of television's all-time forgettable shows,
"The Survivors," had already been announced for Mondays in
the following fall schedule. This lame addition, heralded in
the ABC promotional brochure as "the story of the glamour

and excitement that permeates a power struggle between a sister and brother for control of their father's corporate empire," was to be written by Harold Robbins and would star former sex goddess Lana Turner, George Hamilton, and Kevin McCarthy. The lavish production suffered terminal problems from the start, including, but hardly limited to, the soft focus closeups of Lana Turner necessary to camouflage her wrinkles. Consequently, the show appeared to have been shot through gauze. After four months, the writers, the stars, and then, mercifully, the show, left the air. It was typical of the programming problems ABC experienced regularly with Monday nights.

According to those at ABC, the biggest battle was the one waged between Arledge and the entertainment division of the network. Although other networks scoffed at the idea, Arledge was convinced that Monday night football would go on ABC. Bolstering his argument with the fact that if ABC didn't take Monday night football, the Hughes Sports Network would siphon off ABC's affiliates on Mondays, Arledge fought to persuade his colleagues. Fortunately for ABC, he won the battle.

It was during this period, which was, not coincidentally, one of ABC Television's worst years—they lost $20 million, partly as a result of the economy and a recent merger attempt gone awry and partly because of programming problems—that Rozelle now approached ABC and Hughes.

Both were informed of the NFL's plans and were to get back the first Thursday in May at ten o'clock with their best offer. Dick Bailey was the first to get back to the NFL, coming in early that Thursday morning with his proposals written down in longhand. Although he did not submit his full handwritten proposal, merely his bid, it was obvious to the commissioner that Bailey had not, as yet, acquired "real entities" (a list of station clearances) and that he would have to go out into the marketplace and sell the stations on the package he was attempting to buy. Granted, many stations, including ABC affiliates looking to shore up their sagging Monday night ratings, could be easily cleared, still there were too many imponderables: selling the package to anyone other than the three existing networks presented the real possibility that in several major markets, including Boston, Baltimore, Pittsburgh, and Cleveland, the NFL would lose the V (VHF) capabilities in those markets, to say nothing of the smaller markets.

Next, Commissioner Rozelle and his Broadcast Coordinator Bob Cochran, met with the three representatives of ABC— Roone Arledge, president of ABC Sports; Barry Frank, then his assistant and now sports head at CBS; and their attorney, Dick Zimber—to discuss the same package. During one of the discussions, ABC presented a figure. "How do you like that?" they asked.

Cochran replied, "Well, we're in the football business. But if you were to base it on baseball, I'd say you were at the pitcher's mound, and we're trying to get to the center field wall."

The NFL group left the room and the threesome from ABC recycled their bid and asked them back into the room. This went on one or two more times until at last an agreement was reached for ABC to televise in color thirteen "attractive" regular season games disgorged from the packages sold to NBC and CBS. The price agreed to was $8.5 million per year, or over $25 million for three years, slightly less than the bid by Bailey for the Hughes Sports Network.

That very same day ABC set up a closed circuit feed to the ABC affiliates meeting then being held at the Fairmont Hotel in San Francisco, where the purchase of the package was jointly announced by Rozelle and Arledge. The affiliates, in a question-and-answer session, greeted the plan with a "Next-year-we're-going-to-be-number-one" brand of enthusiasm found in Network. Little did the affiliate members at the Fairmont realize how close to the truth they really were.

Once ABC accepted the call, Monday night was never the same. Until the start of "Monday Night Football," the television show that had made the greatest sociological impact had been "The Milton Berle Show," which is said to have sold more TV sets than Texaco. But with the advent of football on prime time, restaurants closed, theater business fell off, and even doctors refused to deliver babies until the final gun had sounded. The NFL actually received impassioned letters from wives who credited "Monday Night Football" with having saved their marriages, bringing the old man home on Monday nights. And, not incidentally, it created a three-day weekend in many minds. Prime time football became the precursor of other sports specials—something that former CBS President Robert Wussler recently told his affiliates he would be looking toward to boost that network's ratings. It was a monumental breakthrough in programming. But the most important contribution of all was the one it made to the careers of Roone Arledge, Howard Cosell, and Don Meredith. It helped to make them larger-than-life legends. Mondays would never be the same again.

* * *

The first voices heard on "ABC's Monday Night Football" belonged to Howard Cosell, Don Meredith, and Keith Jackson —not listed in alphabetical nor egotistical order, but merely in the order of selection by Roone Arledge as the "talent" for "Monday Night Football." For Arledge, it would transcend a mere football game. It was to be a happening. The NFL had promised him "attractive" games, and through his ability to name whomsoever he wanted in the broadcast booth as talent with no contractual obligation to the NFL for final selection approval, he was out to get the men who could both do the job and get the Nielsen numbers!

During the eleven months succeeding the announcement that ABC had signed a three-year agreement to telecast a Monday night package of NFL games, Arledge went to work putting together his team. Almost immediately, he told Chet Forte, the man who would produce and direct the show, "We want to use Cosell and we want to try three announcers."

Arledge had first encountered Cosell during a pregame show for ABC's "Baseball Game of the Week" back in 1965, a show that was so undistinguished as to soon return to NBC, from whence it had come. Arledge felt that his meeting Cosell was the only good thing "that came out of it." His selection was reenforced by the fact that Cosell was also endorsed by Pete Rozelle, who regarded Cosell as a journalist. He was in the words of Rozelle, "the one man I wanted on this package."

Perhaps Arledge's selection was dictated by mere ratings. Or perhaps it was a more convoluted rationale, based in part on the fact that during the previous four years he had come to grips with a new sophistication. But whatever, he believed Cosell offered more than the simple "they-came-to-play-the-game" pap most announcers then on the air spewed out continually.

Almost immediately, Arledge's choice became catnip for the critics. "What does he know about football—he's a boxing man," they argued, forgetting that they had whistled the same "What-does-he-know?" tune when Cosell moved up from color commentator to blow-by-blow announcer on the fights. But Arledge would not budge.

The first "Monday Night Football" game was between the New York Jets and the Cleveland Browns. As the game progressed, it soon became obvious that Joe Namath and his Jets were outplaying the Browns. The Jets were grinding out more yardage, and, while their score was depressed by a series of mistakes, they held Cleveland's Leroy Kelly to only 44 yards in 28 carries. Cosell mentioned this fact in his patented "tell-it-like-it-is" style saying, "Leroy Kelly has not been a compelling figure out there tonight!" He also pointed out the Jets' mistakes, including Joe Namath's game-losing interception.

That did it for the critics. They crucified Cosell, the nonjock. How dare he? And that did it for thousands of fans who, for the first time, reacted to what they had heard from their broadcasters. Boy did they react! Cosell's remark drew thousands of angry letters from the fans. Some were furious that Cosell had favored the Jets and "slandered" Leroy Kelly; others that he had favored the Browns and "slandered" Joe Namath. Cosell was becoming, as noted in *TV Guide,* "the man middle America loved to hate," which was just fine with Roone. When questioned about the "fan" mail, he replied happily, *"That's* what I'm looking for." At last, somebody out there was paying attention.

From that very first game it has been like that. They have come to view Howard Cosell as a talking psychiatric couch, as they holler at his exotic pronunciamentos, or agree with him, but hardly ever turn off their sets, whatever the score. He was to many viewers the latter-day version of Erich Von Stroheim, also "the man middle America loved to hate." The words he tried on like suits of clothes were foreign to their ears. The kind words they had come to expect from announcers intoning about the on-the-field exploits of the players were not forthcoming. Where never was heard a provocative word, now they were hearing hundreds of them.

Roone Arledge tells the story of the "bar down south where all the regulars put in a few bucks a week and on Monday night they buy an old TV set and a load of buckshot. They then draw lots and the first time Howard's picture comes on the screen, the winners get to blast the TV set to smithereens." Although that bar has never been located, another bar in Valparaiso, Indiana, does exist, which runs a raffle each Monday night. The winner gets to throw an empty bottle through the screen upon the first appearance of Cosell. Similar rituals are performed at bars in Colorado, Michigan, and even in Cosell's native Brooklyn.

And so Arledge's plan to cast Howard as a broadcaster who could always be counted upon to say something interesting or outrageous or both was to be more than successful. But what he now needed was a play-by-play announcer who could give him enough free time during the broadcast to just be himself.

* * *

His first choice had been his old friend and golfing partner Frank Gifford. But Gifford's existing contract with CBS, which would run for one more year, tied him up. Although he did offer a recommendation, it was not one from among the ranks of those announcers then currently on the air. His choice was Don Meredith, formerly of the Dallas Cowboys, who had just signed a contract to participate in 1970 as a color announcer on CBS.

Gifford had seen Meredith on TV several times, but the one appearance that really triggered his recommendation came during a postgame show after the CBS telecast of the 1967 "Frozen Bowl," in which Bart Starr had run in over Jerry Kramer's block in the closing seconds to give the Packers a 21–17 win over Dallas. Gifford conducted the postgame show and interviewed a passing parade of Packers all describing Bart Starr's quarterback sneak.

Sensing that the Cowboys *could* have won the game just as easily and that there was a yawning omission in not interview-

ing at least one of them, Gifford entered Dallas's funereal
locker room in search of Meredith. He found him sitting in
front of his locker, head in hands, beaten and carved up after
having just played his heart out in a game which on any other
day could have given the championship to his team. "Don,
would you come on our postgame show?" asked the slightly
embarrassed Gifford.

Meredith looked up, tears still in his eyes, and asked, "Do
you think I should?"

Gifford, having brought him out of his funk into conversation, wasn't going to lose the momentum now. "Hell, yes, I
think you should. You guys weren't beaten. You're here and
there are fourteen teams at home."

Meredith thought for a moment and then slowly moving his
aching body off the stool, merely said "OK." Pulling a towel
around himself, he went before the cameras to give what Gifford called "a helluva interview."

* * *

If Cosell wasn't the man middle America could identify
with, his sidekick, Don Meredith, was. Arledge's hope was
that Meredith and his "aw shucks" manner would be "humor-
ous and irreverent and could bounce off Howard. I felt that
people would probably not like Howard at first, but they
would tune in hoping to see him fall on his can," he commented. And that hope was embodied in the insouciance of
Meredith. Or at least that's how the script was supposed to
read.

Meredith exuded that good ole boy charm with a drawl that
could only come from "Jeff and Hazel's boy from Mount Ver-
non, Texas." He was, to all who knew him, a free spirit who
had a bracing lack of seriousness and could usually find the
light side in anything. He was one of a kind, a valuable find for
Arledge. After obtaining his release from CBS, Arledge had
two-thirds of the "Monday Night Football" team.

Being a free spirit often worked as much against Meredith as it worked for him. At one point Arledge staged a
full-dress dry run in Detroit in an exhibition game between the
Lions and the Kansas City Chiefs the month before their debut.

Things hadn't gone well for Meredith. He was unsure of himself and his task in the booth. Although Cosell tried often to help him out, Meredith had turned surly and pulled the earpiece out of his ear when Producer-Director Chet Forte had given him continual instructions. That night Meredith called Frank Gifford and complained, "Fuck this. I don't know. The hell with this! I want to get out of here. These guys are all crazy! I can't even hear what they are all talking about." All Gifford could do was to counsel him to "Be yourself."

Back in New York, after watching the tapes of the rehearsal in Detroit, Arledge and Forte were highly critical of Meredith's input. Despite previous pep talks by both Arledge and Forte, Meredith was extremely depressed, justifiably so, for the very next day he was going to institutionalize his little daughter, who had been born blind and retarded. He was not up to such criticism and barked back, "Look fellas, this really isn't my bag, and I don't even know that much about football. I only know the X's and O's Mr. Landry taught me at Dallas. So ah'll just leave."

But Cosell quickly rushed in to try to reason with this latter-day Will Rogers. Taking him across the street to the Warwick Hotel bar, in that avuncular manner he uses when the occasion demands, Cosell launched an impassioned speech and after two hours delivered a summation that would have done justice to Knute Rockne: "Look, Don, I know you're feeling down, but you'd be crazy to leave. I'm going to tell some truths about these goddamned things that have never been told before. People are going to resent it. You played the game, and in the syndrome that the sporting press has created plus your natural personality, you're going to come out a hero. People are going to love you. And I'm going to have to suffer being the villain—The guy who is telling it like it is. I'll get all the heat. You'll get all the light, and in the long run we're both gonna win. You'll wear the white hat and I'll wear the black hat. If you leave now, you're crazy. You can be a star!"

Meredith reflected for a moment on the "win-one-for-the-Dandy" pep talk he had just heard and replied, "By golly, Ha'ard, you're right. I'm with you!"

And from that moment on, Meredith clearly saw his calling in the good-guy–bad-guy scenario that Cosell had laid out for them.

In the very first game, as the teams were introduced, Meredith took delight in the name of the wide receiver Fair Hooker and commented, "What a great name! I've never seen one yet." That was merely the beginning. Now Meredith was warming up. As Namath fumbled and fell on the ball, he exclaimed, "We quarterbacks sure are versatile." And in his own inimitable manner he also threw in a convoluted description of a pass interference call, ending up tangled in his own verbal underwear. He extricated himself masterfully by quipping, "You're not supposed to *do* it. I know that." In time it became a cakewalk for Meredith as he clicked his fingers, cracked his jokes, and broke into song like a Loretta Haggars in shoulder pads.

The moment that gave Meredith lasting immortality took place in 1972. The site was the Houston Astrodome as the Oilers took on the Oakland Raiders before 51,000 people in the domed stadium and millions at home. The Oilers played the worst game in their history, gaining merely 89 yards in total offense. The game, never in doubt, was blown wide open in the fourth quarter, as the Raiders scored 21 points and put the game out of reach of even the most optimistic bettor who had 13 points and Houston. As the crowd filtered out en masse and interest in the game waned, Producer-Director Chet Forte searched the stands for some interesting shots to prove that the viewer at home was not the only one who didn't care. He found one, or thought he had. There in the midst of a thousand fans who were now disguised as empty seats, was a fan, who bore a slight resemblance to Archie Bunker, sound asleep, with his head resting on his hand. He *seemed* to be asleep, that is. As the camera zeroed in on him, he awakened, saw the red light of the camera and gave everyone out there in TVland the ole middle finger. There it was, the first X-rated football game. But responding to a suggestion made by co-producer Denny Lewin, Meredith quickly jumped in and saved the day, proclaiming, "Now thar's a fan who still thinks his team is number one!"

Sometimes "Jeff and Hazel's little boy" could be "just flat beautiful."

* * *

The third member of the team was Keith Jackson, a professional play-by-play announcer from the ABC Sports staff, and a major concession to the football purists in the audience. Announced to the press in April 1970, Arledge's trio of announcers met with less enthusiasm than had greeted the men carrying gold, frankincense, and myrrh. Commissioner Rozelle's office, for one, didn't believe that the three-man concept was workable: They would be "on top of each other," it was felt.

But Arledge had carefully planned and perfectly choreographed his team of announcers. For if three men could be made to work—with the right ingredient called "chemistry"—these were the three who could do it: Keith Jackson, doing play-by-play, albeit functioning somewhat in the role of a PA announcer; Howard Cosell, who would provide his own brand of analysis; and Don Meredith, who would bring color and actual experience to the telecasts. Thus, the most engaging threesome since Porthos, Athos, and Aramis took to the prime time air at 9:00 EDT on September 21, 1970 to mixed reviews —some rabid and some rabied. But all in all, ABC finally had a Monday night program and a Monday night schedule.

* * *

Roone Arledge has always been nonpareil in production and production techniques. Almost all of the innovations that are credited to "Monday Night Football" were first employed when Arledge himself produced the AFL football games on ABC back in the early 1960s. Although, at the time, Arledge probably had that "suppose-you-threw-a-party-and-nobody came" feeling that nobody was watching AFL football when it was programmed against NFL football, he still experimented with innovations that are now used as a matter of course. It was here that Arledge initiated the now-accepted technique of putting the players' names on the screen after a good play and of using the isolated camera. Throughout the intervening years between 1965 and 1970, when ABC had no professional football, he had kept on experimenting at the college level.

Now that he was back in professional football—and on prime time—he expected to better his own efforts. The man he selected to carry out his concept was Chet Forte, the man most people, thanks to Cosell, identify as "the diminutive little guard from Columbia." But Forte is more, much more, than merely the former all-American basketball player from Columbia. He is one of the few men on the ABC Sports staff who is both a producer and a director.

Forte was brought into the Monday night package early. Almost immediately after ABC consummated their deal with the NFL in June 1969, Arledge called Forte into his office. "Chet," he said, after informing him of his decision to make Forte the producer and director of "Monday Night Football," "I'm not going to tell you how many cameras to use, but I want you to go out, do a survey, and get as many cameras as you want. I don't care if it's thirty cameras or four or five cameras. Do it!"

Up until this time both CBS and NBC had used four or five cameras per game. They stood like trees on the fifty-yard line, picking up the passer, the receiver, and the tackler, with approximately a twenty-yard perspective of the field. As one reviewer quipped, all you saw was "the gun, the bullet, and the victim." You had a permanent seat on the fifty, not the forty, the thirty, the twenty, or the ten. Forget that the ball moved. The camera didn't.

The camera is not of itself an imaginative instrument. It is a machine guaranteed to record noncommittally what is there, the incontestable reality of the image on which it focuses. It is the director who provides the inventiveness and the fantasy of the images recorded. Moreover, the flatness, or two-dimensionality, of the cameras brings into play another element. Where three dimensions exist but only two can be photographed, the placement of the camera itself becomes vitally important.

As an acknowledged member of the "scream school" of directing, Forte approaches every game with everything, including his hair, clenched. But if he is psyched for the game, he is also ready. And has been ready for 89 of the 91 Monday night games through the first seven seasons, missing only two—one because of blood poisoning, the other because he was directing a baseball play-off game.

By knowing that the key to any well-photographed game lies in the director-cameraman relationship with the cameraman forever providing the director with potential shots, Forte, with his continual search for better ideas transcended the unimaginative approach traditionally brought to football.

His first survey was conducted at Tiger Stadium in Detroit during a nighttime exhibition, or preseason, game, not televised but used more for baptismal purposes than performance purposes. Forte walked in on Lyall Smith, the public relations man and press liaison of the Lions, and told him he wanted "four cameras at the top, with both end zones"—that's five and six—and "a moving camera on the sidelines" (seven) "and two hand-helds." It was the TV equivalent of "flooding the secondary." The reaction in stadium after stadium when such requests were made was, "Well, CBS puts their cameras here and NBC puts their cameras here. . . ." The obvious intimation was that the ABC people were out of their minds. "They'll gimmick this and gimmick that." Nevertheless, Forte's survey of the stadium indicated that nine or ten cameras were required. This meant more hardware, more space, more people. His request for two hand-held cameras to "personalize"the game —at first—seemed blasphemous. ("We can't have hand-held cameras on the sidelines. We never had it before!")

But Forte, whose underlying philosophy was, "If it moves, cover it," got his cameras, having fought for them not only for ABC, but for CBS and NBC as well, for the acceptance of the cameras worked to the benefit of all those concerned: the three networks and the viewer at home. TV wasn't as good as being there anymore—it was better.

* * *

Howard Cosell continued being, well, Howard. His abrasive and acerbic manner had not only gotten to the viewers at home but to the sportswriters, stations, and the sponsors as well. He had never run for prom king, and his constant hammering on the collective nerves of his audience finally met with the same revulsion that greeted Sir Laurence Olivier's drilling in *Marathon Man*.

"That first year, it was murder, it was unbelievable, the pressure to throw Howard off the show," remembers Roone Arledge. "I used to come in and my office was filled with boxes of mail. I got tired of letters that started 'We the undersigned,' with three hundred signatures after it. I got pressure from virtually all of our stations. Advertisers called and said, 'We think he's terrible. You've got to get him off. A member of my board says he hates him and everybody at the country club hates him.' I just said I'm not going to change it. That it was going to work."

But it almost didn't work. For the Monday after Don Meredith rose to his zenith, Howard fell to his nadir. The two were covering the game between the Philadelphia Eagles and the New York Giants, two also-ran teams, on a cold November evening. Howard also ran. During the warm-ups, he sprinted around the field with John Carlos, the former Olympic sprinter who had, since his black fist days at Mexico City, turned to football and signed with the Eagles. Then, he went back to the announce booth to take a couple of antibiotics and a fortifying drink to ward off the fever he felt coming on. But it came on anyway, maybe as a combination of the two. Soon Cosell found himself unable to even pronounce Philadelphia, which would have made W. C. Fields love him, but not hundreds of sports writers, who intimated he was less under the weather than under the bar stool. By the end of the first half the fever had won, and after throwing up all over Meredith's new cowboy boots, the flu-ridden Cosell went down to the Eagles' dressing room, where the team doctor examined him.

"I was very ill," acknowledged Cosell. "I thought I'd had a stroke and was dying." He took a cab back to New York and went to the hospital, where he was treated for an inner ear infection.

At the time Kermit Alexander of the San Francisco 49ers was watching the game on TV with Frank Gifford. Gifford, who would join the team the following year said, "There's something wrong with Howard." But neither he nor anyone who knew Howard ever used the word *drunk*. (In fact, one of Howard's close friends, commenting on the possibility that he had thrown up as a result of being drunk, tersely commented, "Howard never wastes good booze!") But the press, never a group that had frowned on drinking before, shat all over Cosell, describing his performance as that of an inebriate. One of them, Dick Young of the *New York Daily News*, when told that Howard had indeed had an inner ear infection said, "Yeah. He poured three martinis in his ear." All the symptoms of what reporters had learned from long years of firsthand knowledge were there: the slurring of words, the illness, and the shaking of his right hand. But few checked. One who did was Joe Valerio of the *New York Post*. He was going to do a story mentioning the incident but decided to check it out and is glad he did.

Cosell, astonishingly, wears his sensitivities on his sleeve. He had even brooded earlier that year when Arledge had chided him from the truck on one of his comments; Howard had remained silent the rest of the game. He was normally traumatized by the abuse he received in the press. But the normal abuse was like a state of grace compared to the devastating reports he now read about his performance in Philadelphia. Now he, too, considered quitting.

"I was immature," he now admits in reflecting back on it. By hindsight, it may have worked in Cosell's favor. After all, millions who had heard him on the air and read the purported underlying reasons for his actions now could relate to him, because, after all—even through erroneous reasoning—he was human. When he missed the next-to-last game of the season because of a conflict with an Ali fight, his presence in the booth was suddenly missed by all—including the writers.

While Cosell struggled to survive the attacks of his critics, the third member in the booth, Keith Jackson, was also suffering that first year. The professional yet almost forgettable Jackson, severely circumscribed in his duties by Arledge to act as "nothing more than a public-address announcer," felt like "Charlie Anonymous." He was succinct and kept order and felt that both Meredith and Cosell profited at his expense. He was to say, "With one guy in the booth, you could give the viewers the necessary information and the color stuff, but with three guys, it tends to become a bull session."

* * *

But while individual members squirmed, ABC Sports kept thriving. For thirteen games the "Monday Night Football" game crew paraded into town after town, turning normal games into celebrations. It was a circus, and entire towns turned out to see them. For the first time pro football had something that college football had had from its inception—excitement and spirit. Don Meredith saw enough of it to label it, "a traveling freak show."

Parties were thrown by the governors, mayors, and business-men. It was, to quote Gifford, "one big cocktail party." Per-haps it was the promotion: ABC has always been reputed to do a better job of promoting its wares than other networks, un-doubtedly a throwback to the days when it had no numbers and no programs. Perhaps it was the fact that the broadcasters in the booth had become celebrities in their own right. Or per-haps it was that a truly American game, football, played at night, lent itself to a party atmosphere. Whatever it was, it worked.

All around, further indicia that this was truly a phenom-enon started blossoming. One evening before a game, Producer Chet Forte walked out into the stadium and saw something he had never seen outside of Shea Stadium: banners! And just as in New York, where Mets' fans carried around their banners as a means of communicating and as obvious attempts to get TV exposure, there were hundreds of spent bedsheets hanging over the railings calling attention to ABC, the announcers, and their local heroes. When, for the first time Forte focused his cameras on ones that called out in five-foot painted charac-ters, "Will Rogers Never Met Howard Cosell" or "Miami and ABC are Number One," the message became clear. ABC could get its lively, talk-stimulating shots, and the fans could get on national TV.

Just as the fans were clamoring for recognition, so too were others—those vying for a spot in front of the camera. For now agents and politicians and celebrities—real or imagined—

wanted in on the action. In Washington, they were politicos. In Los Angeles, they were stars of stage, screen, and now, "Monday Night Football." When Ernest Borgnine, Lee Majors, Glenn Ford, and Richard Anderson all lined up outside the booth in Los Angeles one night, it looked like a family portrait straight out of "The Godfather." The players, too, entered into the spirit of the occasion, flexing their muscles on national TV. This was their opportunity, their chance to "star."

P. T. Barnum at his best could not have put on a better show. What had Roone Arledge wrought? This was great theater, presented with an unobstrusive entertainment sheen. But it also was great football. Of the thirteen "attractive" games, nine had been decided in the fourth quarter, four were won by five points or less, and the eight play-off teams had appeared a total number of nine times. For the first year the show that Television Row had pegged to come in with a 24 share—maximum—romped home with a 31 share, second only to Flip Wilson amongst the newcomers. It was an unqualified smash hit no matter how you looked at it. And millions did.

* * *

Tinkering with the chemistry much as an alchemist tinkers with solutions to obtain the formula for producing gold, Arledge was still trying to come up with that perfect combination. Once again he sought out his old pal Frank Gifford, whose contract was now up with CBS. Roone wanted Gifford as much now as he had a year before when Gifford had declined the offer and recommended Meredith instead. But there was the sticky problem of the man in there already, the professional, experienced, but anonymous Keith Jackson, who was being kept under very tight reins by Arledge.

It was on a flight out to California to appear on a show called "Man to Man," hosted by Roman Gabriel and Merlin Olsen with Howard Cosell, that Arledge first broached the idea to Cosell. "How do you feel about replacing Keith Jackson with Frank Gifford?" inquired Arledge.

Cosell responded, "How can you do that to Keith? The man has done everything you told him to do. He was a PA announcer. He was a puppet. Now to replace him doesn't seem right."

"I want Gifford in our stable of announcers," Arledge emphasized. "He has great appeal. Research in New York indicates he's the most popular sportscaster in New York. And I think he'd be great for the football package. Maybe he can provide little insights Jackson can't, based upon his experience as a player."

Howard thought for a moment and then said what Roone wanted to hear, "On a personal basis, I've known Frank for twenty years. He's my friend—more than Keith. But I think Keith is a far more professional announcer. But on a personal basis," Cosell continued, "sure I'd be delighted with Gifford. But you *must* make it up to Keith. And I don't know if you can, morally and ethically."

Deep in his thoughts, Arledge replied, "I'll make it up to him. I'm going to give him the college package and NBA basketball. He'll make more money than he ever made before, and his name will become known for a change."

But if the change was communicated to Howard, it was not communicated to Jackson, who heard rumors about it in early April after he had finished doing one of the Professional Bowlers Tour shows and was on his way to Milwaukee for an NBA basketball game. "I'm no dummy and I could see this thing coming," Jackson remembers. "I knew something was cooking, and I pretty well figured out what it was. When I arrived at my hotel, there was something like forty-four telephone messages in my box." All forty-four were from reporters who had also figured out what was happening, the story having leaked in the *New York Daily News* that Gifford was being brought in. The only person Keith called back was columnist Kay Gardella of the *Daily News*, one of the best fact-getting TV columnists in America. And Keith let loose.

Kay remembers that she "understood they were rating-hunting and that Keith was considered too middle-of-the-road, not a rating-getter." But over and above "the rating manipulations," she wasn't quite sure that "the hand of Howard Cosell wasn't in there somewhere. Gifford at the time was a young boy, not nose-to-nose with Cosell, so Cosell could play Big Poppa and pat him on the back, as he had done with Meredith."

The jilted Jackson, in one startling press interview let it all hang out. When asked if Howard Cosell had gotten him fired, Jackson replied, "No. Howard's my friend. He's on an ego trip. But he doesn't hurt anybody and he's my friend. As for Meredith, he's all bullshit and a yard wide—which is fine if you like that kind of stuff." Several, including Cosell, counseled Jackson to "take it like a man" and "you'll come out the hero on this." Jackson did.

* * *

But if the 1970 "Monday Night Football" series ended as a downer for Jackson, it didn't for one of the other members of the team. For the man who had wanted to quit after the first game and who had harbored self-doubts about his abilities throughout more than half the year, Don Meredith, had warmed the hearts of millions of Americans with his finger-clicking, country-singing, foot-shuffling, free-spirited approach to the game of football. His style of "Just Plain Folks" humor from "Jeff and Hazel's little boy" and his imaginary alter ego, Harley Smydlapp, won out. He had gotten his act together by the end of the year and triumphed over the image of football as America's greatest religion.

Despite Meredith's seeming carefree approach, one that would have him singing "God Didn't Make Honky Tonk Angels" during a crucial huddle, he does care—deeply. When Pete Gent, the author of *Dallas North Forty*, a book Meredith thought never should have been written, was arrested one night in Dallas, he made his one phone call—to Meredith. It just so happened that it was a Monday night and Meredith was in the broadcast booth doing a game during the 1973 season. Meredith immediately responded. He left the booth during the telecast, and when he later returned, Cosell asked, "Is anything wrong?"

Meredith merely said, "I can't tell you about it now." But he cared enough to interrupt his duties' to come to the aid of a friend.

The fans were not alone in their appreciation of Meredith, for his peers in the National Academy of Television Arts and Sciences awarded him an Emmy for his individual "Outstanding achievement in Sports Programming." Meredith was on another "high"—although this one not of his own making.

9
The Madness Continues

By 1974 "Monday Night Football" had hit its stride. Now an established favorite, it had managed to escape TV's annual 70 percent new show mortality rate. As its popularity grew, the show became a real power, knocking off some fairly strong opposition and causing competing shows like "All in the Family" and "Carol Burnett" to move to other time slots in an effort to preserve their ratings.

Moreover, "Monday Night Football" showed none of the program fatigue that normally dooms prime time shows long before they reach the grand old age of five. Each Monday was another match up. But just as the dramatis personae on the field were changing, so too were those in the broadcast booth. First it was Cosell, Meredith, and Jackson. By 1971 it had become Cosell, Meredith, and Gifford. And now Meredith was gone.

* * *

Seventeenth Century author John Dryden, before sitting down to his work, would have himself "blooded and purged." He was not the last one to do so. Another is Frank Gifford. Before appearing on each Monday Night Football game, he carefully studies the previous week's game films of the two scheduled teams. He goes over the team rosters time and again, memorizing the numbers, the hometowns, and the colleges of each player, as well as all of his vital statistics. Gifford talks to his former brethren, the players themselves. Then he prints each player's bio on little tags and hangs them on a board with eleven pegs up and eleven pegs down. Finally, he puts everything in a laundry bag that he will entrust only to spotter Steve Bozeka. Only then is he ready to work the Monday night game.

Frank Gifford was one of those pioneers in broadcasting, the jock-turned-announcer. The Giants of the 50s turned out their share—Huff, Lynch, Patton, Stroud, Webster, Summerall, and Gifford among them. Only Summerall and Gifford made it to network teams as announcers.

Frederick Exley, in his memorable book *A Fan's Notes*, recounts his being at USC at the same time as Gifford: "Frank Gifford was an All-American at USC, and I know of no way of describing this phenomenon short of equating it with being the Pope in the Vatican . . . the USC publicity man, perhaps influenced by the proximity of Hollywood press agents, seemed overly fond of releasing a head-and-shoulder print showing him the apparently proud possessor of long, black . . . perfectly ambrosial locks that came down to caress an alabaster, colossally beauteous face, one that would have aroused envy in Tony Curtis."

As a boy Gifford had traveled all over the world, following his dad as he drilled oil fields, "never finishing one grade in the same school until I got to high school." Then, when his father went to Port Barrow, Alaska, to drill the discovery oil well up there, Gifford "just said 'the hell with it' and stayed" at Bakersfield High School. After one semester at Bakersfield Junior College to pick up a language requirement, he went on to Southern Cal, and the rest, as they say in nearby Hollywood, was history. It was while at Southern Cal that he met his wife-to-be, Maxine, a homecoming queen whom Exley described as possessing a "kind of comeliness—soft, shoulder-length chestnut hair; a sharp beauty mark right at her sensual mouth and a figure that was like a swift, unexpected blow to the diaphragm." In 1948, they were married while Frank was still a teen-ager.

Gifford was the Giants's first-round draft choice in 1952, and they signed him for $8,200. He picked up right where he had left off at Southern Cal, substituting the words "all Pro" for "all America." But in those days of noncontinental communication, his exploits with the Giants were unknown to many, including his friends in California, who asked him upon his return home after the season, "Where have you been?"

In 1958, Ed Scherick asked him to join Sports Programs. Scherick teamed him up with Chris Schenkel, then the Giants's announcer and assigned the pair to a pre-game show on a local channel. Gifford was on his way. Well, almost. He had difficulty pronouncing words with T, Pittsburgh coming out "Pissburgh." He took voice lessons to correct what could be an embarrassing handicap if he ever had to broadcast a Steeler game. The voice lessons not only rid him of his inability to pronounce T's, but also taught him to lower his voice a few decibels, giving him that deep authoritative sound so vital to a sportscaster.

Gifford continued to do his pre-game show through 1960. Then came the Eagles-Giants game on November 27, 1960. Gifford suffered a concussion in a collision with a one-man demolition crew named Chuck Bednarik that put him out of commission for six weeks and out of football for an entire year. Yet, if it was a bad break for Gifford the athlete and the Giants, it was a good break for the aspiring announcer. For during that off-season, the program director of the local CBS radio station gave him a job doing the sports news as a fill-in for Phil Rizzuto. After he got his radio legs, he went over to the television side at CBS and then on to ABC where with hard work he became the best of the jocks-turned-announcers in the business, and won the 1976 Emmy as the Outstanding Sports Personality.

Today Frank Gifford is known as a person with a low key, pleasantly understated personality and as a very private individual who doesn't want his vital statistics to appear in his official ABC bio. Gifford works hard, in his own unannounced way, for causes like multiple sclerosis, which has stricken a member of his own family, and for the special Olympics for retarded children. "Giff" or "Giffer" or "Faultless Frank" is in real life just plain Frank Gifford, a walking advertisement for niceness.

* * *

During football season, each Monday night brought another game, another shoot-out, and another happening.

But the action wasn't always on the field. For barreling through the booth from time to time, like bulls in a china shop, came herds of camera-happy celebrities; Hubert Humphrey, Sargent Shriver, John Denver, Gabriel Kaplan, Olivia Newton-John, Bob Hope, John Wayne, and even Spiro Agnew, sporting, incidentally, according to an on-air remark by Don Meredith, a Howard Cosell watch.

While Chet Forte is always on the lookout for people who will "move" the show, he admits, "I think we make a mistake sometimes. We made a mistake a couple of years ago when we had five or six celebrities on [during the same game]. It must be controlled." In refreshing *mea culpa* fashion, he confesses, "Sometimes we don't control it. Sometimes it gets out of hand."

But if it was bad in the booth at times, the effects of TV's siren call could also be felt on the field.

For example, when Sonny Jurgensen, then quarterback for the Washington Redskins, approached NFL referee Jim Tunney to ask why he had made a given call, Tunney snapped, "Sonny, get out of my way. We're on national TV and you're standing in front of me!"

Meanwhile, down in the stands the banners appeared to be getting bigger and bigger and more succinct. Like Groucho Marx's bobbing little duck, they appeared everywhere at the slightest instigation, festooning the stadium and hanging over railings like do-it-yourself bunting as they proclaimed unabashedly: "Dandy, we know why Landry called the Plays," "Buffalo without O. J. is Like Cosell without a Toupee," and "Cosell is Un-Bear-Able." One three-dimensional banner depicted Cosell's mouth flapping. It was captioned simply "Motormouth."

Roone Arledge has continually told the press that "I suppose we indirectly encourage this when we show the clever ones, but I can guarantee you that we've never paid out a nickel to anybody." But both the banners and the charge that ABC somehow conspired to produce the signs carry on. In truth, ABC interfered only once. It was in San Francisco when Chet

Forte found his main camera confronted with a large, red, hand-lettered banner that screamed out: "Fuck you, Howard." He asked that it be moved.

* * *

Back in the broadcast booth something was happening—the pecking order was subtly changing after Meredith's successful debut. As Arledge described it, "The first year Don was the big hero, mainly because he stuck it into Howard a few times, which people loved." But, according to Roone, "By the second year the people still liked Don, but Don was now clearly the second guy to Howard. Previously Don could do gags about Howard because Howard was so well identified as a villain and an egotist. It was very easy to get laughs. But now there was a change." Howard was becoming the celebrity, the personality in the booth. And Don was slowly becoming the second banana, matching the color of his ABC jacket.

But he could still poke fun—both at Howard and at the situation. During the seventh game of the 1971 season, "Monday Night Football" went to Milwaukee County Stadium for a game between the Lions and the Packers. Played in a steady downpour, the announcers gave the opening scene set from the field, under a huge umbrella that Meredith was given charge of holding. And like that proverbial mischievous boy, he imperceptibly moved it during Cosell's opening remarks so that the rain, once deflected from Cosell's head, now beat steadily on it. And just as surely as "It-don't-rain-in-Indianapolis-in-the-summertime," the rain caused a shift in Cosell's hairpiece; enough to be noticeable. It was the only victory all night as the teams played to a 14–14 tie and a scoreless second half.

In one game between the Giants and the Cowboys, distinguished only by the number of blunders in both teams' backfields, Cosell commented on the "veritable plethora of fumbles" and then set the two former players in the booth up for the zinger: "Gentlemen, neither of your respective teams is showing me much this evening."

Meredith tugged at the brim of his cowboy hat and commented, "Ha'ard, at least we do have respective teams." Score one for the "white hats."

But just then the Producer-Director Chet Forte spoke to Howard through his headset, telling him that the record for most fumbles in one NFL game was held by "guess who?" Chet then instructed his cameraman in the broadcast booth to focus on Meredith while Cosell, deliciously licking his chops, delivered the lines, "Yes, indeed, the very man at whom you are looking held the all-time NFL record for individual futility. It hardly comes as news to any of you that Dandy Don fumbled more times in one game than any other man in the history of the National Football League."

As time passed, Meredith began to feel that there was something "more to life" than "what was going on down on the field." He was confused by the attention he was getting and somewhat startled by the displacement of his values. He couldn't believe he was getting up to $2,000 for a speaking engagement. And more than half of him resented his own success. Resented playing second banana. Resented the entire circus atmosphere. It was the season of his discontent. He was suffering with self-doubts about his position in society. Moreover, his wife, Susan, seemingly had more ambitious ideas about her husband than being a television commentator—albeit an Emmy winner.

Don's complex nature evinced itself occasionally on the telecasts. Instead of playing off Cosell's lines, he would bark back at him. Determined to move on, he had had it with "Monday Night Football." Suddenly his idle threats to quit were no longer idle. During one production meeting he uttered, "Fellas, I shouldn't even be here. I shouldn't of started this season. I'm all talked out. I've got nothing more to say about football. . . ." And this time no amount of reasoning could change his mind or his attitude.

A decision had to be made, and Meredith made it first. After the 1973 season, he signed a two-year personal service contract with NBC that insured him a number of dramatic roles, that he would never be called Dandy Don on the air again, and that he would receive $200,000 a year, more than he was getting from ABC.

And he was gone. It was not until the 1977 season, when Meredith rejoined ABC in what Arledge quipped was "a great leap backwards," that "Monday Night Football" fans again treated to his quick wit and humor.

* * *

Roone Arledge's next trick, finding a replacement for Meredith, seemed impossible. The man whose taste in talent seemed impeccable now found himself poring over list after list of possibilities without success. The NFL sent over a list of seventy-seven names, including Jonathan Winters, Burt Reynolds, Jack Lemmon, and Paul Hornung. But he rejected them all. Arledge even considered a rotation plan that would place a different man in the booth each week. Nothing seemed to work.

There was, however, a name on the NFL list that looked like an interesting possibility. Howard Cosell brought it to Arledge's attention: Fred Williamson.

Cosell had met Fred "the Hammer" Williamson when both had appeared as guests on "The Merv Griffin Show." Williamson, who was then invited to appear on Cosell's radio program, had gained his first bit of notoriety as a defensive member of the Kansas City Chiefs' team that played Green Bay in the first Super Bowl game in 1967. After retiring from football in 1968, Williamson went on to Hollywood, where he appeared as a guest on "Laugh-In" and then as the character Spearchucker in the film M*A*S*H. He later starred as Diahann Carroll's love interest in the TV series "Julia" and began making what *Variety* refers to as "blacksploitation" films, à la *Hell in Harlem, Black Caesar,* and *The Legend of Nigger Charlie.*

Arledge was interested. After listening to Cosell's radio tape and taking a look at *Three the Hard Way,* the movie that Williamson had just completed, Arledge arranged a meeting with his new prospect. After the meeting, as Cosell and Gifford lingered over a game of pool in Arledge's apartment, Arledge and the Hammer emerged from the short consultation and Howard and Frank were asked to "meet your new partner."

At a press conference in the paneled Hunt Room of the 21 Club, Williamson was introduced to the press. "I don't see how I can miss," he stated optimistically. "I'll even take the pressure off Howard because I'll be another target to throw rocks at."

But miss he did. Fred Williamson, gifted and articulate, was trained in the movies with all the security of retakes and scripts. Unfamiliar with even the most basic technicalities of television production and awkward in his new role, he is remembered by Cosell as having had "great difficulty in spontaneously articulating."

Williamson thought he could "wing" it without any preparation at all. It was like walking a tightrope for the first time without a net. He made comments that were, at best, an embarrassment to him, to ABC, to Arledge, and to Cosell. Disconcerting during three preseason games he announced was his repeated remark, "I was hired as a 'color' commentator."

Arledge now had a decision to make. He could stick by his original selection, or he could find a new announcer and accept the inevitable criticism from certain groups over firing a black. He decided to make the change before the regular 1974 season started.

One of those whose name was not found on any list, particularly the NFL's, was Alex Karras. The NFL had felt that "Karras had never said anything nice about the National Football League in the times of his problems with his suspensions." Karras, like Paul Hornung, was suspended for the duration of the 1962 season for betting on the games. During the offseason he had wrestled in the Michigan area and had hosted a television talk show. But the all-pro defensive tackle had never been penitent nor reverential toward football. In light of the fact that the other suspendee, Hornung, had admitted the error of his ways, Karras was less than an NFL favorite. But Karras is one of a kind, a unique man who speaks his mind and acts accordingly. He had come back a year later, in 1963, and reestablished himself as an all pro. Then, following his enforced retirement in 1971, when once again he blasted the NFL and his team, the Detroit Lions, for cutting him, he went into television and lent his name to a betting sheet called "Pro in the Know." It was at this point that he contacted Arledge to apply for the job as the third man in the booth.

Roone had caught Karras's act on Canadian Football League telecasts, where he shared the announcing chores with Jerry Kramer, the former Green Bay Packer great, and in the movie *Blazing Saddles,* where he had played Mongo, the behemoth bully who beat up horses. Arledge liked what he saw—though he thought Karras was miscast as the color analyst in the CFL games—was receptive to Karras's overtures, and invited him to fly in that spring to discuss the job opening.

After a cordial luncheon, which Karras claims cost him $12.95, he suggested Arledge get in touch with his agent, Tommy Vance, to negotiate the matter. It was all set in his mind. Arledge did consider Karras. But he knew that as long as Alex had his name on a betting sheet, he could never hire him. And so, he went with Williamson.

But as it became apparent to all that the Williamson caper was a "total disaster," Arledge began to rethink Karras. And, on the condition that Karras sever all ties with the betting sheet, Arledge offered him the job. Karras was then asked whether he would like to do the opening night in Buffalo. He recalls answering joyously, with the same alacrity he had used to swat down opposing linemen, "Fuck, yeah!"

"Well, we're going to put you on a week-to-week basis," decided Arledge.

"That's O.K. with me," replied the former-jock-turned-Hollywood-star, " 'cause I might not like you either."

And so, after his third exhibition game in Cincinnati, Fred Williamson and ABC mutually agreed to go their separate ways. It had been a mistake from both standpoints, and both admitted it. Williamson—and later, ABC—confessed that he had not been adequately prepared for ad-libbing.

Arledge felt that Karras would appeal to the beer-drinking lineman segment of society. That his humor, his intelligence, and his observations on life were all based on the lineman's perspective. But when Karras started courting some Hollywood starlets and lost fifty pounds to affect his new Don Juan posture, Arledge began to fear that he wouldn't be as funny or identifiable.

But Alex Karras is as funny as he is big. The man who

played a 250-pound twinkle-toed lineman with a "giggle and a slap" carried over his routine. He conducted Alex Karras Golf Classics that included wandering mariachi bands, low-flying planes, and demolished Edsels for first prizes. He was, as several of his cohorts have called the talented actor, "completely off the wall."

Karras made what is probably his most remembered remark on his very first "Monday Night Football" broadcast. The game was between the Western Division Champion Oakland Raiders and the AFC-East's Buffalo Bills. During the game a roving cameraman focused his hand-held camera on Oakland's Otis Sistrunk. Sistrunk, known as the Hitman to his teammates, looks, with his shaved head, like a black Telly Savalas.

The cameraman caught him just after he had removed his helmet and, as the perspiration steamed from his scalp, the Hitman appeared to be surrounded by a nimbus of fog, prompting Karras to remark: "There's Otis Sistrunk from the University of Mars."

* * *

Any number of times during a "Monday Night Football" broadcast you may hear the words: "The clock has been stopped with one minute and thirty-four seconds to go. And that gives us a chance to remind you once again of a great NCAA college football weekend coming up."

The spot is called a *promo*, short for "promotional announcement," and it can be the bane of an announcer's existence—not to mention the viewing audience's.

Promos can be very effective in hyping shows on the network, but they can also make the announcers seem like old-time nostrum salesmen, pushing their snakeroot oil and catarrh cures. When asked how he feels about being used as a shill for other programming products, Howard Cosell comments, "I perform the assignments that my leader, Roone Arledge, gives me. Intellectually, I find it disturbing, I must confess. But I do it, and I stand by what I do."

Even though ABC sometimes falls into the trap of hyping everything just short of its test patterns, on balance they seem to be the least offensive of the three networks when it comes to in-house promotions. On "Monday Night Football," for instance, a conscious effort is made to "pop" (as they call it) only ABC's other sports shows. Entertainment show pops are few and far between. Among other things, this avoids putting the announcers in embarrassing positions. Like the time Tommy Brookshire, after reading a promo for "Executive Suite," an entertainment show on CBS, added, "This is one of my favorite shows, and you can bet I'll be watching it." Since the show was scheduled opposite "Monday Night Football," and since sports was the man's business and passion, most viewers could be forgiven for not exactly taking him at his word.

* * *

In *Fahrenheit 451*, Ray Bradbury spins an imaginative story in which suburban couples save their money to buy 3- and 4-wall television sets, which allow them to totally immerse themselves in soap operalike dramas, holding conversations with the characters and reacting to the situations. But just as life imitates art, "Monday Night Football" had come to imitate Bradbury.

The party that had been created by ABC was beginning to turn Frankensteinian. The cameras had turned the spectators into participants and the audience participation show that resulted made "Let's Make a Deal" look tame by comparison. At first it evinced itself in an innocent enough manner, with banners and men desporting on the turf and shimmying across wires set on high above stadia in enfeebled impersonations of Phillippe Petit. But soon it turned uglier. In Boston's Schaefer Stadium in 1976, midway in the third quarter of a game between the Patriots and the Jets, the excitement begat seven touchdowns, two deaths, and thirty-four arrests. It was a bizarre twilight zone time, as uncontrollable young fans assaulted policemen with their own guns and tackled friends and strangers alike as they descended wildly onto the field. Whiskey bottles were, indeed, as Howard Cosell said, "dangerous instrumentalities." In the hippy vernacular of the day, they "trashed" Schaefer, stealing one of the ABC cameras in a lawless exhibition that might stem from "the-fan-can-do-no-wrong-as-long-as-he-pays-the-admission-price" mentality wedded with the party-like ambience that "Monday Night Football" brings to any town.

The incident, unfortunately, is not an isolated one, for often a few spectators take on a nocturnal metamorphosis and take out their aggressions on the rest of the crowd. The inmates often seem to be running the asylum; the circus now even has an animal act.

In both Buffalo and Philadelphia, cherry bombs have been thrown into the booth with more accuracy in Buffalo than most Bills' quarterbacks could assay, hitting Gifford on the shoulder and Karras on the leg. Both went off, and according to Karras, he went off too, "about thirty feet in the air." Cosell, untouched by the episode, merely turned around and said, "Did you see that Greek? All those cherry bombs and not one touched me."

But somebody was out to do more than merely touch Cosell in Buffalo. He received a death threat and had to be accompanied into the booth by FBI agents. As Gifford remembers the incident, "Cosell received a handwritten note threatening to bomb the booth at 9:30. Both Meredith and I thought that it was real funny until we realized that we would be with Howard at 9:30. At first we suggested that Howard do his commentary from a phone booth across the street, but we decided to stick with him." Gifford added, "You can't imagine how difficult it is to be on camera in front of millions of people and try to keep all your facts and figures straight with something like that in the back of your mind." In jest, Gifford alters the story somewhat for the banquet circuit and lightens up what was actually a very serious moment: "We were all watching the clock and squirming when it came to 9:25 P.M. Then Meredith stood up and said, 'Ha'ard, I'm going to the head.' And Howard went with him." But the last part is for banquet consumption only. It didn't happen that way. They all stood their ground and fortunately the FBI captured the demented fan who had sent the note. He was convicted and sent to jail for ten years—another sorry commentary on the mentality of the fanatic.

* * *

In Miami, Cosell's life was also threatened. But it was over something that Cosell has nothing to do with—the selection of halftime highlights. It seems that the Dolphin fans couldn't get enough of their beloved heroes during their winning years and viewed their omission from halftime highlights as a slight. One of the thousands of letters which poured into Cosell's office was another threat on his life. And once again, several members of the FBI joined the ever-increasing throng in the booth.

From the very first year, Arledge had determined that fans had probably had their fill of the high school bands of America marching this way and that in totally incomprehensible formations tootling "Hey Look Me Over" and "The Theme from S.W.A.T." So, in order to hold the attention of an audience routinized to flushing toilets and opening refrigerator doors during the fifteen-minute period of inactivity on their screens, he arranged with NFL Films in Philadelphia to select the outstanding highlights of those games played the day before for eight minutes of halftime programming. The games highlighted at halftime are selected jointly by ABC's producers and director *after* consultation with NFL Films as to the quality of the film and availability of interesting footage. It was their considered opinion that during the Dolphins' phenomenal undefeated season, few of their games were, in truth, interesting, most being one-sided routs. Cosell's job was to merely lay in the voiceover before the game. But in true Cosell fashion, he had become the lightening conductor for all gripes, large and small.

The Pennsylvania legislature took the matter so seriously that they introduced legislation directed at Cosell to force him to put on the Steelers' highlights during their halycon years. Last year it was the fans of the Denver Broncos. Putting all of Sunday's games on the eight minutes of halftime "Highlights" would have been analogous to writing the Lord's Prayer on the head of a pin, but don't tell that to a football fan. Hell hath no fury like a football fan who's been scorned.

* * *

Nor does the abuse stop when the game ends. Depending upon how their team fared, and it's worse when they lose, there are always people waiting to get a look at Cosell. Usually these are less celebrity-seeking fans than vengeance-seeking malcontents who frequently holler out four- and eight-letter epithets without a verb among them, like Mickey Shaughnessy in the film version of "Don't Go Near the Water." The serious ones sometimes try to get close to Cosell in an attempt to merge their verbal abuse with physical abuse. And although Alex Karras walks out with Cosell, he is not immune to it, which is surprising considering both his size and his reputation.

"You're a fucking disgrace to the Greek community," screamed one vicious patron at Karras after a game in San Francisco. ("And it was a Greek. That's what really riled me," says the somewhat shocked Karras.)

While Karras can usually stem the tide of verbal abuse by putting his finger to his mouth and whispering, "Hush. Hush your mouth," that didn't work once in the parking lot outside Washington, RFK Stadium, where a fan, in an attempt to take out his dimly-perceived aggressions on Karras, swung three times missed by the proverbial mile, and fell on the hood of a car after the third strike—out! To add insult to the non-injury, the same fan sued Karras for the Ali-like sum of $5.3 million, claiming he was "maliciously and premeditatively" assaulted and joined ABC in the matter for hiring such a "volatile and tempermental" person. The lot of the Monday night announcer is not an easy one!

In spite of the detractors and detractions, the "Monday Night Football" extravaganza continued on its merry way, outdrawing the best single game coverage by CBS or NBC by an average of some eight million fans each week. And all the more surprising: More than 36 percent of those forty-five million watching were women! Originally set up to be part of the target audience, the female head of the household was catered to with "personalized" shots of the players, banners, and a "show biz" approach. She was told by Karras what the line of scrimmage was and wasn't bored to tears with the tired litany that had come to punctuate traditional sports commentary were esoteric-expressions like zig-outs and weak-side linebackers replaced by simplistic explanations. And it worked.

Faced with competitive programming on the traditional night of "Rhoda," "Phyllis" and "Maude," ABC was wooing—and wowing—the ladies.

* * *

As Frank Gifford signs off, reading the closing credits with much the same mechanical quality as a high school principal handing out diplomas, the telecast of the Cincinnati Bengals–Los Angeles Rams game comes to a close scant minutes before midnight. The eighty-seventh Monday Night Football game is history. And, in a relative sense, a success, holding its own in television's intramural battle with the greatest ratings-getter yet, "Gone With the Wind," thus insuring Monday Night Football of achieving an all-time audience high for the thirteen-game 1976 season.

But every year has been the same, another success in a long, unbroken string of successes. For, ending its eighth year in 1977, Monday Night Football has not only become an American institution, but also the second-longest running prime time show on television, with sponsors lined up waiting to buy the most expensive commercial minute in TV—$124,000 compared to just $60,000 in 1970. ABC's success doesn't end there, however. The network that once was literally a "Mickey Mouse" network and which carried the games of a similarly-tagged football league, the AFL, back in the early days of televised sports, has become so much of a fixture in prime time sports programming through its innovative Monday Night Football package, that it recently signed an agreement with the NFL to carry not only Monday night games through 1981, but also twenty-two prime time games on Sunday, Tuesday, and Thursday nights during the next four years at a price of over $45 million a year.

The calculated gamble ABC had taken in 1970 had paid off. The dice had come up seven.

10
Sign-Off

Jules Feiffer once drew a subtly powerful cartoon of a typical American couple seated in front of their television set talking to and yet never facing each other as they kept their eyes glued to the screen. The couple, Henry and Florence, gauged everything by the coming and going of TV shows: "Florence, how long has it been now? Since we were married? What? Six years? Seven?"

"When exactly was it, Henry? Let's see. Was it before or after 'I Love Lucy' came on? I think it was between 'I Love Lucy' and 'The Danny Thomas Show,' Henry, isn't that right?"

"Oh yeah, because I remember the night of our first anniversary. I still warm at the glow of it, Florence."

"Yeah, Mary Martin. 'Peter Pan.' And shortly after that our little Wendy was born."

"I remember 'Alfred Hitchcock Presents.' Those were beautiful years, Florence."

Feiffer's incisive cartoon may be exaggerated, but not by much. Out there in TVland are millions of people who mark their lives not by what transpired in them, but by what happened to their twenty-three-inch member of the family, conveniently placed in the most conspicious place in their house. And it's not getting any better. A recent study showed that our national pastime is watching television, something that occupies almost 45 percent of everybody's so-called leisure time.

Six hours a day, day in and day out. We get weather, our news, our entertainment, and our sense of reality from the 525 lines on our screens. No longer is television mere chewing gum for the eyes, it is something on the order of what Karl Marx once called religion—the opium of the people.

And nowhere has it become more of an opiate than in its association with another escape—sports. Last year no less than 1,275 hours, almost two months of a year, were dedicated to sports. On one weekend, the seven New York stations beamed a total of fifty-five hours of sports to pie-eyed aficionados. And that's not counting the late night movie, *Body and Soul,* which had a sports theme for any TV idiot who still had enough energy left to turn the dial and watch it. In Rome, the populace was given bread and circuses to appease them. Now it has become TV and sports.

Ever since the dark ages of television, sporting events have been a prime programming staple. In 1947, with only about 14,000 TV sets in use, something called "Roller Derby" materialized and provided television with what Fred Silverman called "inexpensive programming," saving it from financial ruin. "Roller Derby" was soon joined by another mix between sports and entertainment, wrestling, and once again, no one liked it, except the viewers, who made instant electronic heroes out of Gorgeous George and Antonino Rocco. As television grew into maturity, wrestling and "Roller Derby" were replaced by boxing and baseball, then football, then basketball, and hockey and finally tennis. Even participant sports were becoming spectator sports as more programming was generated to satisfy the public's voracious appetite. Now everybody loved it; advertisers who could reach the male audience, sports promoters who could get in on the entertainment buck, and those faceless people somewhere out there in the hinterlands known familiarly as the audience. It was a mènage-a-quatre that worked all the way around.

But all that was before 1960, which was the watershed year for television sports, Year One of the electronic sports explosion. It was the year NBC decided to jettison their "Friday Night Fights" and Gillette approached ABC with a gigantic war chest, leading to open bidding for television rights among the networks. It was the year the American Football League came into being and instituted a cooperative television plan, with the league negotiating the television contract. It was the year Pete Rozelle became commissioner of the National Football League and structured a similar single bargaining agent, the league itself, dividing the proceeds equally among the member clubs. It was the year of the first televised Olympics. It was the year coast-to-coast jet travel came into widespread use, cutting the time from seven to four hours. It was the year the still embryonic videotape recorder came into its own, allowing television to delay its telecasts of sporting events. And it was the year Roone Arledge came to Sports Programs at ABC. Little after 1960 bore any relationship to what went before.

The first thing that happened to the fragile relationship between the audience, television, advertisers, and sports promoters was that the sports promoters came to view one of their partners, television, as more than a source for extra money; they came to view it as their eminent domain. And they claimed it. Prices skyrocketed as football rights went from $4 million to $14 million a year in the space of just two years. Baseball, historically a slower paced game—both on the field and in the front office—soon caught onto the idea and joined in the triumphant march to get their just dues. Television paid the piper, knowing that the viewer didn't particularly care what network carried sports, just so long as they got their weekly fix to feed their habit.

Television had to turn to advertisers to defray the costs. And advertisers exacted a quid pro quo—control. In a throwback to the days when advertising agencies packaged and controlled radio shows and then provided them to networks, advertisers controlled the sports events, even to the point of ruling out announcers because of product conflicts. For example, to protect the sensitivities of advertisers, when Schlitz sponsored a game from Busch Stadium in St. Louis, much to-do would be made about the game "coming from St. Louis," but nary a word about the name of the stadium. In like manner, during the halcyon days of cigarette advertising, a bowling tournament from Winston-Salem was once announced as coming from "a small town nestled in the foothills of North Carolina." It was the advertisers' ballgame. For the moment.

But two things were working to drastically change the pecking order. The first was the escalating costs the sports promoter faced, as players and their agents, determined to get in on the windfall, suddenly upped their salary demands. The entire structure of sports was now predicated upon television moneys. Where once the promoters had looked to TV as an added source of revenues, it had now become their very financial underpinning. Art Modell, owner of the Cleveland Browns, said it all when he said, "Without it, we'd be out of existence." Costs were also pricing out advertisers.

The other event that was to alter the relationship was the ultimate fruition of two economic precepts that have textbook overtones but very real implications. Television, on the one hand, had by the late fifties and early sixties finally grown to its physical limitation, with the total number of VHF station allocations the maximum the market and the FCC would allow. These five-hundred plus stations will remain the same for the next twenty-five or fifty years. And perhaps forever. It is a monopolistic situation countenanced by the government. Network executives are, in effect, operating under the divine rights of kings theory.

In tandem with this physical evolution was the rapidly developing marketing economy of the sixties, in which oligopolistic advertisers sought to force-feed almost comparable products to the American consumer with heavied-up competitive weights of advertising for fast turnovers and higher profits. They needed an instantaneous medium to accomplish this turnover, and the most instantaneous one was—you guessed it!—television. And so, the supply and demand curves of these two market conditions had by the middle of the seventies formed an incredible seller's market.

Advertisers, who always seek ways of getting aboard the best advertising vehicle available, flocked with money in hand to television. Those who sought a target audience known almost mystically as "men, 18–49" had found in the past that the best way of reaching them had been through prime time action-adventure shows. But, all that has changed. As one advertising executive commented: "Because of the big hue and cry over sex and violence in prime time, advertisers are now moving over into sports to avoid embarassment and publicity."

And so by the mid-1970s, television not only controlled the sports ball game; they also owned the ball.

* * *

How has television acquitted itself in its new capacity as King of the Sports Mountain? Granted that sixty-second World Series commercials now sell for more than double what the gate receipts for the entire first World Series were, they still have not increased above and beyond other price increments in the recent inflationary spiral. In fact, an advertising industry study shows that 1976 network TV cost-per-thousands, based on 1967, have only increased to an index of 143 versus hourly earnings at 185 and consumer prices at 172.

But it was not what they did to the values of their commercials in sports events, over $300 million worth in 1976, which they passed on to the advertiser—who, in turn, passed them on to the fan at home—that mattered. What mattered most were the values of the games they touched. For as television flooded the secondary with commercials, they were accused of destroying everything they touched, a reverse King Midas syndrome, and of doing everything from rescheduling games to calling for times-out.

While television is guilty of many things, it is too easy to blame them for everything. And worse, a cop-out. For it wasn't television that installed artificial turf in stadiums that made every bouncer a bank-shot. Nor was it television that was responsible for the designated hitter, making baseball a ten-man game to be played only by minions. Nor even for night baseball, that was Larry MacPhail. Or night baseball at World Series, that was first introduced by Charles O. Finley. Or the twenty-four second rule in professional basketball; or the two-point conversion in college football.

And yet television *is* responsible for altering the face of sports, although less than its critics would have you believe. For it was television that "persuaded" the Tournament Professional Golfers Association to eliminate match play because it is unsuitable for television. And it was television that initiated the multicolored lines that bedeck the hockey rink, for easier identification. And it was television that dictated that golf deadlocks be played only at the holes where they had cameras. But there are more serious charges than the "tinkering" just described. These include, among other transgressions, scheduling World Series games on cold October nights and calling times-out for commercial breaks during games of soccer and hockey when the momentum of the game favors one of the teams.

The reason for rescheduling and retooling is economics. Each of the three networks and occasionally an independent chain is in a continuing struggle to build circulation, which equates into commercials, ergo dollars. That circulation is built by gaining the rights to events that appeal to the fans— those warm bodies Nielsen turns into a huge body of consumers to be consumed in turn by advertisers. And each Nielsen point accounts for a supposed 712,000 television households—out of more than seventy-one million plus TV homes— and is equal to $1 million in billings each year. So they deliver the best events to gain the largest possible audience. In turn, the viewer, who is much more discriminating about the view he is getting "free" than if he were at the event, must endure the so-called price of admission: commercials. And, all too often, he will absent himself, in tandem with others, from in front of the set while the commercials are being shown to cumulatively lower the water pressure in their local water station by simultaneously flushing toilets.

Football has attempted to subtly intertwine its twenty minutes of commercials, in effect, a fifth quarter, into the matrix of its game. This approach has been effective, although "tinkering" could be charged by the purists. Baseball and boxing get away easier, inserting them into natural breaks in the action, although it has become increasingly difficult to sell commercials in boxing bouts between the fifth and sixth rounds, as there is no guarantee there will be a fifth or sixth round.

Where commercials begin to take their toll is in a game whose action is supposed to be continuous and whose basic appeal is its fluidity. Hockey is such a game. Its continuum is drastically influenced by the breaks in the action, as the head linesman goes over to pick up the puck or some player stops the action to tie his shoelaces, time and again. Commercials break up the cresting and dissipation of waves of action and emotion, leaving it as nothing but a connecting point between commercials. Another game which suffers the same interruption of flow is soccer. Some years ago, the National Professional Soccer League was blessed with a $1 million contract from CBS, and it seemed that the game that had captured the world with its speed and excitement was soon to make inroads into America as well. Excitement, possibly. Speed, never. Especially after one official called twenty-one fouls in one game, eleven of which he later admitted were patently phony and served merely as an excuse for a commercial break. The alternative is to simply break away from the action and perhaps miss the goal, as happened during the 1977 NASL "Soccer Bowl."

Soccer and hockey also suffer intrinsic problems. Without those bogus time-outs, what does one do with all those commercials? And if one can't fit them in, how does one pay for the privilege of televising the event? Eddie Einhorn, president of TVS, an independent sports network, might have the answer. He wistfully says, "I hope that those out-of-bounds balls get lost under the seats for more than two minutes."

Baseball suffers its own set of problems when adapted to television, for baseball is basically a subtle game, one of skill, symmetry, and second guessing. It's the most cerebral of all games. Television, so adept at capturing the action in football, does not seem to translate the actions of those on a baseball diamond onto a twenty-three-inch screen. The field is too broad and the ball too small. The very leisurely pace of baseball, operating within its own peculiar time warp, is distorted by electronics. It is the one sport that is not time oriented, operating on a spatial plane, not a temporal one. Marching to its own drum beat, not television's. The only sport where you do not necessarily follow the ball—which serves merely as the medium of communication between players—baseball's action is more often away from the ball: cut-off men going out into the outfield to take the throw; runners rounding the bases; back-up men scurrying to their positions. No wonder that the tiny sliver of a game shown on the tube tends to be less than exciting; it is less than the whole game. The sport that has so far defied definition by all but a precious few poets like Roger Angell has also defied television.

Director Chet Forte admits that "out of the ten or fifteen home runs hit at the beginning of our first year, we probably saw four of them go into the stands." This was partially because baseball is a difficult sport for a novice to cover and partially because as Forte, Barnathan, Arledge, and everyone admitted, ABC's first year of baseball came on the heels of their coverage of two Olympics and the allocation of cameramen to the political conventions. It was "not our finest hour," said Arledge. But then, again, baseball is not television's finest hour.

The continuity of a game and the slowing down of that fabled and oft-mentioned invisible twelfth man, "Mo Mentum," has been handled differently in the coverage of football. At one time a production assistant was stationed conspicuously along the sidelines, set off from everyone else by a red hat, which he took off when instructed by the producer. But not only did his taking off of his red hat clue the referee to take a break in the action at the first "natural" point in time so that those magical words, "And now a word from our sponsor," could come across millions of sets, but it also inspired thousands of fans to take aim at the red hat and pelt the wearer with beer cans.

So much for the red hat approach. It was back to the drawing board. Now the production assistant, situated on the sidelines—with a liaison official in college football, without one in pro—merely indicates to the official that "at the next opportunity" they are going to take a break by crossing his hands across his chest. After he gets the official's acknowledgment, usually a finger pointed straight down at the ground, he keeps one hand across his chest to show "we're away." This salute happens twenty-one times during a college game and twenty during a pro. Still, it's less interruptive and intrusive than it could be—and foots the bill.

Only once has a request ever been denied for a commercial time-out. Some years back when Bill Russell was coaching the Boston Celtics, he refused to call an ordered time-out while his team was rallying against the Philadelphia 76ers. For that he received a $50 fine from the league's front office. But Russell is practically alone in nay-saying the networks.

Another television practice that could be classified as "tinkering" is the rearranging of the games and the rupturing of the traditional seasonality of some sports. Basketball now ends in June. Hockey has ended as late as May, with players skating around the ice waving towels in the air to clear the vapors rising from the warm ice so they can continue play. However, extending the season can be laid just as much at the door of the sports promoters and team owners. They want their games shown to as many people as possible, and this results in scheduling on weekends and avoiding intervening playing dates. Major-league baseball has agreed to schedule night World Series games in nippy fall weather as a concession to television's big bucks. The National Football League has sold the Super Bowl game as an evening event for $500,000 and not as a mere favor to TV. Even some of the promoters and owners have begun to cry "enough," rebelling at the Frankenstein they have created. One, Ray Kroc, owner of the San Diego Padres, recently said, "Baseball has prostituted itself. We're making a mistake always going for more money."

It remains a difficult situation, because if television does cut back sports programming, how does it deal with the fans, who not only want it when they want it, but will complain in droves when a moon shot interrupts their cherished ball game?

But if television is only partially to blame for rescheduling, it shoulders more responsibility for other things that have crept into sports. For example, no longer are winner-take-all tennis matches as television has advertised them. A split or guarantee has been made beforehand. Television has also ballyhooed players of golf matches who have not only failed to qualify for the final televised rounds on Saturday and Sunday but never even entered the tournament. And how many times have you, the fan, stayed tuned for the postgame scoreboard because the announcers withheld scores during the final quarters of the preceding games?

Sports no longer operates in a vacuum. With more than $400 million in gross revenues generated by the more than 1,400 hours in sports programming on the three networks, even Congress is now interested in the networks' clout. The House Subcommittee on Communications recently concluded its own investigation into network sports programming, attempting to determine to what extent the networks control the sports they are covering. Areas of specific interest included CBS's "Winner-Take-All" heavyweight tennis match-ups, with hidden guarantees unbeknownst to the viewer; NBC's purchase of the rights to the Moscow Olympics for $85 million; and ABC's U.S. Boxing Championships, as well as whether exclusive telecasts are in the public interest.

Perhaps TV sports' greatest problem now—and in the future—is that the high state of visual art has left the audio portion far behind. Many of the announcers are reduced to mere rehashers of what the viewers have already seen. For television has made our eyes into ears and the announcers into radio commentators attempting to explain what we have just witnessed.

Another problem is the color or celebrity commentator. These ex-athletes who pulled themselves up by their jock straps have literally invaded the airwaves. By repeating pseudo-scientific phrases like "zig out" and "post pattern," they often fail in their primary mission: to make the telecast more informative and interesting. There are now so many of them that they're beginning to shoulder the professionals out of the booth. But it is not their fault, it's the fault of the TV executives who parade them in front of the mikes as if they have something important to say. (A few years ago one announced that Redskin Herb Mul-Key had gone to No-Name University. Pat Summerall had to correct him, telling him that the "No-Name" he saw on his fact sheet meant that Mul-Key had not gone to college.)

Keith Jackson, who talks to communications students at many of the universities he goes to on his NCAA assignments, finds the toughest question he has to answer is one which goes, "I want to be a sports announcer. How am I going to get a job when the athletes get all the jobs? We don't have, in effect, that mountain to climb. Taking that away from us, what is going to be our goal?"

There is no readily available answer, especially from the color commentators who are one of the two groups who can get a job with little or no training. Even those who are not ex-jocks but hired because of other attributes, like Phyllis George, experience difficulties. Before her first game she looked over at Irv Cross and said, "What's a quarterback?" Maybe she can ask one of the color commentators, but don't bother us, we're trying to watch a game.

* * *

More and more sports are demanded not only by the fans but by the advertisers and the affiliates. After NBC announced they would devote 150 hours to the 1980 Olympics at an affiliates meeting, the local stations clamored for more. Bob Wussler, president of CBS, told a CBS gathering that although the Evel Knievel special was an "embarrassment," they would be devoting more of their prime time to sports. What sports? The supply is limited and relatively inelastic.

And although CBS once tried to have its own bowl game, the Santa Bowl, sanctioned by the NCAA, the answer might lie in something ABC pioneered in, just as they pioneered television's affiliation with movies back in 1954—the ersatz event. From the Billie Jean King-Bobby Riggs "Battle of the Sexes" to the "Superstars," ABC has brought a new dimension to televised sports—the made-for-television event. Served up more as entertainment than sports, they are what Roone Arledge calls "a gimmick." But they still are good programming as long as we view them as entertainment and not sports. For to hold them out as sports would certainly drive what we now view as sports out of our viewing diet; just as confections have a tendency to drive nutritional foods out of the diet of many who cannot discern the difference.

* * *

If television has had one redeeming moment, one moment when it gainsaid William Holden's line in *Network* that "television destroys everything it touches," that moment came at an exhibition the day after the 1972 Ice Skating World Championships at Alberta, Canada.

Trixie Shuba, the larged-boned Austrian who was the perennial World Champion and 1972 Olympic champion, had won again. Her victory was based almost entirely on her perfect compulsory school figures, something in which she was virtually nonpareil and which counted then for 60 percent of her mark. She had finished, as usual, sixth or seventh, at best, in the free-skating portion of her program. When the last day came, after the competitions, everyone was to do a number for the spectators—a fun exhibition that everyone, spectators and performers alike, looked forward to. As Shuba took her position on the ice, the third to last skater, everyone in the arena hushed, not sure what they were going to see. They were obviously not looking forward to seeing her do her freestyle routine since it was only adequate. Moreover, most ice skating aficionados had come to view her as the villainess because of the grace and beauty of other skaters, most notably Janet Lynn and Dorothy Hamill.

As she went through her routine, even falling down and hurting herself, Joe Aceti, the associate director for the "Wide World" crew that was taping the event, thought back to the time when she excelled in the school-figure competition in Lyon, France. Aceti got on the private line and said to Producer Doug Wilson, "You know what she should do— compulsories."

Immediately Wilson got on the private line and called down to Dick Button, who was standing next to the exit area, and told him to tell her to go back out on the ice and do her compulsories. She heeded Button's advice and returned to the middle of the ice. The crowd, waiting for the dance pair scheduled next to appear, began to shift uneasily in their seats, not believing the presumptuousness of this young woman. Her just completed freestyle performance had failed to excite them, and they were anxious to see the more graceful skaters. But instead of doing her compulsories, she went into a musical encore, which also failed to move the audience. Again she exited, and Wilson could see Button talking to her. Once again she went out and took her place at center ice. The crowd couldn't believe it.

Now she looked over at the official who ran the music and the public address system, thinking he was cued in on what she was going to do. But only Aceti, Wilson, Button, and the other announcer, Bill Flemming, knew. Or, rather, what she should do. But she seemed uneasy and confused. For a moment she just stood there and the crowd greeted her third appearance with a deafening hush. Then slowly she started doing her school figures. And the applause began to build. As she finished she received a thundering ovation, the first time she ever had experienced that most welcomed indicia of appreciation any athlete can experience. As she came off the ice, she was overwhelmed and could only say, "Oh, Mein Gott!" She was Paderewski, doing what they knew she did best, and if those men in the television crew, Aceti and Wilson, had slightly tampered with the prepared event, it was well worth it.

* * *

Ever since Bill Stern hurried out to Columbia's Baker Field to announce the very first sporting event ever televised—the Columbia-Princeton baseball game in 1939—and lost his toupee, sports have been an integral part of television. The relationship between the promoters and television has grown so fast that much has been lost in the process. Those in control of the games admit that television has the upper hand, much as Bear Bryant did when he said, "TV exposure is so important that we will schedule ourselves to fit the medium. I'll play at midnight if that's what TV wants." Also lost is the viewer: he sits in front of the set in a semistupor demanding little more than that something move in front of him, hollering "Pour it to me."

The little box that grew from a curiosity piece in our living rooms to a constant companion in our lives now beams out more than 1,400 hours of sports a year over the airwaves—a *blitzkrieg* ten times that shown in 1960 and double the sports programming of 1970. This has created a gigantic maw, which must repeatedly be fed by new and juicy morsels on an average of four hours a day.

It is a combination of this yawning chasm plus inter- and intranetwork competition that now threatens another loss: Also in danger of being lost is ABC's supremacy in sports. Where once ABC pioneered in presenting an artform of their own making, a sports show on weekends, they are now confronted by CBS and NBC bringing the same type of show to the screens. CBS has resuscitated "Sports Spectacular," even outbidding "Wide World" for one of its longtime staples, the Demotion Derby from Islip, New York. (And thereby, in the words of one sportswriter, "raising the standards of both programs.") NBC has unceremoniously dropped its tepid Grandstand format to also get into the fray. The bidding for events and quasi-events has risen to a level unthinkable in the past. As the money paid for rights goes up and up and the number of events that would make good television fare goes down and down, ABC may well be hard pressed to continue to lap the field as it has in the past.

On another front, ABC has already lost the Olympics to NBC for 1980, an event they had single-handedly molded into a made-for-television global attraction. NBC, much as ABC in years past, saddled with the number three position among networks, bought the rights more for prestige than for potential profit, as witnessed by the NBC affiliates already demanding more than the 100-plus hours of Olympic programming promised them by their network. ABC faces other challenges by CBS and NBC in future years, networks that once were described as "easy to run around," but which now have two ABC alumni as heads of their sports departments.

ABC Sports, even on the home front, may experience some further difficulties. The one department that gave ABC its initial credibility has suddenly been eclipsed by the success of Entertainment under Fred Silverman. Will they be able to retain their favored department status? Chet Forte feels that "we've been kind of carrying the network for a while. And all of a sudden with nighttime entertainment doing well, there is the possibility that where we could get X amount of dollars to bid on an event, maybe they don't want that now because nighttime entertainment wants that time for their own program. Maybe they won't want to do a championship fight in prime time because they feel that we can now get a 40 share, can you give us a 45?"

The only sure thing is that ABC will have to scramble to keep its number one position in sports. That scrambling will take the form of developing new programming, new events, and new time slots. For sports is one staple whose prime time has come, and more and more sports will be shown on prime time in the future. Again, the network that gave America its first sports night with "Monday Night Football" and "Monday Night Baseball" will undoubtedly be in the forefront, just as they were in presenting such specials as the Riggs-King match.

After all is said, the man who took ABC to the top of the sports mountain, Roone Arledge, is still there, still in charge of ABC Sports, and still as capable of performing his magic to keep it there. Only it will be more difficult—far more difficult—to stay there than it was to get there. For you can only ambush someone once. Stay tuned to this station for further developments. . . .

Index